The State Economic Handbook

The State Economic Handbook
2009 Edition

Anderson Economic Group, LLC
Scott D. Watkins, Editor
Patrick L. Anderson, Editor

palgrave
macmillan

THE STATE ECONOMIC HANDBOOK 2009

First published in 2008 by
PALGRAVE MACMILLAN®
in the US—a division of St. Martin's Press LLC,
175 Fifth Avenue, New York, NY10010.

Where this book is distributed in the UK, Europe and the rest of the world, this is by Palgrave Macmillan, a division of Macmillan Publishers Limited, registered in England, company number 785998, of Houndmills, Basingstoke, Hampshire RG21 6XS.

Palgrave Macmillan is the global academic imprint of the above companies and has companies and representatives throughout the world.

ISBN-13: 978–0–230–60955–6
ISBN-10: 0–230–60955–4
ISSN: 1938–4939

A catalog record of the book is available from the Library of Congress.

A catalogue record of the book is available from the British Library.

Design by Newgen Imaging Systems (P) Ltd., Chennai, India.

First edition: September 2008

10 9 8 7 6 5 4 3 2 1

Printed in the United States of America.

Table of Contents

Acknowledgments

This book could not have been completed if not for the assistance of the staff at Anderson Economic Group, LLC who spent time collecting and organizing data, maintaining databases, analyzing and checking figures, and researching each of the 50 states.

The editors wish to particularly thank Tyler Marie Theile for her assistance in the collection and organization of the data, as well as in writing the state profiles. Also deserving of recognition is Cameron VanWyngarden for creating the maps used in the book and assisting in the review process. Also assisting in the review process were Ilhan Geckil, Lauren Hathaway, Darci Keyes, Alex Rosean, and Jeff Smith. Becky Scott of PS Publications in Lansing, Michigan, is thanked for her assistance in developing the XML scripts used to automate much of the data formatting and publishing.

Introduction

Many of our most important decisions center on "where?" Where is the best market for my services? Where should my family move? Where will my target customers be located 20 years from now? And the list goes on.

The experts at Anderson Economic Group, LLC have assembled this 2009 edition of *The State Economic Handbook* to help navigate the troves of data available for use in making informed location decisions. This handbook is intended to serve both as a quick reference for top-level decisions, and as a starting point for more in-depth research. It includes carefully selected variables that give a broad picture of the economic, demographic, and political environments in each state. It also carefully documents the sources of the information, allowing you to access the original source if necessary.

Just as in the 2008 edition, we present important information on each state about population, workforce and industry, voter behavior, taxation, and more. In this edition, we have added 29 additional data points for each state, providing an additional year of comparative information on demographics, socioeconomics, and workforce and industry data. We have also added a new measure of state business climate from the American Legislative Exchange Council (ALEC).

These data, which come from various federal agencies, Forbes Magazine, Anderson Economic Group, the American Legislative Exchange Council, the Tax Foundation, and other such sources are not assembled in any other single volume. We selected the data in this book based on what our business, government, and nonprofit clients actually use to make decisions in real-world situations.

Organization of the Book

This book provides a concise look at key economic, demographic, and political information for each of America's 50 states. Data is presented on a state-by-state basis, and the states are ordered alphabetically, from Alabama to Wyoming. There is also a State Ranking section toward the end of the book to present a clear look at how the states compare. Following the ranking section is a brief discussion on the data sources used in the book, as well as a glossary of terms that provides a clear understanding of what each variable presented really means.

Each state's section begins with a map of the state showing its major population centers, the main road network, the capital city, and where the state is located relative to others. A narrative is provided to highlight key demographic and economic trends, and to assess the state's economy and demography relative to the nation as a whole.

In addition to the maps and the narrative there are five data sections for each state. First is demographic and socioeconomic data from 2000, 2005, and 2006, including population and income figures. This is followed by a section on workforce and industry, which covers the labor force, education attainment, and employment and payroll information. It also includes a listing of the state's top ten industries in terms of 2005 employment, with comparison information for 1998.

The third data section for each state presents tax and business climate information. Tax revenues, by type of tax, are presented for the 2003–4 and the 2004–5 fiscal years. Business climate rankings, as reported by Anderson Economic Group, LLC; Forbes Magazine; the American Legislative Exchange Council, and the Tax Foundation are also provided. The number of firm births and terminations in 2003–4, as reported by the Census Bureau, is also included in this section.

Voting behavior and elected officials is the next data section for each state. Included is voter turnout, popular vote, and electoral vote data for the last four presidential elections. Information on Gubernatorial and Congressional office holders is also provided.

The last data section for each state presents the names and websites for four business and economic agencies in the state. The agencies selected for listing were the state-level chamber of commerce, the state's economic development agency, the state office or agency for small business development and assistance, and the state office for business and corporate registrations.

About Anderson Economic Group, LLC

This book was prepared by Anderson Economic Group, LLC, a consulting firm specializing in economics, finance, business valuation, public policy, and land use economics. The firm assists businesses, state and local governments, and nonprofits with location analyses, market strategies, economic development, and policy analyses, often relying on the data presented in this book.

Scott D. Watkins, a consultant with Anderson Economic Group, is the editor of this publication. His work focuses on economic, public policy, and education finance. Recent reports by Mr. Watkins include

"Automation Alley's Annual Technology Industry Report" 2007 edition, "Benchmarking for Success: Education Performance among the American States," and "Economic Impact of Big Ten Football Games in Michigan." Mr. Watkins holds an MBA from the Eli Broad College of Business at Michigan State University. He also has a bachelor's degree in international relations from the James Madison College at Michigan State University.

Patrick L. Anderson, Principal and CEO at Anderson Economic Group, is this book's executive editor. Mr. Anderson is the author of more than 100 published works on economics, finance, and public policy, and his views are often cited in news reports throughout the United States. His first book, *Business Economics and Finance*, was published in 2004, and his paper on "Pocketbook Issues and the Presidency" was awarded the Edmund Mennis Award for the best contributed paper in 2004 by the National Association for Business Economics.

Prior to founding Anderson Economic Group, Mr. Anderson served as the Chief of Staff of the Michigan Department of State, and as Deputy Budget Director for the State of Michigan. He is a graduate of the University of Michigan, where he earned a master's degree in public policy and a bachelor's degree in political science. The Michigan Chamber of Commerce awarded Mr. Anderson its 2006 *Leadership Michigan Distinguished Alumni* award for his civic and professional accomplishments.

Contacting Anderson Economic Group

For more information on Anderson Economic Group please visit the company's website at http://www.AndersonEconomicGroup.com.

To offer suggestions for future editions of *The State Economic Handbook,* or to notify us of a typographical or data error, please e-mail statehandbook@AndersonEconomicGroup.com. Any errata or significant data notes will be available on the State Economic Handbook page at http://www.AndersonEconomicGroup.com. Please note that minor data revisions, especially of demographic data, occur regularly and may be the cause of small differences in data reported at a later date.

Alabama

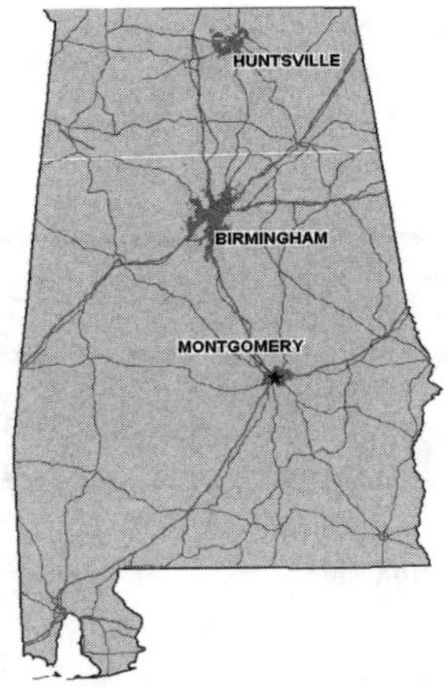

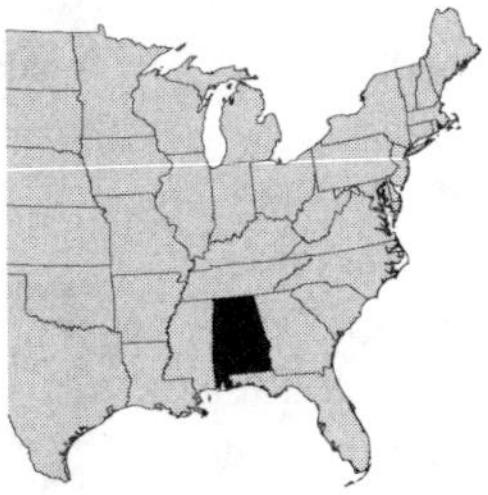

★ State Capitol

Major Urban Area

Major Roadway

Alabama, located in the East South Central region of the United States, had a population of 4.6 million people in 2006, making it the twenty-third most populous state. The state's population increased by 151,930 people from 2000 to 2006, and is projected to increase to 4.8 million by 2025. This 0.2% projected annual growth rate compares to the projected national average of 0.8%. Per capita personal income in Alabama was $30,841 in 2006, up from $29,255 in 2005. For 2006, this was ninth lowest in the country and $5,788 below the national average. From 2000 to 2006, per capita income in Alabama grew at an average annual rate of 4.4%, compared to 3.5% nationally.

In 2005, the state's largest industry in terms of employment was manufacturing, followed by retail trade. The fastest growing industry was professional, scientific, and technical services, with 5.6% annual employment growth from 1998 to 2005. The state's workforce is generally less educated than other states—80.1% of the adult population has graduated from high school, compared to an 84.1% national average. Nationally, an average of

Demographic and Socioeconomic Profile

Demographics and Socioeconomic Figures			
Population and Households	**2000**	**2005**	**2006**
Total Population	4,447,100	4,442,558	4,599,030
Number of Households	1,737,080	1,788,692	1,796,058
Average Household Size	2.5	2.5	2.5
Age and Ethnicity			
Median Age	35.8	37.4	37.2
Population 18 Years of Age and Older	3,324,488	3,356,850	3,483,362
Population 65 Years of Age and Older	580,028	572,684	610,371
Caucasian Population	3,161,671	3,153,627	3,237,958
African-American Population	1,153,044	1,144,330	1,209,321
Hispanic Population	72,627	99,040	111,432
Asian Population	29,908	38,444	45,882
Foreign-Born Population (%)	2.0	2.7	2.8
Income			
Per Capita Personal Income (USD)	$23,764	$29,255	$30,841
Median Household Income (USD)	$34,135	$36,879	$38,783
Individuals Below Poverty Level	16.1%	17.0%	16.6%

Data: U.S. Census, American Community Survey; U.S. Department of Commerce, Bureau of Economic Analysis

27.0% hold a bachelor degree or higher, compared to 21.1% in Alabama, and 9.9% hold professional or graduate degrees, compared to 7.7% in Alabama.

In fiscal year 2004–5, Alabama had total tax revenues of $11.7 billion. The largest share was generated from sales and gross receipts taxes, followed by individual income taxes. The per capita tax burden in Alabama was $2,574 for 2004–5, some $1,131 below the national average. In terms of business taxes, the state ranked fourteenth in a study from Anderson Economic Group. Forbes Magazine and the Tax Foundation ranked the state's business climate thirty-fifth and twenty-first, respectively, while ALEC ranked Alabama eighteenth in its state competitiveness index. One is considered best for each ranking.

Population Projections

Year	2010	2015	2020	2025
Total Population	4,596,330	4,663,111	4,728,915	4,800,092
Median Age	38.5	39.4	40.3	40.9
Population 18 Years of Age and Older	3,504,146	3,574,114	3,642,576	3,706,831
Population 65 Years of Age and Older	648,889	739,580	842,607	953,727

Data: U.S. Census Bureau

Workforce and Industry Profile

Workforce

	2000	2005	2006
Civilian Labor Force	2,154,545	2,140,229	2,199,562
Labor Force Participation Rate	63.7%	61.2%	62.1%
Unemployment Rate	4.1%	3.9%	3.6%
Average Wage Per Job (USD)	$29,041	$32,310	$33,440
Education Attainment (Population 25 Years and Older)	**(%)**	**(%)**	**(%)**
High School Graduate or Higher	75.3	80.3	80.1
Bachelors Degree or Higher	19.0	21.4	21.1
Graduate or Professional Degree	6.9	7.9	7.7

Data: U.S. Census Bureau, American Community Survey; U.S. Department of Commerce, Bureau of Economic Analysis; U.S. Department of Labor, Bureau of Labor Statistics

Industry Overview

	1998	2004	2005
Total Employees	1,604,110	1,629,141	1,667,526
Total Payroll ($1,000s)	$40,330,597	$49,772,829	$53,365,320
Total Establishments	100,316	100,802	101,976
Establishments with 1–19 Employees	86,193	85,838	86,944
Establishments with 20–49 Employees	8,791	9,429	9,420
Establishments with 50–249 Employees	4,558	4,778	4,836
Establishments with 250–999 Employees	674	657	667
Establishments with 1,000+ Employees	100	100	109

Data: U.S. Census Bureau, County Business Patterns

Major Industries (Ranked by 2005 Employment; Payroll in $1,000s)				
Industry	1998 Employment	2005 Employment	1998 Payroll	2005 Payroll
Manufacturing	352,422	282,136	10,341,656	10,526,271
Retail Trade	226,485	237,503	3,651,939	4,846,484
Health Care and Social Assistance	201,111	228,797	5,738,000	7,920,889
Accommodation and Food Services	127,254	145,447	1,175,671	1,591,435
Admin., Support, Waste Mngt., Remediation Services	100,378	118,430	1,706,594	2,616,279
Construction	101,007	105,850	2,635,107	3,597,814
Professional, Scientific, Technical Services	65,195	95,543	2,519,999	4,919,444
Other Services (except Public Admin.)	80,060	83,752	1,219,639	1,612,088
Wholesale Trade	79,147	78,099	2,540,100	3,259,343
Finance and Insurance	67,933	77,144	2,554,861	4,040,625

Data: U.S. Census Bureau, County Business Patterns

Taxes and Business Climate

State and Local Taxes		
Combined Revenues ($1,000s)	2003–4	2004–5
Revenue from Property Taxes	1,661,855	1,792,320
Revenue from Sales and Gross Receipts Taxes	5,217,009	5,732,583
Revenue from Individual Income Taxes	2,344,266	2,644,726
Revenue from Corporate Income Taxes	292,051	397,308
Revenue from Other Taxes	1,020,185	1,119,738
Total Tax Revenue	10,535,366	11,686,675
Per Capita Taxes		
Property Tax Per Capita	367	395
Sales and Gross Receipts Tax Per Capita	1,153	1,263
Individual Income Tax Per Capita	518	583
Corporate Income Tax Per Capita	65	88
Other Taxes Per Capita	225	247
Total Taxes Per Capita	2,328	2,574

Data: U.S. Census Bureau; Anderson Economic Group, LLC

Business Climate Measures

Anderson Economic Group: 2007 Business Tax Ranking (1 is Best)	14
Forbes Magazine: 2007 Best States for Business Ranking (1 is Best)	35
Tax Foundation: 2008 Business Tax Climate Ranking (1 is Best)	21
ALEC-Laffer 2007 Economic Competitiveness Ranking (1 is Best)	18
2003–4 Employer Firm Births	9,564
2003–4 Employer Firm Terminations	8,803

Data: Anderson Economic Group; Tax Foundation; Forbes Magazine; U.S. Census, Statistics of U.S. Businesses; American Legislative Exchange Council

Voting Behavior and Elected Officials

Voter Registration and Turnout (%)

	1992	1996	2000	2004
Registered Voters Who Voted	76.4	62.1	66.1	72.5
Citizens Age 18+ Who Voted	55.2	47.7	50.3	55.5

Data: Dave Leip's Atlas of U.S. Presidential Elections

Presidential Election Results (Nationwide Winner Listed First)

2004	Popular Vote (%)	Electoral Votes
George W. Bush (Republican, Incumbent)	62.5	9
John Kerry (Democrat)	36.8	0
Other	0.7	0
2000		
George W. Bush (Republican)	56.5	9
Albert Gore (Democrat)	41.6	0
Ralph Nader (Green)	1.1	0
Other	0.8	0
1996		
William Clinton (Democrat, Incumbent)	43.2	0
Robert Dole (Republican)	50.1	9
H. Ross Perot (Reformist)	6.0	0
Other	0.7	0
1992		
William Clinton (Democrat)	40.9	0
George H. W. Bush (Republican, Incumbent)	47.7	9
H. Ross Perot (Independent)	10.9	0
Other	0.6	0

Data: Dave Leip's Atlas of U.S. Presidential Elections

Governor and U.S. Congressional Seats				
Governor	**Party**	**Year Term Began**	**Term**	**Max. Consecutive Terms**
Bob Riley	R	2007	Second	2
U.S. Senators	**Party**	**Year Elected**	**Term Expires**	
Jeff Sessions	R	1996	2009	
Richard C. Shelby	R	1986	2011	
U.S. Representatives		**Republican**	**Democrat**	**Other**
		5	2	0

Data: National Governors Association; U.S. Senate, Office of the Clerk; U.S. House of Representatives

Business and Economic Agencies

Agency	Website Address
Business Council of Alabama	www.bcatoday.org
Alabama Development Office	www.ado.state.al.us
Alabama Small Business Dev. Consortium	www.asbdc.org
Alabama Secretary of State	www.sos.state.al.us

Data: Various agency websites

Alaska

With a population of 670,053 people, Alaska was the fourth least populous state in the United States in 2006. From 2000 to 2006 the state's population increased by 43,121 people, and is projected to increase to 820,881 by 2025. This 1.1% projected annual growth rate compares to the projected national average of 0.8%. The state's 2006 per capita personal income of $38,622 was higher compared to $36,636 in 2005 and fourteenth highest in the United States, some $1,993 above the national average. Per capita income in Alaska grew at an average annual rate of 4.3% from 2000 to 2006, compared to 3.5% nationally.

Alaska's largest industry in terms of 2005 employment was health care and social assistance. The fastest growing industry was administration, support, waste management, and remediation services, with 8.1% annual employment growth from 1998 to 2005. The second fastest growing industry was construction. The state's workforce is generally slightly less educated than other states—89.7% of the state's adult population has graduated from high school, compared to an 84.1% national average; 26.9% hold a bachelor degree or higher

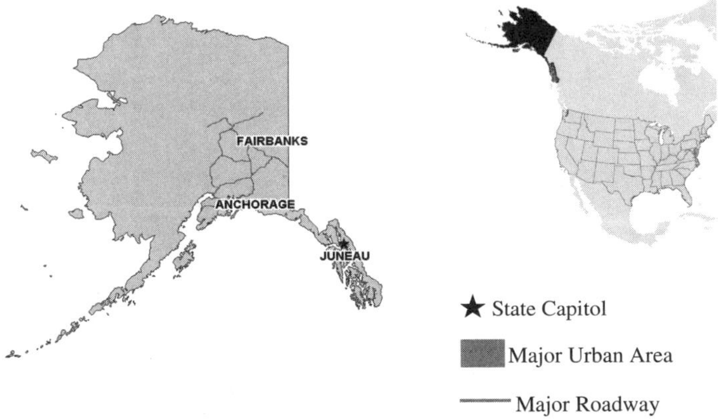

Demographic and Socioeconomic Profile

Demographics and Socioeconomic Figures

Population and Households	2000	2005	2006
Total Population	626,932	641,724	670,053
Number of Households	221,600	233,252	229,878
Average Household Size	2.7	2.8	2.8
Age and Ethnicity			
Median Age	32.4	33.9	33.5
Population 18 Years of Age and Older	436,425	454,226	490,366
Population 65 Years of Age and Older	35,093	42,156	44,035
Caucasian Population	434,225	443,874	460,170
African-American Population	21,968	22,103	21,476
Hispanic Population	25,765	30,843	37,498
Asian Population	25,496	28,838	30,151
Foreign-Born Population (%)	5.9	5.4	7.0
Income			
Per Capita Personal Income (USD)	$29,867	$36,636	$38,622
Median Household Income (USD)	$51,571	$56,234	$59,393
Individuals Below Poverty Level	9.4%	11.2%	10.9%

Data: U.S. Census, American Community Survey; U.S. Department of Commerce, Bureau of Economic Analysis

(national average is 27.0%); and 9.5% hold professional or graduate degrees compared to the national average of 9.9%.

Alaska's total tax revenue was $2.9 billion for fiscal year 2004–5, up from the 2003–4 total revenue of $2.4 billion. The largest share of tax revenue in 2004–5 was generated from the other taxes category, followed by property taxes. On a per capita basis, residents of Alaska paid taxes of $4,402, compared to the national average of $3,705 for 2004–5. In terms of business taxes, the state ranked forty-seventh in a study from Anderson Economic Group. Forbes Magazine and the Tax Foundation ranked the state's business climate forty-seventh and fourth, respectively, while ALEC ranked Alaska thirty-eighth in its state competitiveness index. One is considered best for each ranking.

Population Projections

Year	2010	2015	2020	2025
Total Population	694,109	732,544	774,421	820,881
Median Age	32.5	32.3	32.9	33.3
Population 18 Years of Age and Older	510,126	533,371	555,795	584,703
Population 65 Years of Age and Older	56,548	75,023	96,388	115,135

Data: U.S. Census Bureau

Workforce and Industry Profile

Workforce

	2000	2005	2006
Civilian Labor Force	319,002	342,032	346,769
Labor Force Participation Rate	73.1%	71.7%	71.6%
Unemployment Rate	6.2%	6.9%	6.7%
Average Wage Per Job (USD)	$35,142	$42,740	$43,920
Education Attainment (Population 25 Years and Older)	**(%)**	**(%)**	**(%)**
High School Graduate or Higher	88.3	91.0	89.7
Bachelors Degree or Higher	24.7	27.3	26.9
Graduate or Professional Degree	8.6	10.1	9.5

Data: U.S. Census Bureau, American Community Survey; U.S. Department of Commerce, Bureau of Economic Analysis; U.S. Department of Labor, Bureau of Labor Statistics

Industry Overview

	1998	2004	2005
Total Employees	196,135	223,153	231,088
Total Payroll ($1,000s)	$6,883,920	$9,124,830	$9,774,285
Total Establishments	18,212	19,387	19,808
Establishments with 1–19 Employees	16,424	17,317	17,723
Establishments with 20–49 Employees	1,212	1,402	1,393
Establishments with 50–249 Employees	486	573	588
Establishments with 250–999 Employees	85	83	90
Establishments with 1,000+ Employees	5	12	14

Data: U.S. Census Bureau, County Business Patterns

Major Industries (Ranked by 2005 Employment; Payroll in $1,000s)				
Industry	1998 Employment	2005 Employment	1998 Payroll	2005 Payroll
Health Care and Social Assistance	28,919	37,476	1,061,078	1,627,019
Retail Trade	32,186	34,897	743,092	911,704
Accommodation and Food Services	20,086	23,939	343,467	483,353
Construction	12,915	19,353	642,928	1,272,040
Transportation and Warehousing	17,005	18,549	745,246	961,489
Admin., Support, Waste Mngt., Remediation Services	9,881	17,003	289,675	649,505
Professional, Scientific, Technical Services	9,497	12,014	446,785	676,383
Other Services (except Public Admin.)	9,991	10,209	211,565	269,630
Manufacturing	12,117	9,860	352,818	402,806
Wholesale Trade	7,040	8,239	275,492	386,296

Data: U.S. Census Bureau, County Business Patterns

Taxes and Business Climate

State and Local Taxes		
Combined Revenues ($1,000s)	2003–4	2004–5
Revenue from Property Taxes	859,056	892,307
Revenue from Sales and Gross Receipts Taxes	358,186	400,070
Revenue from Individual Income Taxes	0	0
Revenue from Corporate Income Taxes	339,564	588,694
Revenue from Other Taxes	818,825	1,065,963
Total Tax Revenue	2,375,631	2,947,034
Per Capita Taxes		
Property Tax Per Capita	1,306	1,333
Sales and Gross Receipts Tax Per Capita	544	598
Individual Income Tax Per Capita	0	0
Corporate Income Tax Per Capita	516	879
Other Taxes Per Capita	1,244	1,592
Total Taxes Per Capita	3,610	4,402

Data: U.S. Census Bureau; Anderson Economic Group, LLC

Business Climate Measures	
Anderson Economic Group: 2007 Business Tax Ranking (1 is Best)	47
Forbes Magazine: 2007 Best States for Business Ranking (1 is Best)	47
Tax Foundation: 2008 Business Tax Climate Ranking (1 is Best)	4
ALEC-Laffer 2007 Economic Competitiveness Ranking (1 is Best)	38
2003–4 Employer Firm Births	1,963
2003–4 Employer Firm Terminations	1,686

Data: Anderson Economic Group; Tax Foundation; Forbes Magazine; U.S. Census, Statistics of U.S. Businesses; American Legislative Exchange Council

Voting Behavior and Elected Officials

Voter Registration and Turnout (%)

	1992	1996	2000	2004
Registered Voters Who Voted	82.1	58.2	60.3	66.2
Citizens Age 18+ Who Voted	65.4	56.9	65.4	68.0

Data: Dave Leip's Atlas of U.S. Presidential Elections

Presidential Election Results (Nationwide Winner Listed First)

2004	Popular Vote (%)	Electoral Votes
George W. Bush (Republican, Incumbent)	61.1	3
John Kerry (Democrat)	35.5	0
Other	3.4	0
2000		
George W. Bush (Republican)	58.6	3
Albert Gore (Democrat)	27.7	0
Ralph Nader (Green)	10.1	0
Other	3.6	0
1996		
William Clinton (Democrat, Incumbent)	33.3	0
Robert Dole (Republican)	50.8	3
H. Ross Perot (Reformist)	10.9	0
Other	5.0	0
1992		
William Clinton (Democrat)	30.3	0
George H. W. Bush (Republican, Incumbent)	39.5	3
H. Ross Perot (Independent)	28.4	0
Other	1.8%	0

Data: Dave Leip's Atlas of U.S. Presidential Elections

Governor and U.S. Congressional Seats

Governor	Party	Year Term Began	Term	Max. Consecutive Terms
Sarah Palin	R	2007	First	2
U.S. Senators	**Party**	**Year Elected**	**Term Expires**	
Ted Stevens	R	1970	2009	
Lisa Murkowski	R	2002	2011	
U.S. Representatives		**Republican**	**Democrat**	**Other**
		1	0	0

Data: National Governors Association; U.S. Senate, Office of the Clerk; U.S. House of Representatives

Business and Economic Agencies

Agency	Website Address
Alaska State Chamber	www.alaskachamber.com
Alaska Department of Commerce, Community & Economic Development	www.dced.state.ak.us
Alaska Small Business Dev. Center	www.aksbdc.org
Division of Corporations, Business, and Professional Licensing	www.dced.state.ak.us/occ

Data: Various agency websites

Arizona

In 2006, Arizona had a population of 6.2 million people, making it the thirty-fifth most populous state. The state's population increased by 1,035,686 people from 2000 to 2006, and is projected to increase to 9.5 million by 2025. This 2.3% projected annual growth rate is above the national average of 0.8%. Per capita personal income in Arizona was $31,949 in 2006, up from $30,384 in 2005. For 2006, this was $4,680 below the national average and the thirteenth lowest in the country. The state's per capita income grew at an average annual rate of 3.7% from 2000 to 2006, compared to 3.5% nationally.

The state's workforce generally has slightly less education than other states—83.8% of the state's adult population has graduated from high school, compared to an 84.1% national average; 25.5% hold a bachelor degree or higher (national average is 27.0%); and 9.2% hold professional or graduate degrees (national average is 9.9%). In 2005, the state's largest industry in terms of employment was retail trade, followed by health care and social assistance. The fastest growing industry was construction,

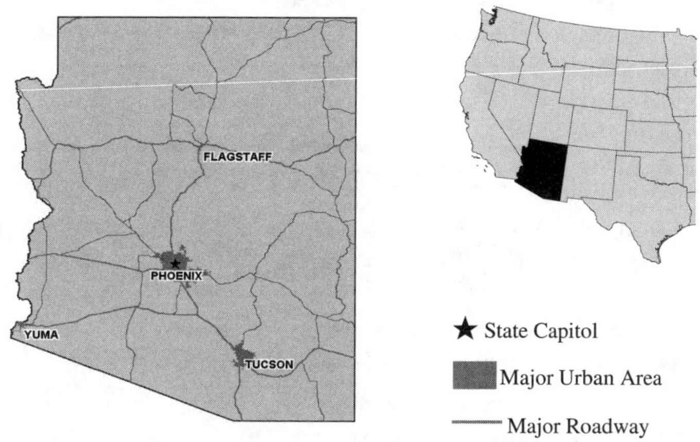

Demographic and Socioeconomic Profile

Demographics and Socioeconomic Figures			
Population and Households	**2000**	**2005**	**2006**
Total Population	5,130,632	5,829,839	6,166,318
Number of Households	1,901,327	2,204,013	2,224,992
Average Household Size	2.6	2.7	2.7
Age and Ethnicity			
Median Age	34.2	34.5	34.6
Population 18 Years of Age and Older	3,767,931	4,255,951	4,539,463
Population 65 Years of Age and Older	667,607	735,397	789,751
Caucasian Population	3,871,715	4,440,804	4,741,310
African-American Population	154,316	180,769	207,837
Hispanic Population	1,295,317	1,668,524	1,803,377
Asian Population	91,223	129,197	144,858
Foreign-Born Population (%)	12.8	14.5	15.1
Income			
Per Capita Personal Income (USD)	$25,660	$30,384	$31,949
Median Household Income (USD)	$40,558	$44,282	$47,265
Individuals Below Poverty Level	13.9%	14.2%	14.2%

Data: U.S. Census, American Community Survey; U.S. Department of Commerce, Bureau of Economic Analysis

with 5.7% annual employment growth from 1998 to 2005.

In fiscal year 2004–5, Arizona had total tax revenues of $18.3 billion. The largest share was generated from sales and gross receipts taxes, followed by property taxes. The per capita tax burden in Arizona was $3,080 for 2004–5, some $625 below the national average, and a $209 increase from 2003–4. In terms of business taxes, Arizona ranked thirty-first in a study from Anderson Economic Group. The state's business climate was ranked eighteenth by Forbes Magazine and twenty-fifth by the Tax Foundation. Arizona was ranked second by ALEC in its state competitiveness index. One is considered best for each ranking.

Population Projections

Year	2010	2015	2020	2025
Total Population	6,637,381	7,495,238	8,456,448	9,531,537
Median Age	36.4	37.3	38.2	38.8
Population 18 Years of Age and Older	4,948,917	5,602,941	6,328,068	7,170,395
Population 65 Years of Age and Older	922,010	1,181,358	1,520,622	1,940,356

Data: U.S. Census Bureau

Workforce and Industry Profile

Workforce

	2000	2005	2006
Civilian Labor Force	2,505,306	2,859,490	2,977,094
Labor Force Participation Rate	65.1%	64.2%	64.4%
Unemployment Rate	4.0%	4.6%	4.1%
Average Wage Per Job (USD)	$32,610	$34,940	$36,260
Education Attainment (Population 25 Years and Older)	**(%)**	**(%)**	**(%)**
High School Graduate or Higher	81.0	83.8	83.8
Bachelors Degree or Higher	23.5	25.6	25.5
Graduate or Professional Degree	8.4	9.3	9.2

Data: U.S. Census Bureau, American Community Survey; U.S. Department of Commerce, Bureau of Economic Analysis; U.S. Department of Labor, Bureau of Labor Statistics

Industry Overview

	1998	2004	2005
Total Employees	1,763,508	2,044,134	2,159,823
Total Payroll ($1,000s)	$49,052,246	$69,160,754	$76,340,525
Total Establishments	110,245	125,693	131,651
Establishments with 1–19 Employees	94,264	106,797	111,990
Establishments with 20–49 Employees	9,997	11,700	12,060
Establishments with 50–249 Employees	5,221	6,278	6,613
Establishments with 250–999 Employees	656	805	872
Establishments with 1,000+ Employees	107	113	116

Data: U.S. Census Bureau, County Business Patterns

Major Industries (Ranked by 2005 Employment; Payroll in $1,000s)				
Industry	1998 Employment	2005 Employment	1998 Payroll	2005 Payroll
Retail Trade	241,092	306,113	4,734,716	7,311,713
Health Care and Social Assistance	190,110	252,401	5,572,775	9,831,310
Accommodation and Food Services	187,762	238,838	2,091,494	3,238,141
Admin., Support, Waste Mngt., Remediation Services	178,828	221,178	3,566,564	5,836,677
Construction	143,373	211,584	4,191,730	7,954,878
Manufacturing	199,616	167,886	7,565,451	7,827,619
Finance and Insurance	92,132	131,283	3,647,327	7,004,350
Professional, Scientific, Technical Services	98,547	118,943	3,636,335	6,193,259
Wholesale Trade	84,631	95,027	3,175,460	4,437,410
Other Services (except Public Admin.)	73,577	83,496	1,386,582	1,906,080

Data: U.S. Census Bureau, County Business Patterns

Taxes and Business Climate

State and Local Taxes		
Combined Revenues ($1,000s)	2003–4	2004–5
Revenue from Property Taxes	4,867,990	5,126,076
Revenue from Sales and Gross Receipts Taxes	7,989,125	8,749,977
Revenue from Individual Income Taxes	2,315,865	2,848,450
Revenue from Corporate Income Taxes	525,650	701,859
Revenue from Other Taxes	782,544	904,755
Total Tax Revenue	16,481,174	18,331,117
Per Capita Taxes		
Property Tax Per Capita	848	861
Sales and Gross Receipts Tax Per Capita	1,392	1,470
Individual Income Tax Per Capita	403	479
Corporate Income Tax Per Capita	92	118
Other Taxes Per Capita	136	152
Total Taxes Per Capita	2,871	3,080

Data: U.S. Census Bureau; Anderson Economic Group, LLC

Business Climate Measures	
Anderson Economic Group: 2007 Business Tax Ranking (1 is Best)	31
Forbes Magazine: 2007 Best States for Business Ranking (1 is Best)	18
Tax Foundation: 2008 Business Tax Climate Ranking (1 is Best)	25
ALEC-Laffer 2007 Economic Competitiveness Ranking (1 is Best)	2
2003–4 Employer Firm Births	14,740
2003–4 Employer Firm Terminations	12,009

Data: Anderson Economic Group; Tax Foundation; Forbes Magazine; U.S. Census, Statistics of U.S. Businesses; American Legislative Exchange Council

Voting Behavior and Elected Officials

Voter Registration and Turnout (%)

	1992	1996	2000	2004
Registered Voters Who Voted	75.7	62.6	70.6	76.1
Citizens Age 18+ Who Voted	54.1	44.7	40.7	49.6

Data: Dave Leip's Atlas of U.S. Presidential Elections

Presidential Election Results (Nationwide Winner Listed First)

2004	Popular Vote (%)	Electoral Votes
George W. Bush (Republican, Incumbent)	54.8	10
John Kerry (Democrat)	44.4	0
Other	0.8	0
2000		
George W. Bush (Republican)	51.0	8
Albert Gore (Democrat)	44.7	0
Ralph Nader (Green)	3.0	0
Other	1.2	0
1996		
William Clinton (Democrat, Incumbent)	46.5	8
Robert Dole (Republican)	44.3	0
H. Ross Perot (Reformist)	8.0	0
Other	1.2	0
1992		
William Clinton (Democrat)	36.5	0
George H. W. Bush (Republican, Incumbent)	38.5	8
H. Ross Perot (Independent)	23.8	0
Other	1.2	0

Data: Dave Leip's Atlas of U.S. Presidential Elections

Governor and U.S. Congressional Seats				
Governor	**Party**	**Year Term Began**	**Term**	**Max. Consecutive Terms**
Janet Napolitano	D	2007	Second	2
U.S. Senators	**Party**	**Year Elected**	**Term Expires**	
Jon Kyl	R	1994	2013	
John McCain	R	1986	2011	
U.S. Representatives		**Republican**	**Democrat**	**Other**
		4	4	0

Data: National Governors Association; U.S. Senate, Office of the Clerk; U.S. House of Representatives

Business and Economic Agencies

Agency	Website Address
Arizona Chamber of Commerce	www.azchamber.com
Arizona Department of Commerce	www.azcommerce.com
Arizona Small Business Dev. Center	www.maricopa.edu/sbdc
Arizona Secretary of State	www.azsos.gov/business_services

Data: Various agency websites

Arkansas

Arkansas, located in the West South Central region of the United States, had a population of 2.8 million people in 2006, making it the nineteenth least populous state. The state's population increased by 137,472 people from 2000 to 2006, and is projected to increase to 3.2 million by 2025. This 0.6% projected annual growth rate compares to the projected national average of 0.8%. Per capita personal income in Arkansas was $28,444 in 2006, up from $26,961 in 2005. For 2006, this was third lowest in the country and $8,185 below the national average. From 2000 to 2006 per capita income in Arkansas grew at an average annual rate of 4.4%, compared to 3.5% nationally.

In 2005, the state's largest industry in terms of employment was manufacturing, followed by health care and social assistance. The fastest growing industry was transportation and warehousing, with 6.6% annual employment growth from 1998 to 2005. The state's workforce is generally less educated than other states—80.5% of the state's adult population has graduated from high school, compared to an 84.1% national average. Nationally, an average of 27.0% hold a bachelor degree

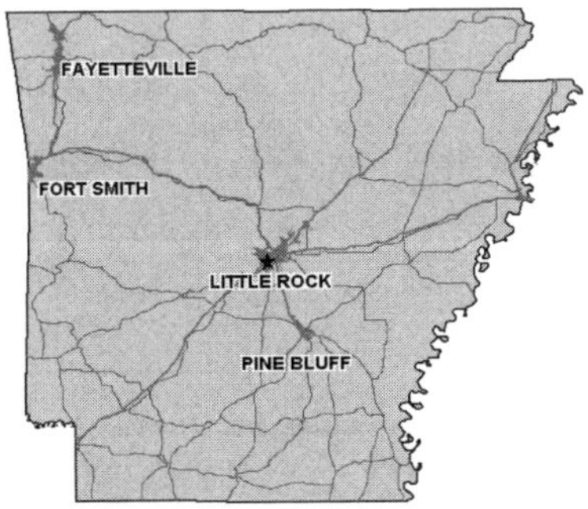

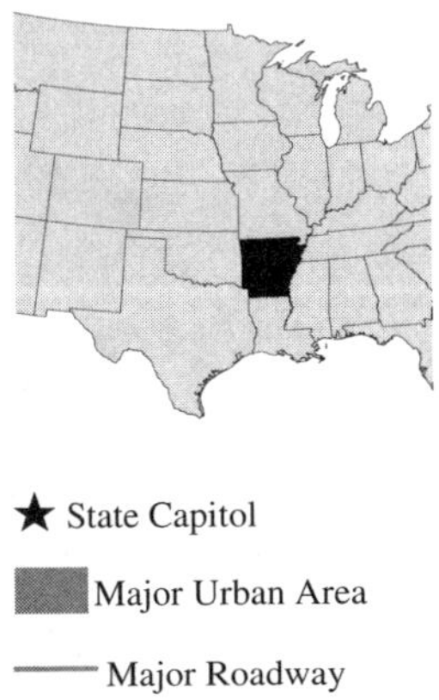

Demographic and Socioeconomic Profile

Demographics and Socioeconomic Figures			
Population and Households	**2000**	**2005**	**2006**
Total Population	2,673,400	2,701,431	2,810,872
Number of Households	1,042,696	1,087,542	1,103,428
Average Household Size	2.5	2.5	2.5
Age and Ethnicity			
Median Age	36.0	37.0	37.1
Population 18 Years of Age and Older	1,993,342	2,029,097	2,117,836
Population 65 Years of Age and Older	374,729	363,641	388,860
Caucasian Population	2,137,166	2,135,069	2,208,224
African-American Population	417,881	414,260	437,680
Hispanic Population	85,576	126,932	138,283
Asian Population	19,081	25,249	28,168
Foreign-Born Population (%)	2.8	3.7	3.8
Income			
Per Capita Personal Income (USD)	$21,925	$26,961	$28,444
Median Household Income (USD)	$32,182	$34,999	$36,599
Individuals Below Poverty Level	15.8%	17.2%	17.3%

Data: U.S. Census, American Community Survey; U.S. Department of Commerce, Bureau of Economic Analysis

or higher compared to 18.2% in Arkansas. Nationally, 9.9% hold professional or graduate degrees compared to 6.3% in Arkansas.

In fiscal year 2004–5, Arkansas had total tax revenues of $8.1 billion. The largest share was generated from sales and gross receipts taxes, followed by individual income taxes. The per capita tax burden in Arkansas was $2,905 for 2004–5, some $800 below the national average. In terms of business taxes, the state ranked fifteenth in a study from Anderson Economic Group. Forbes Magazine and the Tax Foundation ranked the state's business climate twenty-first and thirty-fifth, respectively, while ALEC ranked Arkansas fifteenth in its state competitiveness index. One is considered best for each ranking.

Population Projections

Year	2010	2015	2020	2025
Total Population	2,875,039	2,968,913	3,060,219	3,151,005
Median Age	37.9	38.6	39.4	39.8
Population 18 Years of Age and Older	2,172,383	2,247,849	2,322,453	2,395,591
Population 65 Years of Age and Older	412,152	467,880	531,028	599,028

Data: U.S. Census Bureau

Workforce and Industry Profile

Workforce

	2000	2005	2006
Civilian Labor Force	1,260,256	1,345,318	1,364,646
Labor Force Participation Rate	62.2%	63.5%	63.5%
Unemployment Rate	4.2%	5.1%	5.3%
Average Wage Per Job (USD)	$26,317	$29,750	$30,870
Education Attainment (Population 25 Years and Older)	**(%)**	**(%)**	**(%)**
High School Graduate or Higher	75.3	81.0	80.5
Bachelors Degree or Higher	16.6	18.9	18.2
Graduate or Professional Degree	5.7	6.3	6.3

Data: U.S. Census Bureau, American Community Survey; U.S. Department of Commerce, Bureau of Economic Analysis; U.S. Department of Labor, Bureau of Labor Statistics

Industry Overview

	1998	2004	2005
Total Employees	944,935	1,007,512	1,017,424
Total Payroll ($1,000s)	$21,764,625	$28,670,925	$30,185,779
Total Establishments	62,353	65,291	66,039
Establishments with 1–19 Employees	54,335	56,547	57,236
Establishments with 20–49 Employees	4,974	5,546	5,594
Establishments with 50–249 Employees	2,547	2,738	2,712
Establishments with 250–999 Employees	435	397	432
Establishments with 1,000+ Employees	62	63	65

Data: U.S. Census Bureau, County Business Patterns

Major Industries (Ranked by 2005 Employment; Payroll in $1,000s)				
Industry	1998 Employment	2005 Employment	1998 Payroll	2005 Payroll
Manufacturing	232,671	198,288	6,121,981	6,577,058
Health Care and Social Assistance	130,129	154,792	3,187,490	5,001,545
Retail Trade	134,134	140,465	2,072,154	2,724,653
Accommodation and Food Services	73,562	86,916	657,263	890,819
Transportation and Warehousing	39,313	61,474	1,180,877	2,037,033
Admin., Support, Waste Mngt., Remediation Services	51,425	50,044	819,087	985,672
Construction	43,475	49,959	1,097,864	1,634,994
Wholesale Trade	42,470	49,206	1,231,247	1,904,796
Other Services (except Public Admin.)	39,816	44,474	579,680	855,644
Finance and Insurance	32,334	37,092	1,045,075	1,496,807

Data: U.S. Census Bureau, County Business Patterns

Taxes and Business Climate

State and Local Taxes		
Combined Revenues ($1,000s)	2003–4	2004–5
Revenue from Property Taxes	1,100,938	1,172,261
Revenue from Sales and Gross Receipts Taxes	3,714,211	4,315,049
Revenue from Individual Income Taxes	1,688,156	1,875,065
Revenue from Corporate Income Taxes	181,830	277,315
Revenue from Other Taxes	288,030	414,236
Total Tax Revenue	6,973,165	8,053,926
Per Capita Taxes		
Property Tax Per Capita	400	423
Sales and Gross Receipts Tax Per Capita	1,351	1,557
Individual Income Tax Per Capita	614	676
Corporate Income Tax Per Capita	66	100
Other Taxes Per Capita	105	149
Total Taxes Per Capita	2,536	2,905

Data: U.S. Census Bureau; Anderson Economic Group, LLC

Business Climate Measures	
Anderson Economic Group: 2007 Business Tax Ranking (1 is Best)	15
Forbes Magazine: 2007 Best States for Business Ranking (1 is Best)	21
Tax Foundation: 2008 Business Tax Climate Ranking (1 is Best)	35
ALEC-Laffer 2007 Economic Competitiveness Ranking (1 is Best)	15
2003-04 Employer Firm Births	6,305
2003-04 Employer Firm Terminations	5,665

Data: Anderson Economic Group; Tax Foundation; Forbes Magazine; U.S. Census, Statistics of U.S. Businesses; American Legislative Exchange Council

Voting Behavior and Elected Officials

Voter Registration and Turnout (%)

	1992	1996	2000	2004
Registered Voters Who Voted	72.1	64.6	59.2	62.6
Citizens Age 18+ Who Voted	53.8	47.2	46.2	51.6

Data: Dave Leip's Atlas of U.S. Presidential Elections

Presidential Election Results (Nationwide Winner Listed First)

2004	Popular Vote (%)	Electoral Votes
George W. Bush (Republican, Incumbent)	54.3	6
John Kerry (Democrat)	44.6	0
Other	1.2	0
2000		
George W. Bush (Republican)	51.3	6
Albert Gore (Democrat)	45.9	0
Ralph Nader (Green)	1.5	0
Other	1.4	0
1996		
William Clinton (Democrat, Incumbent)	53.7	6
Robert Dole (Republican)	36.8	0
H. Ross Perot (Reformist)	7.9	0
Other	1.6	0
1992		
William Clinton (Democrat)	53.2	6
George H. W. Bush (Republican, Incumbent)	35.5	0
H. Ross Perot (Independent)	10.4	0
Other	0.9	0

Data: Dave Leip's Atlas of U.S. Presidential Elections

Governor and U.S. Congressional Seats				
Governor	**Party**	**Year Term Began**	**Term**	**Max. Consecutive Terms**
Mike Beebe	D	2007	First	2
U.S. Senators	**Party**	**Year Elected**	**Term Expires**	
Mark Pryor	D	2002	2009	
Blanche Lincoln	D	1998	2011	
U.S. Representatives		**Republican**	**Democrat**	**Other**
		1	3	0

Data: National Governors Association; U.S. Senate, Office of the Clerk; U.S. House of Representatives

Business and Economic Agencies

Agency	Website Address
Arkansas State Chamber of Commerce	www.statechamber-aia.dina.org
Arkansas Department of Economic Development	www.1800arkansas.com
Arkansas Small Business Dev. Center	www.asbdc.ualr.edu
Arkansas Secretary of State	www.sos.arkansas.gov/corp_ucc.html

Data: Various agency websites

California

With a population of 36.5 million people, California was the most populous state in the United States in 2006. From 2000 to 2006 the state's population increased by 2,585,901 and is projected to increase to 44.3 million by 2025. This 1.0% projected annual growth rate compares to the projected national average of 0.8%. The state's 2006 per capita personal income of $39,358 was higher compared to $37,283 in 2005 and tenth highest in the United States, some $2,729 above the national average. Per capita income in California grew at an average annual rate of 3.2% from 2000 to 2006, compared to 3.5% nationally.

California's largest industry in terms of 2005 employment was retail trade. The fastest growing industry was construction, with 4.8% annual employment growth from 1998 to 2005. The second fastest growing industry was professional, scientific, and technical services. The state's workforce is generally more educated than other states—80.1% of the state's adult population has graduated from high school, compared to an 84.1% national average; 29.0% hold a bachelor degree or higher (national average is 27.0%); and 10.4%

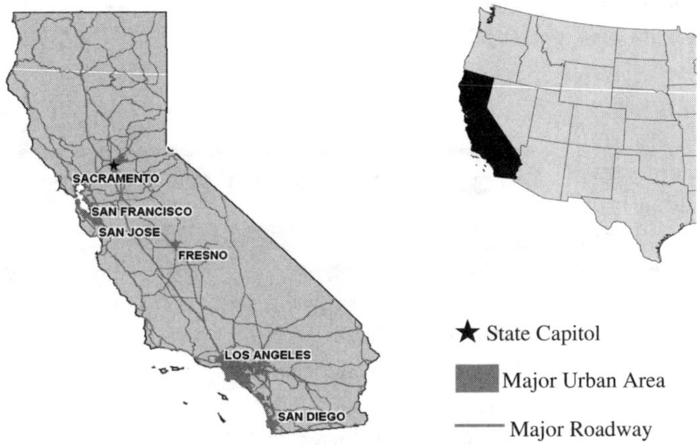

Demographic and Socioeconomic Profile

Demographics and Socioeconomic Figures			
Population and Households	**2000**	**2005**	**2006**
Total Population	33,871,648	35,278,768	36,457,549
Number of Households	11,502,870	12,097,894	12,151,227
Average Household Size	2.9	2.9	2.9
Age and Ethnicity			
Median Age	33.3	34.4	34.4
Population 18 Years of Age and Older	24,650,185	25,623,626	26,926,503
Population 65 Years of Age and Older	3,586,794	3,701,104	3,927,830
Caucasian Population	20,122,959	21,491,336	21,810,156
African-American Population	2,219,190	2,163,530	2,260,648
Hispanic Population	10,969,132	12,523,379	13,074,155
Asian Population	3,682,975	4,365,548	4,483,252
Foreign-Born Population (%)	26.2	27.2	27.2
Income			
Per Capita Personal Income (USD)	$32,463	$37,283	$39,358
Median Household Income (USD)	$47,493	$53,629	$56,645
Individuals Below Poverty Level	14.2%	13.3%	13.1%

Data: U.S. Census, American Community Survey; U.S. Department of Commerce, Bureau of Economic Analysis

hold professional or graduate degrees compared to the national average of 9.9%.

California's total tax revenue was $146.6 billion for fiscal year 2004–5, up from the 2003–4 total revenue of $133.9 billion. The largest share of tax revenue in 2004–5 was generated from sales and gross receipts taxes, followed by individual income taxes. On a per capita basis, residents of California paid taxes of $4,074, compared to the national average of $3,705 for 2004–5. In terms of business taxes, the state ranked twenty-eighth in a study from Anderson Economic Group. Forbes Magazine and the Tax Foundation ranked the state's business climate thirty-fourth and forty-seventh, respectively, while ALEC ranked California at forty-first in its state competitiveness index. One is considered best for each ranking.

Population Projections

Year	2010	2015	2020	2025
Total Population	38,067,134	40,123,232	42,206,743	44,305,177
Median Age	34.9	35.2	35.7	36.5
Population 18 Years of Age and Older	28,570,156	30,303,080	31,792,635	33,473,509
Population 65 Years of Age and Older	4,392,708	5,227,964	6,199,126	7,284,978

Data: U.S. Census Bureau

Workforce and Industry Profile

Workforce

	2000	2005	2006
Civilian Labor Force	16,857,578	17,740,379	17,901,874
Labor Force Participation Rate	67.1%	65.5%	65.2%
Unemployment Rate	4.9%	5.4%	4.9%
Average Wage Per Job (USD)	$41,186	$42,510	$44,180
Education Attainment (Population 25 Years and Older)	**(%)**	**(%)**	**(%)**
High School Graduate or Higher	76.8	80.1	80.1
Bachelors Degree or Higher	26.6	29.5	29.0
Graduate or Professional Degree	9.5	10.6	10.4

Data: U.S. Census Bureau, American Community Survey; U.S. Department of Commerce, Bureau of Economic Analysis; U.S. Department of Labor, Bureau of Labor Statistics

Industry Overview

	1998	2004	2005
Total Employees	12,026,989	13,264,918	13,382,470
Total Payroll ($1,000s)	$406,481,070	$554,736,012	$588,450,315
Total Establishments	773,925	841,774	860,866
Establishments with 1–19 Employees	662,920	719,347	738,392
Establishments with 20–49 Employees	69,203	76,375	75,940
Establishments with 50–249 Employees	36,809	40,554	40,949
Establishments with 250–999 Employees	4,372	4,755	4,837
Establishments with 1,000+ Employees	621	743	748

Data: U.S. Census Bureau, County Business Patterns

Major Industries (Ranked by 2005 Employment; Payroll in $1,000s)				
Industry	1998 Employment	2005 Employment	1998 Payroll	2005 Payroll
Retail Trade	1,382,460	1,651,973	29,103,980	43,416,017
Health Care and Social Assistance	1,269,893	1,507,717	39,962,820	63,344,431
Manufacturing	1,827,350	1,450,372	73,353,460	71,776,365
Accommodation and Food Services	1,052,065	1,285,138	13,134,254	19,887,731
Professional, Scientific, Technical Services	923,030	1,192,324	42,291,124	74,611,098
Admin., Support, Waste Mngt., Remediation Services	992,229	1,061,489	21,527,208	31,252,773
Construction	621,722	865,810	22,673,205	39,863,707
Wholesale Trade	769,617	816,186	32,448,343	47,831,555
Finance and Insurance	599,859	703,282	32,773,849	54,895,842
Other Services (except Public Admin.)	517,331	569,480	10,684,352	14,905,895

Data: U.S. Census Bureau, County Business Patterns

Taxes and Business Climate

State and Local Taxes		
Combined Revenues ($1,000s)	**2003–4**	**2004–5**
Revenue from Property Taxes	34,499,304	34,058,299
Revenue from Sales and Gross Receipts Taxes	45,193,487	49,026,218
Revenue from Individual Income Taxes	36,398,983	42,992,007
Revenue from Corporate Income Taxes	6,925,916	8,670,066
Revenue from Other Taxes	10,875,934	11,870,297
Total Tax Revenue	133,893,624	146,616,887
Per Capita Taxes		
Property Tax Per Capita	963	946
Sales and Gross Receipts Tax Per Capita	1,261	1,362
Individual Income Tax Per Capita	1,016	1,195
Corporate Income Tax Per Capita	193	241
Other Taxes Per Capita	303	330
Total Taxes Per Capita	3,736	4,074

Data: U.S. Census Bureau; Anderson Economic Group, LLC

Business Climate Measures	
Anderson Economic Group: 2007 Business Tax Ranking (1 is Best)	28
Forbes Magazine: 2007 Best States for Business Ranking (1 is Best)	34
Tax Foundation: 2008 Business Tax Climate Ranking (1 is Best)	47
ALEC-Laffer 2007 Economic Competitiveness Ranking (1 is Best)	41
2003–4 Employer Firm Births	91,201
2003–4 Employer Firm Terminations	83,731

Data: Anderson Economic Group; Tax Foundation; Forbes Magazine; U.S. Census, Statistics of U.S. Businesses; American Legislative Exchange Council

Voting Behavior and Elected Officials

Voter Registration and Turnout (%)

	1992	1996	2000	2004
Registered Voters Who Voted	73.7	64.0	69.8	75.0
Citizens Age 18+ Who Voted	49.1	43.9	44.5	47.7

Data: Dave Leip's Atlas of U.S. Presidential Elections

Presidential Election Results (Nationwide Winner Listed First)

2004	Popular Vote (%)	Electoral Votes
George W. Bush (Republican, Incumbent)	44.4	0
John Kerry (Democrat)	54.3	55
Other	1.3	0
2000		
George W. Bush (Republican)	41.7	0
Albert Gore (Democrat)	53.5	54
Ralph Nader (Green)	3.8	0
Other	1.1	0
1996		
William Clinton (Democrat, Incumbent)	51.1	54
Robert Dole (Republican)	38.2	0
H. Ross Perot (Reformist)	7.0	0
Other	3.7	0
1992		
William Clinton (Democrat)	46.0	54
George H. W. Bush (Republican, Incumbent)	32.6	0
H. Ross Perot (Independent)	20.6	0
Other	0.8	0

Data: Dave Leip's Atlas of U.S. Presidential Elections

Governor and U.S. Congressional Seats				
Governor	**Party**	**Year Term Began**	**Term**	**Max. Consecutive Terms**
Arnold Schwarzenegger	R	2007	Second	2
U.S. Senators	**Party**	**Year Elected**	**Term Expires**	
Barbara Boxer	D	1992	2011	
Dianne Feinstein	D	1992	2013	
U.S. Representatives		**Republican**	**Democrat**	**Other**
		19	34	0

Data: National Governors Association; U.S. Senate, Office of the Clerk; U.S. House of Representatives

Business and Economic Agencies

Agency	Website Address
California Chamber of Commerce	www.calchamber.com
California Association for Local Economic Development	www.caled.org
California Small Business Dev. Center	sbdc.ucmerced.edu
California Secretary of State	www.ss.ca.gov

Data: Various agency websites

Colorado

In 2006, Colorado had a population of 4.8 million people, making it the eighth most populous state in the country. The state's population increased by 452,116 people from 2000 to 2006, and is projected to increase to 5.5 million by 2025. The 0.8% projected annual growth rate is equal to the national average. Per capita personal income in Colorado was $39,587 in 2006, up from $37,702 in 2005. For 2006, this was $2,958 above the national average and the eighth highest in the country. The state's per capita income grew at an average annual rate of 2.9% from 2000 to 2006, compared to 3.5% nationally.

The state's workforce generally has more education than other states—88.1% of the state's adult population has graduated from high school, compared to an 84.1% national average; 34.4% hold a bachelor degree or higher (national average is 27.0%); and 12.4% hold professional or graduate degrees (national average is 9.9%). In 2005, the state's largest industry in terms of employment was retail trade, followed by accommodation and food services. The fastest growing industry was professional, scientific, and technical services, with 4.0%

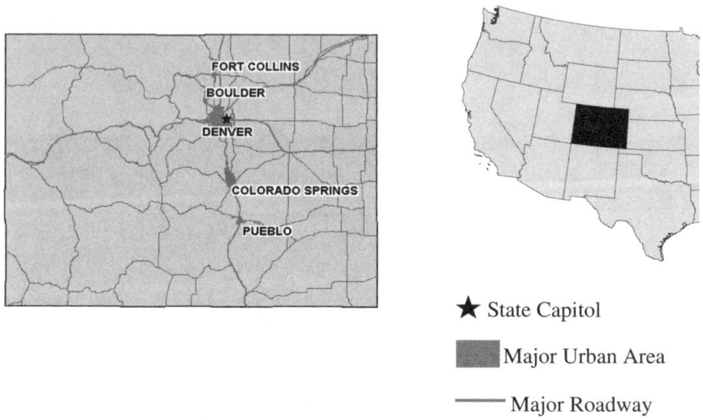

Demographic and Socioeconomic Profile

Demographics and Socioeconomic Figures			
Population and Households	**2000**	**2005**	**2006**
Total Population	4,301,261	4,562,244	4,753,377
Number of Households	1,658,238	1,819,037	1,846,988
Average Household Size	2.5	2.5	2.5
Age and Ethnicity			
Median Age	34.3	34.7	35.4
Population 18 Years of Age and Older	3,204,471	3,386,081	3,583,734
Population 65 Years of Age and Older	415,782	442,897	476,885
Caucasian Population	3,558,579	3,809,054	3,934,971
African-American Population	159,279	165,729	177,902
Hispanic Population	735,099	891,614	934,410
Asian Population	93,306	117,506	133,079
Foreign-Born Population (%)	8.6	10.1	10.3
Income			
Per Capita Personal Income (USD)	$33,371	$37,702	$39,587
Median Household Income (USD)	$47,203	$50,652	$52,015
Individuals Below Poverty Level	9.3%	11.1%	12.0%

Data: U.S. Census, American Community Survey; U.S. Department of Commerce, Bureau of Economic Analysis

annual employment growth from 1998 to 2005.

In fiscal year 2004–5, Colorado had total tax revenues of $15.7 billion. The largest share was generated from sales and gross receipts taxes, followed by property taxes. The per capita tax burden in Colorado was $3,355 for 2004–5, some $350 below the national average, and a $186 increase from 2003–4. In terms of business taxes, Colorado ranked thirteenth in a study from Anderson Economic Group. The state's business climate was ranked eighth by Forbes Magazine and thirteenth by the Tax Foundation. Colorado was ranked seventh by ALEC in its state competitiveness index. One is considered best for each ranking.

Population Projections

Year	2010	2015	2020	2025
Total Population	4,831,554	5,049,493	5,278,867	5,522,803
Median Age	35.7	35.9	36.0	36.0
Population 18 Years of Age and Older	3,642,971	3,793,139	3,951,400	4,128,803
Population 65 Years of Age and Older	517,419	627,408	750,903	869,646

Data: U.S. Census Bureau

Workforce and Industry Profile

Workforce

	2000	2005	2006
Civilian Labor Force	2,364,990	2,568,101	2,651,718
Labor Force Participation Rate	72.5%	72.3%	73.1%
Unemployment Rate	2.7%	5.1%	4.3%
Average Wage Per Job (USD)	$37,168	$40,280	$41,450
Education Attainment (population 25 years and older)	**(%)**	**(%)**	**(%)**
High School Graduate or Higher	86.9	88.7	88.1
Bachelors Degree or Higher	32.7	35.5	34.4
Graduate or Professional Degree	11.1	12.3	12.4

Data: U.S. Census Bureau, American Community Survey; U.S. Department of Commerce, Bureau of Economic Analysis; U.S. Department of Labor, Bureau of Labor Statistics

Industry Overview

	1998	2004	2005
Total Employees	1,757,628	1,908,508	1,936,264
Total Payroll ($1,000s)	$53,790,978	$71,579,086	$75,525,841
Total Establishments	130,354	147,314	151,070
Establishments with 1–19 Employees	114,141	129,662	133,125
Establishments with 20–49 Employees	10,144	11,156	11,317
Establishments with 50–249 Employees	5,370	5,753	5,876
Establishments with 250–999 Employees	602	638	648
Establishments with 1,000+ Employees	97	105	104

Data: U.S. Census Bureau, County Business Patterns

Major Industries (Ranked by 2005 Employment; Payroll in $1,000s)				
Industry	1998 Employment	2005 Employment	1998 Payroll	2005 Payroll
Retail Trade	232,581	249,433	4,667,472	6,046,900
Accommodation and Food Services	192,632	222,283	2,208,219	3,136,250
Health Care and Social Assistance	180,801	221,956	5,267,467	8,294,247
Admin., Support, Waste Mngt., Remediation Services	150,768	170,950	3,550,768	5,258,194
Professional, Scientific, Technical Services	117,740	155,267	5,631,574	9,458,401
Construction	132,921	152,212	4,582,355	6,620,283
Manufacturing	173,403	135,832	6,555,826	6,279,451
Finance and Insurance	97,679	102,599	4,292,298	6,280,715
Wholesale Trade	92,992	98,511	3,735,494	5,635,317
Other Services (except Public Admin.)	83,161	94,085	1,666,738	2,272,356

Data: U.S. Census Bureau, County Business Patterns

Taxes and Business Climate

State and Local Taxes		
Combined Revenues ($1,000s)	2003–4	2004–5
Revenue from Property Taxes	4,722,286	4,940,398
Revenue from Sales and Gross Receipts Taxes	5,390,069	5,696,742
Revenue from Individual Income Taxes	3,413,891	3,770,736
Revenue from Corporate Income Taxes	239,591	315,834
Revenue from Other Taxes	815,725	957,111
Total Tax Revenue	14,581,562	15,680,821
Per Capita Taxes		
Property Tax Per Capita	1,026	1,057
Sales and Gross Receipts Tax Per Capita	1,171	1,219
Individual Income Tax Per Capita	742	807
Corporate Income Tax Per Capita	52	68
Other Taxes Per Capita	177	205
Total Taxes Per Capita	3,169	3,355

Data: U.S. Census Bureau; Anderson Economic Group, LLC

Business Climate Measures	
Anderson Economic Group: 2007 Business Tax Ranking (1 is Best)	13
Forbes Magazine: 2007 Best States for Business Ranking (1 is Best)	8
Tax Foundation: 2008 Business Tax Climate Ranking (1 is Best)	13
ALEC-Laffer 2007 Economic Competitiveness Ranking (1 is Best)	7
2003–4 Employer Firm Births	16,771
2003–4 Employer Firm Terminations	14,690

Data: Anderson Economic Group; Tax Foundation; Forbes Magazine; U.S. Census, Statistics of U.S. Businesses; American Legislative Exchange Council

Voting Behavior and Elected Officials

Voter Registration and Turnout (%)

	1992	1996	2000	2004
Registered Voters Who Voted	78.3	66.1	65.9	88.6
Citizens Age 18+ Who Voted	62.7	52.8	54.3	62.7

Data: Dave Leip's Atlas of U.S. Presidential Elections

Presidential Election Results (Nationwide Winner Listed First)

2004	Popular Vote (%)	Electoral Votes
George W. Bush (Republican, Incumbent)	51.7	9
John Kerry (Democrat)	47.0	0
Other	1.3	0
2000		
George W. Bush (Republican)	50.8	8
Albert Gore (Democrat)	42.4	0
Ralph Nader (Green)	5.3	0
Other	1.6	0
1996		
William Clinton (Democrat, Incumbent)	44.4	0
Robert Dole (Republican)	45.8	8
H. Ross Perot (Reformist)	6.6	0
Other	3.2	0
1992		
William Clinton (Democrat)	40.1	8
George H. W. Bush (Republican, Incumbent)	35.9	0
H. Ross Perot (Independent)	23.3	0
Other	0.7	0

Data: Dave Leip's Atlas of U.S. Presidential Elections

Governor and U.S. Congressional Seats				
Governor	**Party**	**Year Term Began**	**Term**	**Max. Consecutive Terms**
Bill Ritter Jr.	D	2007	First	2
U.S. Senators	**Party**	**Year Elected**	**Term Expires**	
Wayne Allard	R	1996	2009	
Ken Salazar	D	2004	2011	
U.S. Representatives		**Republican**	**Democrat**	**Other**
		3	4	0

Data: National Governors Association; U.S. Senate, Office of the Clerk; U.S. House of Representatives

Business and Economic Agencies

Agency	Website Address
Colorado Association of Commerce and Industry	www.cochamber.com
Colorado Office of Economic Development	www.state.co.us/oed
Colorado Small Business Dev. Center	www.coloradosbdc.org
Colorado Secretary of State	www.sos.state.co.us

Data: Various agency websites

Connecticut

Connecticut, located in the New England region of the United States, had a population of 3.5 million people in 2006, making it the twenty-second most populous state. The state's population increased by 99,224 people from 2000 to 2006, and is projected to increase to 3.7 million by 2025. This 0.27% projected annual growth rate compares to the projected national average of 0.8%. Per capita personal income in Connecticut was $50,787 in 2006, up from $47,701 in 2005. For 2006, this was the highest in the country and $14,158 above the national average. From 2000 to 2006 per capita income in Connecticut grew at an average annual rate of 3.5%, equal to the national growth rate.

In 2005, the state's largest industry in terms of employment was health care and social assistance, followed by retail trade. The fastest growing industry was accommodation and food services, with 4.3% annual employment growth from 1998 to 2005. The state's workforce is generally more educated than other states—88.0% of the state's adult population has graduated from high school, compared to an 84.1%

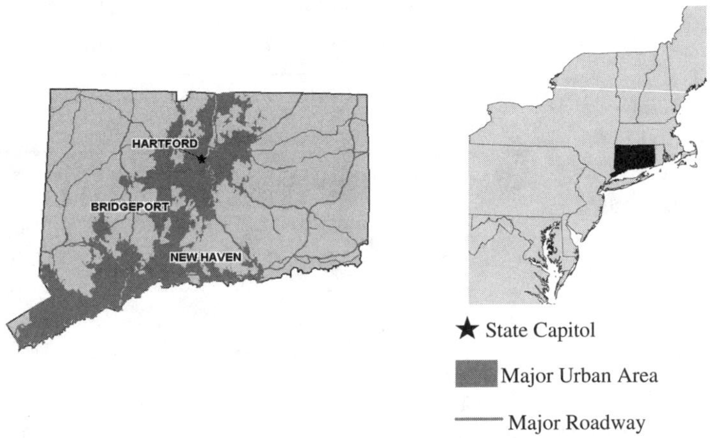

Demographic and Socioeconomic Profile

Demographics and Socioeconomic Figures			
Population and Households	**2000**	**2005**	**2006**
Total Population	3,405,565	3,394,751	3,504,809
Number of Households	1,301,670	1,323,838	1,325,443
Average Household Size	2.5	2.6	2.6
Age and Ethnicity			
Median Age	37.4	39.3	39.1
Population 18 Years of Age and Older	2,565,991	2,563,861	2,686,943
Population 65 Years of Age and Older	469,287	442,579	470,465
Caucasian Population	2,777,794	2,756,081	2,800,344
African-American Population	305,902	309,769	332,711
Hispanic Population	318,947	371,425	391,935
Asian Population	82,277	108,644	117,054
Foreign-Born Population (%)	10.9	12.5	12.9
Income			
Per Capita Personal Income (USD)	$41,489	$47,701	$50,787
Median Household Income (USD)	$53,935	$60,941	$63,422
Individuals Below Poverty Level	7.9%	8.3%	8.3%

Data: U.S. Census, American Community Survey; U.S. Department of Commerce, Bureau of Economic Analysis

national average. Nationally, an average of 27.0% hold a bachelor degree or higher compared to 33.7% in Connecticut. Nationally, 9.9% hold professional or graduate degrees compared to 14.4% in Connecticut.

In fiscal year 2004–5, Connecticut had total tax revenues of $18.9 billion. The largest share was generated from property taxes, followed by sales and gross receipts taxes. The per capita tax burden in Connecticut was $5,420 for 2004–5, some $1,715 above the national average. In terms of business taxes, the state ranked fifth in a study from Anderson Economic Group. Forbes Magazine and the Tax Foundation ranked the state's business climate thirty-first and thirty-eighth, respectively, while ALEC ranked Connecticut thirty-ninth in its state competitiveness index. One is considered best for each ranking.

Population Projections

Year	2010	2015	2020	2025
Total Population	3,577,490	3,635,414	3,675,650	3,691,016
Median Age	39.6	39.6	39.7	40.3
Population 18 Years of Age and Older	2,763,482	2,828,539	2,859,305	2,864,095
Population 65 Years of Age and Older	515,621	577,083	642,541	723,326

Data: U.S. Census Bureau

Workforce and Industry Profile

Workforce

	2000	2005	2006
Civilian Labor Force	1,736,831	1,822,874	1,844,235
Labor Force Participation Rate	66.9%	67.3%	67.6%
Unemployment Rate	2.3%	4.9%	4.3%
Average Wage Per Job (USD)	$45,486	$44,860	$45,970
Education Attainment (Population 25 Years and Older)	**(%)**	**(%)**	**(%)**
High School Graduate or Higher	84.0	87.9	88.0
Bachelors Degree or Higher	31.4	34.9	33.7
Graduate or Professional Degree	13.3	15.0	14.4

Data: U.S. Census Bureau, American Community Survey; U.S. Department of Commerce, Bureau of Economic Analysis; U.S. Department of Labor, Bureau of Labor Statistics

Industry Overview

	1998	2004	2005
Total Employees	1,493,964	1,537,461	1,529,827
Total Payroll ($1,000s)	$58,225,763	$72,848,717	$75,605,605
Total Establishments	92,362	91,611	93,561
Establishments with 1–19 Employees	79,965	79,887	80,422
Establishments with 20–49 Employees	7,451	8,035	7,992
Establishments with 50–249 Employees	4,315	4,492	4,549
Establishments with 250–999 Employees	538	498	508
Establishments with 1,000+ Employees	93	99	90

Data: U.S. Census Bureau, County Business Patterns

Major Industries (Ranked by 2005 Employment; Payroll in $1,000s)				
Industry	1998 Employment	2005 Employment	1998 Payroll	2005 Payroll
Health Care and Social Assistance	211,359	238,784	6,617,997	9,326,294
Retail Trade	189,957	198,459	3,989,688	5,083,890
Manufacturing	246,125	185,259	10,779,212	9,766,644
Finance and Insurance	122,463	133,285	9,087,074	15,586,173
Accommodation and Food Services	95,866	128,777	1,208,849	2,374,481
Admin., Support, Waste Mngt., Remediation Services	98,890	102,454	2,434,799	3,185,310
Professional, Scientific, Technical Services	78,060	99,651	4,410,149	6,581,420
Wholesale Trade	73,082	80,024	3,804,026	4,873,666
Other Services (except Public Admin.)	61,578	63,487	1,356,837	1,673,759
Construction	60,041	62,362	2,531,796	3,385,312

Data: U.S. Census Bureau, County Business Patterns

Taxes and Business Climate

State and Local Taxes		
Combined Revenues ($1,000s)	**2003–4**	**2004–5**
Revenue from Property Taxes	6,801,676	7,155,644
Revenue from Sales and Gross Receipts Taxes	4,900,376	5,128,163
Revenue from Individual Income Taxes	4,319,546	5,033,442
Revenue from Corporate Income Taxes	379,822	574,984
Revenue from Other Taxes	818,694	1,004,579
Total Tax Revenue	17,220,114	18,896,812
Per Capita Taxes		
Property Tax Per Capita	1,944	2,052
Sales and Gross Receipts Tax Per Capita	1,401	1,471
Individual Income Tax Per Capita	1,235	1,444
Corporate Income Tax Per Capita	109	165
Other Taxes Per Capita	234	288
Total Taxes Per Capita	4,921	5,420

Data: U.S. Census Bureau; Anderson Economic Group, LLC

Business Climate Measures

Anderson Economic Group: 2007 Business Tax Ranking (1 is Best)	5
Forbes Magazine: 2007 Best States for Business Ranking (1 is Best)	31
Tax Foundation: 2008 Business Tax Climate Ranking (1 is Best)	38
ALEC-Laffer 2007 Economic Competitiveness Ranking (1 is Best)	39
2003–4 Employer Firm Births	8,024
2003–4 Employer Firm Terminations	7,215

Data: Anderson Economic Group; Tax Foundation; Forbes Magazine; U.S. Census, Statistics of U.S. Businesses; American Legislative Exchange Council

Voting Behavior and Elected Officials

Voter Registration and Turnout (%)

	1992	1996	2000	2004
Registered Voters Who Voted	82.4	74.0	76.8	77.2
Citizens Age 18+ Who Voted	63.8	56.2	56.9	59.6

Data: Dave Leip's Atlas of U.S. Presidential Elections

Presidential Election Results (Nationwide Winner Listed First)

2004	Popular Vote (%)	Electoral Votes
George W. Bush (Republican, Incumbent)	44.0	0
John Kerry (Democrat)	54.3	7
Other	1.7	0
2000		
George W. Bush (Republican)	38.4	0
Albert Gore (Democrat)	55.9	8
Ralph Nader (Green)	4.4	0
Other	1.2	0
1996		
William Clinton (Democrat, Incumbent)	52.8	8
Robert Dole (Republican)	34.7	0
H. Ross Perot (Reformist)	10.0	0
Other	2.5	0
1992		
William Clinton (Democrat)	42.2	8
George H. W. Bush (Republican, Incumbent)	35.8	0
H. Ross Perot (Independent)	21.6	0
Other	0.4	0

Data: Dave Leip's Atlas of U.S. Presidential Elections

Governor and U.S. Congressional Seats				
Governor	Party	Year Term Began	Term	Max. Consecutive Terms
M. Jodi Rell	R	2007	Second	No limit
U.S. Senators	Party	Year Elected	Term Expires	
Christopher Dodd	D	1980	2011	
Joseph Lieberman	D	1988	2013	
U.S. Representatives		Republican	Democrat	Other
		1	4	0

Data: National Governors Association; U.S. Senate, Office of the Clerk; U.S. House of Representatives

Business and Economic Agencies

Agency	Website Address
Connecticut Business and Industry Association, Inc.	www.cbia.com
Department of Economic and Community Development	www.ct.gov/ecd
Connecticut Small Business Dev. Center	www.sbdc.uconn.edu
Connecticut Secretary of State, Commercial Recording Division	www.sots.ct.gov/CommercialRecording/Crdindex.html

Data: Various agency websites

Delaware

With a population of 853,476 people, Delaware was the sixth least populous state in the United States in 2006. From 2000 to 2006 the state's population increased by 69,876 people, and is projected to increase to 990,694 by 2025. This 0.8% projected annual growth rate is equal to the projected national average. The state's 2006 per capita personal income of $39,984 was higher compared to $37,702 in 2005 and twelfth highest in the United States, some $2,355 above the national average. Per capita income in Delaware grew at an average annual rate of 4.0% from 2000 to 2006, compared to 3.5% nationally.

Delaware's largest industry in terms of 2005 employment was retail trade. The fastest growing industry was professional, scientific, and technical services, with 6.9% annual employment growth from 1998 to 2005. The second fastest growing industry was wholesale trade. The state's workforce is generally more educated than other states—85.5% of the state's adult population has graduated from high school, compared to an 84.1% national average; 27% hold a bachelor degree or higher (equal to the national average); and 10.5% hold professional or graduate

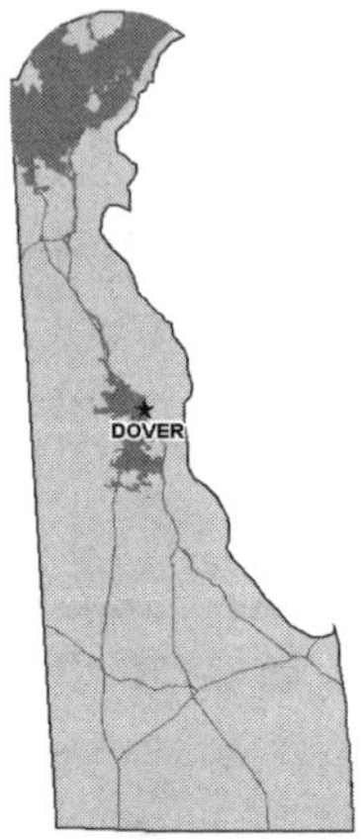

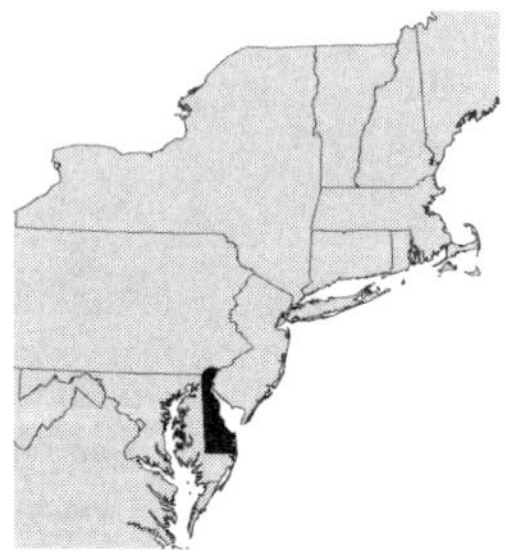

★ State Capitol

Major Urban Area

Major Roadway

Demographic and Socioeconomic Profile

Demographics and Socioeconomic Figures			
Population and Households	**2000**	**2005**	**2006**
Total Population	783,600	818,587	853,476
Number of Households	298,736	317,640	320,110
Average Household Size	2.5	2.6	2.6
Age and Ethnicity			
Median Age	36.0	37.9	37.5
Population 18 Years of Age and Older	589,638	623,124	649,740
Population 65 Years of Age and Older	101,670	106,791	114,554
Caucasian Population	584,684	602,213	615,638
African-American Population	148,823	163,052	176,845
Hispanic Population	37,321	50,218	53,836
Asian Population	16,053	22,376	24,413
Foreign-Born Population (%)	5.7	7.7	8.1
Income			
Per Capita Personal Income (USD)	$30,869	$37,080	$38,984
Median Household Income (USD)	$47,381	$52,499	$52,833
Individuals Below Poverty Level	9.2%	10.4%	11.1%

Data: U.S. Census, American Community Survey; U.S. Department of Commerce, Bureau of Economic Analysis

degrees compared to the national average of 9.9%.

Delaware's total tax revenue was $3.3 billion for fiscal year 2004–5, up from the 2003–4 total revenue of $3.0 billion. The largest share of tax revenue in 2004–5 was generated from taxes other than property, sales, gross receipts, individual income, and corporate income taxes, followed by individual income taxes. On a per capita basis, residents of Delaware paid taxes of $3,899, compared to the national average of $3,705 for 2004–5. In terms of business taxes, the state ranked first in a study from Anderson Economic Group. Forbes Magazine and the Tax Foundation ranked the state's business climate eleventh and ninth, respectively, while ALEC ranked Delaware twenty-second in its state competitiveness index. One is considered best for each ranking.

Population Projections

Year	2010	2015	2020	2025
Total Population	884,342	927,400	963,209	990,694
Median Age	39.4	40.5	41.5	42.8
Population 18 Years of Age and Older	682,134	717,862	747,886	772,682
Population 65 Years of Age and Older	124,972	148,682	176,121	208,599

Data: U.S. Census Bureau

Workforce and Industry Profile

Workforce

	2000	2005	2006
Civilian Labor Force	416,503	432,977	440,322
Labor Force Participation Rate	69.7%	66.9%	66.8%
Unemployment Rate	3.3%	4.0%	3.6%
Average Wage Per Job (USD)	$36,533	$39,190	$41,680
Education Attainment (Population 25 Years and Older)	**(%)**	**(%)**	**(%)**
High School Graduate or Higher	82.6	85.6	85.5
Bachelors Degree or Higher	25.0	27.6	27.0
Graduate or Professional Degree	9.4	11.1	10.5

Data: U.S. Census Bureau, American Community Survey; U.S. Department of Commerce, Bureau of Economic Analysis; U.S. Department of Labor, Bureau of Labor Statistics

Industry Overview

	1998	2004	2005
Total Employees	354,643	391,682	392,840
Total Payroll ($1,000s)	$11,831,134	$16,074,764	$16,875,311
Total Establishments	22,871	25,391	25,319
Establishments with 1–19 Employees	19,941	22,040	21,983
Establishments with 20–49 Employees	1,777	2,078	2,047
Establishments with 50–249 Employees	985	1,103	1,118
Establishments with 250–999 Employees	146	136	139
Establishments with 1,000+ Employees	22	34	32

Data: U.S. Census Bureau, County Business Patterns

Major Industries (Ranked by 2005 Employment; Payroll in $1,000s)				
Industry	1998 Employment	2005 Employment	1998 Payroll	2005 Payroll
Retail Trade	47,631	54,524	871,384	1,298,046
Health Care and Social Assistance	41,202	51,444	1,279,822	2,085,645
Finance and Insurance	41,611	40,894	1,909,720	2,896,158
Manufacturing	43,511	35,624	1,632,155	1,661,304
Accommodation and Food Services	25,867	31,094	313,948	483,637
Professional, Scientific, Technical Services	17,043	27,202	824,062	1,895,569
Admin., Support, Waste Mngt., Remediation Services	26,117	24,941	488,195	654,180
Construction	20,367	23,925	676,309	1,003,802
Wholesale Trade	14,839	20,040	789,212	1,399,099
Mngt. of Companies and Enterprises	20,243	18,164	1,288,596	1,307,311

Data: U.S. Census Bureau, County Business Patterns

Taxes and Business Climate

State and Local Taxes		
Combined Revenues ($1,000s)	**2003–4**	**2004–5**
Revenue from Property Taxes	453,198	485,848
Revenue from Sales and Gross Receipts Taxes	394,434	405,451
Revenue from Individual Income Taxes	827,984	932,254
Revenue from Corporate Income Taxes	217,768	248,869
Revenue from Other Taxes	1,100,944	1,204,965
Total Tax Revenue	2,994,328	3,277,387
Per Capita Taxes		
Property Tax Per Capita	546	578
Sales and Gross Receipts Tax Per Capita	475	482
Individual Income Tax Per Capita	998	1,109
Corporate Income Tax Per Capita	262	296
Other Taxes Per Capita	1,326	1,434
Total Taxes Per Capita	3,608	3,899

Data: U.S. Census Bureau; Anderson Economic Group, LLC

Business Climate Measures

Anderson Economic Group: 2007 Business Tax Ranking (1 is Best)	1
Forbes Magazine: 2007 Best States for Business Ranking (1 is Best)	11
Tax Foundation: 2008 Business Tax Climate Ranking (1 is Best)	9
ALEC-Laffer 2007 Economic Competitiveness Ranking (1 is Best)	22
2003–4 Employer Firm Births	2,682
2003–4 Employer Firm Terminations	2,160

Data: Anderson Economic Group; Tax Foundation; Forbes Magazine; U.S. Census, Statistics of U.S. Businesses; American Legislative Exchange Council

Voting Behavior and Elected Officials

Voter Registration and Turnout (%)

	1992	1996	2000	2004
Registered Voters Who Voted	84.7	64.2	65.1	67.7
Citizens Age 18+ Who Voted	55.2	49.4	55.6	60.6

Data: Dave Leip's Atlas of U.S. Presidential Elections

Presidential Election Results (Nationwide Winner Listed First)

2004	Popular Vote (%)	Electoral Votes
George W. Bush (Republican, Incumbent)	45.8	0
John Kerry (Democrat)	53.4	3
Other	0.9	0
2000		
George W. Bush (Republican)	41.9	0
Albert Gore (Democrat)	55.0	3
Ralph Nader (Green)	2.5	0
Other	0.6	0
1996		
William Clinton (Democrat, Incumbent)	51.8	3
Robert Dole (Republican)	36.6	0
H. Ross Perot (Reformist)	10.6	0
Other	1.0	0
1992		
William Clinton (Democrat)	43.5	3
George H. W. Bush (Republican, Incumbent)	35.3	0
H. Ross Perot (Independent)	20.4	0
Other	0.7	0

Data: Dave Leip's Atlas of U.S. Presidential Elections

Governor and U.S. Congressional Seats

Governor	Party	Year Term Began	Term	Max. Consecutive Terms
Ruth Ann Minner	D	2005	Second	2
U.S. Senators	**Party**	**Year Elected**	**Term Expires**	
Joseph R. Biden Jr.	D	1972	2009	
Thomas Carper	D	2000	2013	
U.S. Representatives		**Republican**	**Democrat**	**Other**
		1	0	0

Data: National Governors Association; U.S. Senate, Office of the Clerk; U.S. House of Representatives

Business and Economic Agencies

Agency	Website Address
Delaware State Chamber of Commerce	www.dscc.com
Delaware Economic Development Office	www.state.de.us/dedo/default.shtml
Delaware Small Business Dev. Center	www.delawaresbdc.org
Delaware Division of Corporations	www.state.de.us/corp

Data: Various agency websites

Florida

Florida is located in the Southeast region of the United States and had a population of 18 million people in 2006, making it the fourth most populous state. The state's population increased by 2,107,511 people from 2000 to 2006, and is projected to increase to 25.9 million by 2025. This 1.9% projected annual growth rate is above the national average of 0.8%. Per capita personal income in Florida was $36,665 in 2006, up from $34,712 in 2005. For 2006, this was $36 above the national average and the twentieth highest in the country. The state's per capita income grew at an average annual rate of 4.3% from 2000 to 2006, compared to 3.5% nationally.

The state's workforce generally has less education than other states—84.6% of the state's adult population has graduated from high school, compared to an 84.1% national average; 25.3% hold a bachelor degree or higher (national average is 27.0%); and 8.9% hold professional or graduate degrees (national average is 9.9%). In 2005, the state's largest industry in terms of employment was administration, support, waste management,

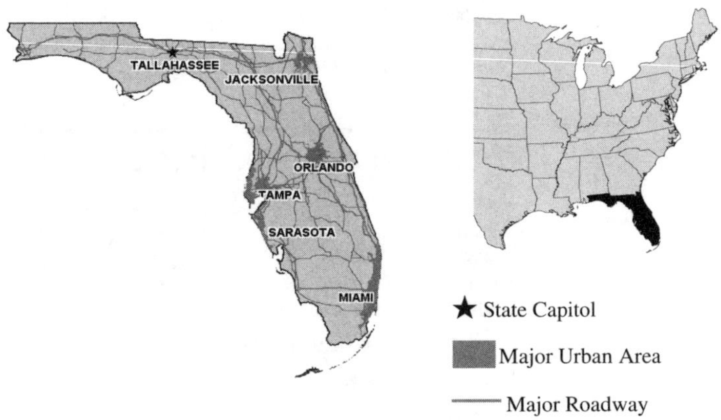

Demographic and Socioeconomic Profile

Demographics and Socioeconomic Figures			
Population and Households	**2000**	**2005**	**2006**
Total Population	15,982,378	17,382,511	18,089,889
Number of Households	6,337,929	7,048,800	7,106,042
Average Household Size	2.5	2.5	2.5
Age and Ethnicity			
Median Age	38.7	39.5	39.8
Population 18 Years of Age and Older	12,347,806	13,335,661	14,071,245
Population 65 Years of Age and Older	2,806,137	2,881,213	3,034,117
Caucasian Population	12,463,302	13,341,532	13,767,248
African-American Population	2,312,105	2,613,628	2,778,549
Hispanic Population	2,680,314	3,414,414	3,642,989
Asian Population	264,377	371,385	393,427
Foreign-Born Population (%)	16.7	18.5	18.9
Income			
Per Capita Personal Income (USD)	$28,509	$34,712	$36,665
Median Household Income (USD)	$38,819	$42,433	$45,495
Individuals Below Poverty Level	12.5%	12.8%	12.6%

Data: U.S. Census, American Community Survey; U.S. Department of Commerce, Bureau of Economic Analysis

and remediation services, followed by retail trade. The fastest growing industry was also administration, support, waste management, and remediation services, with 8.4% annual growth from 1998 to 2005.

In fiscal year 2004–5, Florida had total tax revenues of $59.9 billion. The largest share was generated from sales and gross receipts taxes, followed by property taxes. The per capita tax burden in Florida was $3,375 for 2004–5, some $330 below the national average, and a $281 increase from 2003–4. In terms of business taxes, Florida ranked forty-first in a study from Anderson Economic Group. The state's business climate was ranked seventh by Forbes Magazine and fifth by the Tax Foundation. Florida was ranked fourteenth by ALEC in its state competitiveness index. One is considered best for each ranking.

Population Projections

Year	2010	2015	2020	2025
Total Population	19,251,691	21,204,132	23,406,525	25,912,458
Median Age	41.9	43.2	44.1	44.8
Population 18 Years of Age and Older	15,165,568	16,749,420	18,518,914	20,611,286
Population 65 Years of Age and Older	3,418,697	4,133,945	5,106,857	6,387,843

Data: U.S. Census Bureau

Workforce and Industry Profile

Workforce

	2000	2005	2006
Civilian Labor Force	7,869,690	8,710,827	8,988,611
Labor Force Participation Rate	63.0%	62.5%	63.2%
Unemployment Rate	3.8%	3.8%	3.3%
Average Wage Per Job (USD)	$30,560	$34,420	$35,820
Education Attainment (Population 25 Years and Older)	**(%)**	**(%)**	**(%)**
High School Graduate or Higher	79.9	84.6	84.6
Bachelors Degree or Higher	22.3	25.1	25.3
Graduate or Professional Degree	8.1	8.8	8.9

Data: U.S. Census Bureau, American Community Survey; U.S. Department of Commerce, Bureau of Economic Analysis; U.S. Department of Labor, Bureau of Labor Statistics

Industry Overview

	1998	2004	2005
Total Employees	5,756,353	6,864,987	7,107,378
Total Payroll ($1,000s)	$149,936,849	$219,794,114	$239,197,889
Total Establishments	420,638	484,938	504,662
Establishments with 1–19 Employees	371,384	429,069	447,764
Establishments with 20–49 Employees	29,930	33,891	34,320
Establishments with 50–249 Employees	17,086	19,351	19,890
Establishments with 250–999 Employees	1,890	2,242	2,291
Establishments with 1,000+ Employees	348	385	397

Data: U.S. Census Bureau, County Business Patterns

Major Industries (Ranked by 2005 Employment; Payroll in $1,000s)				
Industry	1998 Employment	2005 Employment	1998 Payroll	2005 Payroll
Admin., Support, Waste Mngt., Remediation Services	705,898	1,239,827	13,287,683	33,734,241
Retail Trade	872,391	987,307	15,636,653	23,452,267
Health Care and Social Assistance	740,828	866,420	21,829,102	32,749,098
Accommodation and Food Services	596,481	724,791	6,994,893	10,738,660
Construction	341,673	477,670	9,674,731	18,452,509
Professional, Scientific, Technical Services	318,814	422,953	13,047,144	21,899,141
Manufacturing	428,642	371,432	13,514,960	14,906,536
Finance and Insurance	302,704	370,990	12,522,788	20,227,493
Wholesale Trade	298,551	311,270	10,388,706	13,996,062
Other Services (except Public Admin.)	288,705	308,134	5,192,259	6,798,269

Data: U.S. Census Bureau, County Business Patterns

Taxes and Business Climate

State and Local Taxes		
Combined Revenues ($1,000s)	**2003–4**	**2004–5**
Revenue from Property Taxes	18,500,291	20,389,149
Revenue from Sales and Gross Receipts Taxes	27,407,756	29,785,839
Revenue from Individual Income Taxes	0	0
Revenue from Corporate Income Taxes	1,441,338	1,785,623
Revenue from Other Taxes	6,440,069	7,903,273
Total Tax Revenue	53,789,454	59,863,884
Per Capita Taxes		
Property Tax Per Capita	1,064	1,150
Sales and Gross Receipts Tax Per Capita	1,577	1,679
Individual Income Tax Per Capita	0	0
Corporate Income Tax Per Capita	83	101
Other Taxes Per Capita	370	446
Total Taxes Per Capita	3,094	3,375

Data: U.S. Census Bureau; Anderson Economic Group, LLC

Business Climate Measures	
Anderson Economic Group: 2007 Business Tax Ranking (1 is Best)	41
Forbes Magazine: 2007 Best States for Business Ranking (1 is Best)	7
Tax Foundation: 2008 Business Tax Climate Ranking (1 is Best)	5
ALEC-Laffer 2007 Economic Competitiveness Ranking (1 is Best)	14
2003–4 Employer Firm Births	65,983
2003–4 Employer Firm Terminations	48,429

Data: Anderson Economic Group; Tax Foundation; Forbes Magazine; U.S. Census, Statistics of U.S. Businesses; American Legislative Exchange Council

Voting Behavior and Elected Officials

Voter Registration and Turnout (%)

	1992	1996	2000	2004
Registered Voters Who Voted	81.2	65.7	68.1	73.9
Citizens Age 18+ Who Voted	50.2	48.0	48.3	58.1

Data: Dave Leip's Atlas of U.S. Presidential Elections

Presidential Election Results (Nationwide Winner Listed First)

2004	Popular Vote (%)	Electoral Votes
George W. Bush (Republican, Incumbent)	52.1	27
John Kerry (Democrat)	47.1	0
Other	0.8	0
2000		
George W. Bush (Republican)	48.9	25
Albert Gore (Democrat)	48.8	0
Ralph Nader (Green)	1.6	0
Other	0.7	0
1996		
William Clinton (Democrat, Incumbent)	48.0	25
Robert Dole (Republican)	42.3	0
H. Ross Perot (Reformist)	9.1	0
Other	0.5	0
1992		
William Clinton (Democrat)	39.0	0
George H. W. Bush (Republican, Incumbent)	40.9	25
H. Ross Perot (Independent)	19.8	0
Other	0.3	0

Data: Dave Leip's Atlas of U.S. Presidential Elections

Governor and U.S. Congressional Seats				
Governor	Party	Year Term Began	Term	Max. Consecutive Terms
Charlie Crist	R	2007	First	2
U.S. Senators	Party	Year Elected	Term Expires	
Mel Martinez	R	2004	2011	
Bill Nelson	D	2000	2013	
U.S. Representatives		Republican	Democrat	Other
		16	9	0

Data: National Governors Association; U.S. Senate, Office of the Clerk; U.S. House of Representatives

Business and Economic Agencies

Agency	Website Address
Florida Chamber of Commerce	www.flchamber.com
Governor's Office of Trade, Tourism, and Economic Development	www.flgov.com/otted_home
Florida Small Business Dev. Center	www.floridasbdc.com
Florida Department of State, Division of Corporations	www.sunbiz.org

Data: Various agency websites

Georgia

Georgia located in the South Atlantic region of the United States, had a population of 9.4 million people, making it the ninth most populous state in 2006. The state's population increased by 1,177,488 people from 2000 to 2006, and is projected to increase to 11.4 million by 2025. This 1.1% projected annual growth rate compares to the projected national average of 0.8%. Per capita personal income in Georgia was $32,025 in 2006, up from $31,088 in 2005. For 2006, this was fourteenth lowest in the country and $4,604 below the national average. From 2000 to 2006 per capita income in Georgia grew at an average annual rate of 2.3%, compared to 3.5% nationally.

In 2005, the state's largest industry in terms of employment was retail trade, followed by manufacturing. The fastest growing industry was professional, scientific, and technical services, with 3.3% annual employment growth from 1998 to 2005. The state's workforce is generally less educated than other states—82.2% of the state's adult population has graduated from high school, compared to an 84.1% national average. Nationally, an average of 27.0% hold a bachelor degree or higher compared to

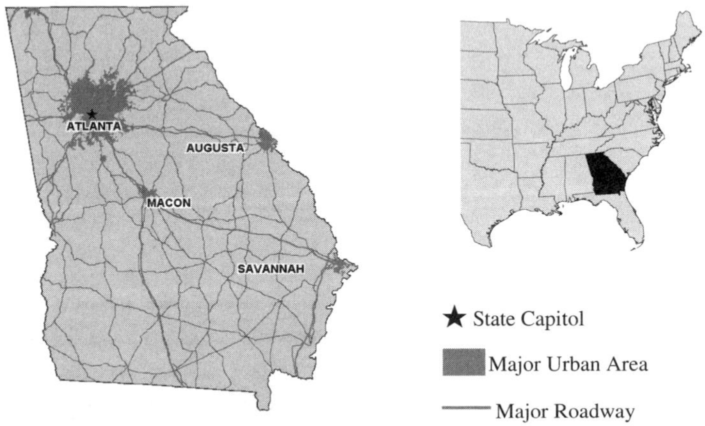

Demographic and Socioeconomic Profile

Demographics and Socioeconomic Figures

Population and Households	2000	2005	2006
Total Population	8,186,453	8,821,142	9,363,941
Number of Households	3,006,369	3,320,278	3,376,763
Average Household Size	2.6	2.7	2.7
Age and Ethnicity			
Median Age	33.4	34.3	34.6
Population 18 Years of Age and Older	6,020,679	6,468,467	6,911,716
Population 65 Years of Age and Older	787,906	811,503	906,879
Caucasian Population	5,327,175	5,516,920	5,816,513
African-American Population	2,342,110	2,571,396	2,794,300
Hispanic Population	429,976	625,028	696,146
Asian Population	171,463	240,832	254,899
Foreign-Born Population (%)	7.1	9.0	9.2
Income			
Per Capita Personal Income (USD)	$27,989	$31,088	$32,025
Median Household Income (USD)	$42,433	$45,604	$46,832
Individuals Below Poverty Level	13.0%	14.4%	14.7%

Data: U.S. Census, American Community Survey; U.S. Department of Commerce, Bureau of Economic Analysis

26.6% in Georgia. Nationally, 9.9% hold professional or graduate degrees compared to 9.2 in Georgia.

In fiscal year 2004–5, Georgia had total tax revenues of $27.5 billion. The largest share was generated from sales and gross receipts taxes, followed by property taxes. The per capita tax burden in Georgia was $3,018 for 2004–5, some $687 below the national average. In terms of business taxes, the state ranked tenth in a study from Anderson Economic Group. Forbes Magazine and the Tax Foundation ranked the state's business climate fifteenth and twentieth, respectively, while ALEC ranked Georgia eighth in its state competitiveness index. One is considered best for each ranking.

Population Projections

Year	2010	2015	2020	2025
Total Population	9,589,080	10,230,578	10,843,753	11,438,622
Median Age	34.7	35.1	35.4	35.5
Population 18 Years of Age and Older	7,086,694	7,551,789	8,006,490	8,453,077
Population 65 Years of Age and Older	980,824	1,187,576	1,409,923	1,659,679

Data: U.S. Census Bureau

Workforce and Industry Profile

Workforce

	2000	2005	2006
Civilian Labor Force	4,242,889	4,622,105	4,741,860
Labor Force Participation Rate	69.6%	68.1%	68.0%
Unemployment Rate	3.5%	5.2%	4.6%
Average Wage Per Job (USD)	$34,214	$36,290	$37,150
Education Attainment (Population 25 Years and Older)	**(%)**	**(%)**	**(%)**
High School Graduate or Higher	78.6	82.8	82.2
Bachelors Degree or Higher	24.3	27.1	26.6
Graduate or Professional Degree	8.3	9.5	9.2

Data: U.S. Census Bureau, American Community Survey; U.S. Department of Commerce, Bureau of Economic Analysis; U.S. Department of Labor, Bureau of Labor Statistics

Industry Overview

	1998	2004	2005
Total Employees	3,198,950	3,452,451	3,489,046
Total Payroll ($1,000s)	$94,687,270	$121,341,653	$128,827,270
Total Establishments	194,213	214,714	220,528
Establishments with 1–19 Employees	166,186	183,593	189,331
Establishments with 20–49 Employees	17,122	19,120	19,192
Establishments with 50–249 Employees	9,306	10,399	10,363
Establishments with 250–999 Employees	1,403	1,395	1,442
Establishments with 1,000+ Employees	196	207	200

Data: U.S. Census Bureau, County Business Patterns

Major Industries (Ranked by 2005 Employment; Payroll in $1,000s)				
Industry	1998 Employment	2005 Employment	1998 Payroll	2005 Payroll
Retail Trade	431,806	474,458	7,798,334	10,225,754
Manufacturing	535,051	428,467	16,722,306	16,218,823
Health Care and Social Assistance	331,889	398,607	9,810,907	14,800,306
Accommodation and Food Services	273,389	336,804	3,035,725	4,341,413
Admin., Support, Waste Mngt., Remediation Services	261,555	318,109	5,596,097	8,823,966
Professional, Scientific, Technical Services	166,535	209,548	7,679,090	11,815,810
Construction	174,774	201,496	5,527,052	7,901,149
Wholesale Trade	193,112	200,693	8,167,514	10,510,976
Finance and Insurance	154,798	174,282	6,662,088	10,044,949
Other Services (except Public Admin.)	135,530	152,895	2,539,172	3,441,859

Data: U.S. Census Bureau, County Business Patterns

Taxes and Business Climate

State and Local Taxes		
Combined Revenues ($1,000s)	2003–4	2004–5
Revenue from Property Taxes	7,844,826	8,214,542
Revenue from Sales and Gross Receipts Taxes	9,422,758	10,137,348
Revenue from Individual Income Taxes	6,830,486	7,326,225
Revenue from Corporate Income Taxes	494,701	712,310
Revenue from Other Taxes	1,061,989	1,095,684
Total Tax Revenue	25,654,760	27,486,109
Per Capita Taxes		
Property Tax Per Capita	880	902
Sales and Gross Receipts Tax Per Capita	1,057	1,113
Individual Income Tax Per Capita	766	804
Corporate Income Tax Per Capita	55	78
Other Taxes Per Capita	119	120
Total Taxes Per Capita	2,877	3,018

Data: U.S. Census Bureau; Anderson Economic Group, LLC

Business Climate Measures

Anderson Economic Group: 2007 Business Tax Ranking (1 is Best)	10
Forbes Magazine: 2007 Best States for Business Ranking (1 is Best)	15
Tax Foundation: 2008 Business Tax Climate Ranking (1 is Best)	20
ALEC-Laffer 2007 Economic Competitiveness Ranking (1 is Best)	8
2003–4 Employer Firm Births	24,198
2003–4 Employer Firm Terminations	19,826

Data: Anderson Economic Group; Tax Foundation; Forbes Magazine; U.S. Census, Statistics of U.S. Businesses; American Legislative Exchange Council

Voting Behavior and Elected Officials

Voter Registration and Turnout (%)

	1992	1996	2000	2004
Registered Voters Who Voted	73.1	60.3	67.3	79.4
Citizens Age 18+ Who Voted	46.9	42.4	43.1	51.7

Data: Dave Leip's Atlas of U.S. Presidential Elections

Presidential Election Results (Nationwide Winner Listed First)

2004	Popular Vote (%)	Electoral Votes
George W. Bush (Republican, Incumbent)	58.0	15
John Kerry (Democrat)	41.4	0
Other	0.7	0
2000		
George W. Bush (Republican)	54.7	13
Albert Gore (Democrat)	43.0	0
Ralph Nader (Green)	0.5	0
Other	1.8	0
1996		
William Clinton (Democrat, Incumbent)	45.8	0
Robert Dole (Republican)	47.0	13
H. Ross Perot (Reformist)	6.4	0
Other	0.8	0
1992		
William Clinton (Democrat)	43.5	13
George H. W. Bush (Republican, Incumbent)	42.9	0
H. Ross Perot (Independent)	13.3	0
Other	0.3	0

Data: Dave Leip's Atlas of U.S. Presidential Elections

Governor and U.S. Congressional Seats				
Governor	**Party**	**Year Term Began**	**Term**	**Max. Consecutive Terms**
Sonny Perdue	R	2007	Second	2
U.S. Senators	**Party**	**Year Elected**	**Term Expires**	
Saxby Chambliss	R	2002	2009	
Johnny Isakson	R	2005	2011	
U.S. Representatives		**Republican**	**Democrat**	**Other**
		7	6	0

Data: National Governors Association; U.S. Senate, Office of the Clerk; U.S. House of Representatives

Business and Economic Agencies

Agency	Website Address
Georgia Chamber of Commerce	www.gachamber.com
Georgia Department of Economic Development	www.georgia.org
Georgia Small Business Dev. Center	www.sbdc.uga.edu
Georgia Secretary of State, Corporations Division	www.sos.state.ga.us/corporations

Data: Various agency websites

Hawaii

With a population of 1.3 million people, Hawaii was the ninth least populous state in the United States in 2006. From 2000 to 2006 the state's population increased by 73,961 people, and is projected to increase to 1.4 million by 2025. This 0.6% projected annual growth rate compares to the projected national average of 0.8%. The state's 2006 per capita personal income of $36,826 was higher compared to $34,818 in 2005 and eighteenth highest in the United States, some $197 above the national average. Per capita income in Hawaii grew at an average annual rate of 4.4% from 2000 to 2006, compared to 3.5% nationally.

Hawaii's largest industry in terms of 2005 employment was accommodation and food services. The fastest growing industry was professional, scientific, and technical services, with 5.4% annual employment growth from 1998 to 2005. The second fastest growing industry was construction. The state's workforce is generally more educated than other states—89.0% of the state's adult population has graduated from high school, compared to an 84.1% national average; 29.7% hold a bachelor degree

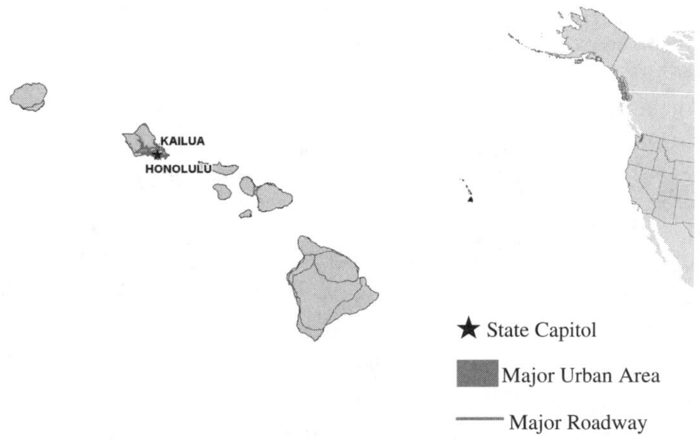

Demographic and Socioeconomic Profile

Demographics and Socioeconomic Figures			
Population and Households	**2000**	**2005**	**2006**
Total Population	1,211,537	1,238,158	1,285,498
Number of Households	403,240	430,007	432,632
Average Household Size	2.9	2.9	2.9
Age and Ethnicity			
Median Age	36.2	38.5	37.2
Population 18 Years of Age and Older	917,212	939,587	988,265
Population 65 Years of Age and Older	161,141	168,895	179,012
Caucasian Population	292,457	308,912	337,507
African-American Population	20,945	24,239	28,062
Hispanic Population	87,582	98,699	99,664
Asian Population	503,950	520,564	512,995
Foreign-Born Population (%)	17.5	17.2	16.3
Income			
Per Capita Personal Income (USD)	$28,422	$34,818	$36,826
Median Household Income (USD)	$49,820	$58,112	$61,160
Individuals Below Poverty Level	10.7%	9.8%	9.3%

Data: U.S. Census, American Community Survey; U.S. Department of Commerce, Bureau of Economic Analysis

or higher (national average is 27.0%); and 9.8% hold professional or graduate degrees compared to the national average of 9.9%.

Hawaii's total tax revenue was $5.5 billion for fiscal year 2004–5, up from the 2003–4 total revenue of $4.8 billion. The largest share of tax revenue in 2004–5 was generated from sales and gross receipts taxes, followed by individual income taxes. On a per capita basis, residents of Hawaii paid taxes of $4,358, compared to the national average of $3,705 for 2004–5. In terms of business taxes, the state ranked forty-fifth in a report by Anderson Economic Group. Forbes Magazine and the Tax Foundation ranked the state's business climate thirty-seventh and twenty-second respectively. ALEC ranked Hawaii forty-fifth in its state competitiveness index. One is considered best for each ranking.

Population Projections

Year	2010	2015	2020	2025
Total Population	1,340,674	1,385,952	1,412,373	1,438,720
Median Age	37.4	37.3	37.5	38.1
Population 18 Years of Age and Older	1,024,411	1,055,684	1,073,236	1,105,783
Population 65 Years of Age and Older	191,065	226,189	264,527	300,743

Data: U.S. Census Bureau

Workforce and Industry Profile

Workforce

	2000	2005	2006
Civilian Labor Force	609,018	631,298	643,486
Labor Force Participation Rate	67.6%	66.1%	66.4%
Unemployment Rate	4.0%	2.7%	2.4%
Average Wage Per Job (USD)	$30,628	$37,050	$38,630
Education Attainment (Population 25 Years and Older)	**(%)**	**(%)**	**(%)**
High School Graduate or Higher	84.6	88.1	89.0
Bachelors Degree or Higher	26.2	27.9	29.7
Graduate or Professional Degree	8.4	9.1	9.8

Data: U.S. Census Bureau, American Community Survey; U.S. Department of Commerce, Bureau of Economic Analysis; U.S. Department of Labor, Bureau of Labor Statistics

Industry Overview

	1998	2004	2005
Total Employees	416,571	473,500	490,682
Total Payroll ($1,000s)	$11,291,978	$15,074,629	$16,163,137
Total Establishments	29,603	31,605	32,244
Establishments with 1–19 Employees	25,653	27,142	27,711
Establishments with 20–49 Employees	2,498	2,766	2,730
Establishments with 50–249 Employees	1,287	1,491	1,581
Establishments with 250–999 Employees	142	179	194
Establishments with 1,000+ Employees	23	27	28

Data: U.S. Census Bureau, County Business Patterns

Major Industries (Ranked by 2005 Employment; Payroll in $1,000s)				
Industry	1998 Employment	2005 Employment	1998 Payroll	2005 Payroll
Accommodation and Food Services	83,261	99,886	1,519,689	2,308,858
Retail Trade	60,620	69,323	1,179,640	1,645,587
Health Care and Social Assistance	47,389	61,005	1,670,402	2,358,932
Admin., Support, Waste Mngt., Remediation Services	31,342	38,021	649,096	973,291
Construction	21,265	29,480	862,290	1,556,880
Transportation and Warehousing	23,635	26,490	773,653	926,945
Professional, Scientific, Technical Services	17,140	24,724	690,001	1,218,103
Other Services (except Public Admin.)	22,790	24,304	456,924	588,160
Wholesale Trade	18,442	19,978	602,585	763,702
Finance and Insurance	20,050	19,707	807,310	1,060,036

Data: U.S. Census Bureau, County Business Patterns

Taxes and Business Climate

State and Local Taxes		
Combined Revenues ($1,000s)	**2003–4**	**2004–5**
Revenue from Property Taxes	720,798	818,239
Revenue from Sales and Gross Receipts Taxes	2,605,694	2,895,269
Revenue from Individual Income Taxes	1,169,205	1,381,481
Revenue from Corporate Income Taxes	58,119	124,125
Revenue from Other Taxes	258,240	304,633
Total Tax Revenue	4,812,056	5,523,747
Per Capita Taxes		
Property Tax Per Capita	571	646
Sales and Gross Receipts Tax Per Capita	2,065	2,284
Individual Income Tax Per Capita	926	1,090
Corporate Income Tax Per Capita	46	98
Other Taxes Per Capita	205	240
Total Taxes Per Capita	3,813	4,358

Data: U.S. Census Bureau; Anderson Economic Group, LLC

Business Climate Measures	
Anderson Economic Group: 2007 Business Tax Ranking (1 is Best)	45
Forbes Magazine: 2007 Best States for Business Ranking (1 is Best)	37
Tax Foundation: 2008 Business Tax Climate Ranking (1 is Best)	22
ALEC-Laffer 2007 Economic Competitiveness Ranking (1 is Best)	45
2003–4 Employer Firm Births	2,926
2003–4 Employer Firm Terminations	2,440

Data: Anderson Economic Group; Tax Foundation; Forbes Magazine; U.S. Census, Statistics of U.S. Businesses; American Legislative Exchange Council

Voting Behavior and Elected Officials

Voter Registration and Turnout (%)

	1992	1996	2000	2004
Registered Voters Who Voted	80.3	66.1	57.7	66.3
Citizens Age 18+ Who Voted	41.9	40.5	40.1	44.7

Data: Dave Leip's Atlas of U.S. Presidential Elections

Presidential Election Results (Nationwide Winner Listed First)

2004	Popular Vote (%)	Electoral Votes
George W. Bush (Republican, Incumbent)	45.3	0
John Kerry (Democrat)	54.0	4
Other	0.7	0
2000		
George W. Bush (Republican)	37.5	0
Albert Gore (Democrat)	55.8	4
Ralph Nader (Green)	5.9	0
Other	0.9	0
1996		
William Clinton (Democrat, Incumbent)	56.9	4
Robert Dole (Republican)	31.6	0
H. Ross Perot (Reformist)	7.6	0
Other	3.8	0
1992		
William Clinton (Democrat)	48.1	4
George H. W. Bush (Republican, Incumbent)	36.7	0
H. Ross Perot (Independent)	14.2	0
Other	1.0	0

Data: Dave Leip's Atlas of U.S. Presidential Elections

Governor and U.S. Congressional Seats				
Governor	Party	Year Term Began	Term	Max. Consecutive Terms
Linda Lingle	R	2006	Second	2
U.S. Senators	Party	Year Elected	Term Expires	
Daniel K. Akaka	D	1990	2013	
Daniel K. Inouye	D	1962	2011	
U.S. Representatives		Republican	Democrat	Other
		0	2	0

Data: National Governors Association; U.S. Senate, Office of the Clerk; U.S. House of Representatives

Business and Economic Agencies

Agency	Website Address
Chamber of Commerce of Hawaii	www.cochawaii.com
Department of Business, Economic Development & Tourism	www.hawaii.gov/dbedt
Hawaii Small Business Dev. Center	www.hawaii-sbdc.org
Department of Commerce and Consumer Affairs	www.hawaii.gov/dcca

Data: Various agency websites

Idaho

In 2006, Idaho had a population of 1.5 million people, making it the twelfth least populous state in the country. The state's population increased by 172,512 people from 2000 to 2006, and is projected to increase to 1.9 million by 2025. This 1.24% projected annual growth rate is above the national average of 0.8%. Per capita personal income in Idaho was $29,948 in 2006, up from $28,274 in 2005. For 2006, this was $6,681 below the national average and the eighth lowest in the country. The state's per capita income grew at an average annual rate of 3.7% from 2000 to 2006, compared to 3.5% nationally.

The state's workforce generally has less education than other states—87.3% of the state's adult population has graduated from high school, compared to an 84.1% national average; 23.3% hold a bachelor degree or higher (national average is 27.0%); and 7.1% hold professional or graduate degrees (national average is 9.9%). In 2005, the state's largest industry in terms of employment was retail trade, followed by health care and social assistance. The fastest growing industry was administration, support, waste management, and remediation services, with 9.2% annual

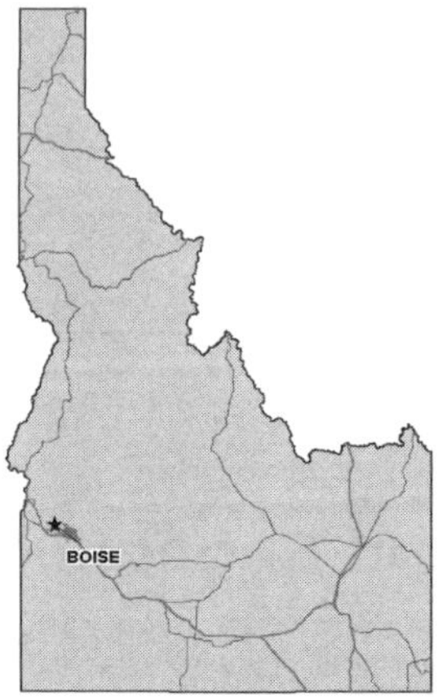

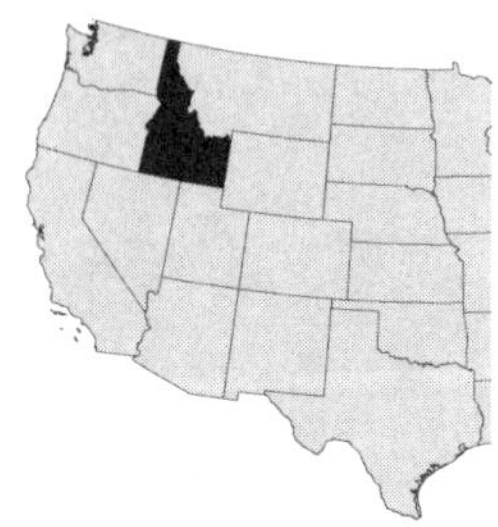

★ State Capitol

Major Urban Area

Major Roadway

Demographic and Socioeconomic Profile

Demographics and Socioeconomic Figures			
Population and Households	**2000**	**2005**	**2006**
Total Population	1,293,953	1,395,634	1,466,465
Number of Households	469,645	532,135	548,555
Average Household Size	2.7	2.6	2.6
Age and Ethnicity			
Median Age	33.2	34.6	34.3
Population 18 Years of Age and Older	925,822	1,022,698	1,072,150
Population 65 Years of Age and Older	145,945	156,720	169,391
Caucasian Population	1,176,568	1,281,279	1,357,129
African-American Population	5,244	5,931	6,842
Hispanic Population	101,594	126,785	138,871
Asian Population	11,321	15,117	15,335
Foreign-Born Population (%)	5.0	5.5	5.6
Income			
Per Capita Personal Income (USD)	$24,075	$28,274	$29,948
Median Household Income (USD)	$37,572	$41,443	$42,865
Individuals Below Poverty Level	11.8%	13.9%	12.6%

Data: U.S. Census, American Community Survey; U.S. Department of Commerce, Bureau of Economic Analysis

employment growth from 1998 to 2005.

In fiscal year 2004–5, Idaho had total tax revenues of $4.2 billion. The largest share was generated from sales and gross receipts taxes, followed by property taxes. The per capita tax burden in Idaho was $2,933 for 2004–5, some $772 below the national average, and a $205 increase from 2003–4. In terms of business taxes, Idaho ranked fortieth in a study from Anderson Economic Group. The state's business climate was ranked sixth by Forbes Magazine and thirty-first by the Tax Foundation. Idaho was ranked ninth by ALEC in its state competitiveness index. One is considered best for each ranking.

Population Projections

Year	2010	2015	2020	2025
Total Population	1,517,291	1,630,045	1,741,333	1,852,627
Median Age	34.8	35.9	37.5	38.6
Population 18 Years of Age and Older	1,117,054	1,202,945	1,292,913	1,385,569
Population 65 Years of Age and Older	181,416	220,113	269,439	320,205

Data: U.S. Census Bureau

Workforce and Industry Profile

Workforce

	2000	2005	2006
Civilian Labor Force	662,958	727,463	749,244
Labor Force Participation Rate	69.7%	68.5%	68.5%
Unemployment Rate	4.6%	4.0%	3.4%
Average Wage Per Job (USD)	$27,701	$33,050	$34,810
Education Attainment (Population 25 Years and Older)	**(%)**	**(%)**	**(%)**
High School Graduate or Higher	84.7	86.7	87.3
Bachelors Degree or Higher	21.7	23.3	23.3
Graduate or Professional Degree	6.8	7.4	7.1

Data: U.S. Census Bureau, American Community Survey; U.S. Department of Commerce, Bureau of Economic Analysis; U.S. Department of Labor, Bureau of Labor Statistics

Industry Overview

	1998	2004	2005
Total Employees	423,615	488,676	519,319
Total Payroll ($1,000s)	$10,595,285	$14,207,992	$15,397,889
Total Establishments	35,961	41,336	43,346
Establishments with 1–19 Employees	32,152	36,960	38,744
Establishments with 20–49 Employees	2,562	2,923	3,061
Establishments with 50–249 Employees	1,105	1,280	1,349
Establishments with 250–999 Employees	125	152	168
Establishments with 1,000+ Employees	17	21	24

Data: U.S. Census Bureau, County Business Patterns

Major Industries (Ranked by 2005 Employment; Payroll in $1,000s)				
Industry	1998 Employment	2005 Employment	1998 Payroll	2005 Payroll
Retail Trade	65,665	75,716	1,173,071	1,673,120
Health Care and Social Assistance	50,674	68,820	1,285,725	2,146,695
Manufacturing	66,719	61,167	2,214,164	2,393,039
Accommodation and Food Services	44,106	51,670	389,942	571,584
Admin., Support, Waste Mngt., Remediation Services	25,398	47,096	452,844	965,124
Construction	35,446	44,658	1,064,026	1,622,096
Professional, Scientific, Technical Services	22,338	35,126	902,270	1,411,856
Wholesale Trade	23,488	23,602	699,924	907,831
Finance and Insurance	16,285	20,924	531,207	907,058
Other Services (except Public Admin.)	16,899	18,503	249,420	361,511

Data: U.S. Census Bureau, County Business Patterns

Taxes and Business Climate

State and Local Taxes		
Combined Revenues ($1,000s)	2003–4	2004–5
Revenue from Property Taxes	1,084,470	1,153,841
Revenue from Sales and Gross Receipts Taxes	1,426,827	1,523,808
Revenue from Individual Income Taxes	907,795	1,040,512
Revenue from Corporate Income Taxes	103,784	140,585
Revenue from Other Taxes	282,951	323,800
Total Tax Revenue	3,805,827	4,182,546
Per Capita Taxes		
Property Tax Per Capita	777	809
Sales and Gross Receipts Tax Per Capita	1,023	1,069
Individual Income Tax Per Capita	651	730
Corporate Income Tax Per Capita	74	99
Other Taxes Per Capita	203	227
Total Taxes Per Capita	2,728	2,933

Data: U.S. Census Bureau; Anderson Economic Group, LLC

Business Climate Measures	
Anderson Economic Group: 2007 Business Tax Ranking (1 is Best)	40
Forbes Magazine: 2007 Best States for Business Ranking (1 is Best)	6
Tax Foundation: 2008 Business Tax Climate Ranking (1 is Best)	31
ALEC-Laffer 2007 Economic Competitiveness Ranking (1 is Best)	9
2003–4 Employer Firm Births	4,640
2003–4 Employer Firm Terminations	3,581

Data: Anderson Economic Group; Tax Foundation; Forbes Magazine; U.S. Census, Statistics of U.S. Businesses; American Legislative Exchange Council

Voting Behavior and Elected Officials

Voter Registration and Turnout (%)

	1992	1996	2000	2004
Registered Voters Who Voted	78.9	70.2	68.9	75.0
Citizens Age 18+ Who Voted	65.2	57.3	54.2	60.2

Data: Dave Leip's Atlas of U.S. Presidential Elections

Presidential Election Results (Nationwide Winner Listed First)

2004	Popular Vote (%)	Electoral Votes
George W. Bush (Republican, Incumbent)	68.4	4
John Kerry (Democrat)	30.3	0
Other	1.4	0
2000		
George W. Bush (Republican)	67.2	4
Albert Gore (Democrat)	27.6	0
Ralph Nader (Green)	2.5	0
Other	2.7	0
1996		
William Clinton (Democrat, Incumbent)	33.7	0
Robert Dole (Republican)	52.2	4
H. Ross Perot (Reformist)	12.7	0
Other	1.5	0
1992		
William Clinton (Democrat)	28.4	0
George H. W. Bush (Republican, Incumbent)	42.0	4
H. Ross Perot (Independent)	27.0	0
Other	2.5	0

Data: Dave Leip's Atlas of U.S. Presidential Elections

Governor and U.S. Congressional Seats				
Governor	**Party**	**Year Term Began**	**Term**	**Max. Consecutive Terms**
C.L. "Butch" Otter	R	2007	First	2
U.S. Senators	**Party**	**Year Elected**	**Term Expires**	
Larry E. Craig	R	1990	2009	
Michael Crapo	R	1998	2011	
U.S. Representatives		**Republican**	**Democrat**	**Other**
		2	0	0

Data: National Governors Association; U.S. Senate, Office of the Clerk; U.S. House of Representatives

Business and Economic Agencies

Agency	Website Address
Boise Metro Chamber of Commerce	www.boisechamber.org
Idaho Department of Commerce and Labor	www.cl.idaho.gov
Idaho Small Business Dev. Center	www.idahosbdc.org
Idaho Secretary of State	www.idsos.state.id.us

Data: Various agency websites

Illinois

Illinois, located in the Middle West region of the United States, and had a population of 12.8 million people in 2006, making it the fifth most populous state. The state's population increased by 412,677 people from 2000 to 2006, and is projected to increase to 13.3 million by 2025. This 0.2% projected annual growth rate compares to the projected national average of 0.8%. Per capita personal income in Illinois was $38,297 in 2006, up from $36,361 in 2005. For 2006, this was fifteenth highest in the country and $1,668 above the national average. From 2000 to 2006 per capita income in Illinois grew at an average annual rate of 2.9%, compared to 3.5% nationally.

In 2005, the state's largest industry in terms of employment was health care and social assistance, followed by manufacturing. The fastest growing industry was accommodation and food services, with 1.8% annual employment growth from 1998 to 2005. The state's workforce is generally more educated than other states—85.0% of the state's adult population has graduated from high school, compared to an 84.1% national average. Nationally, an average of

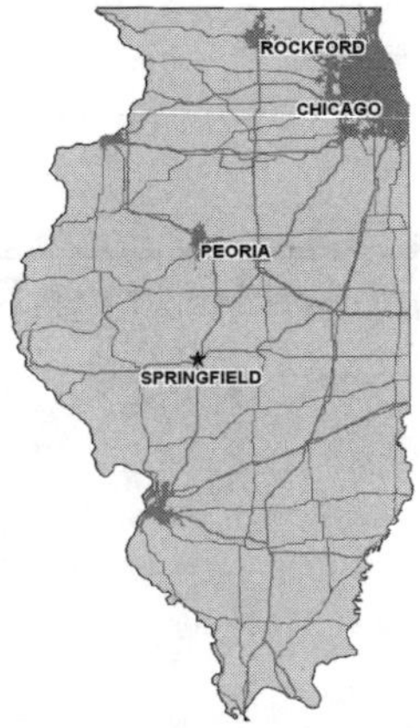

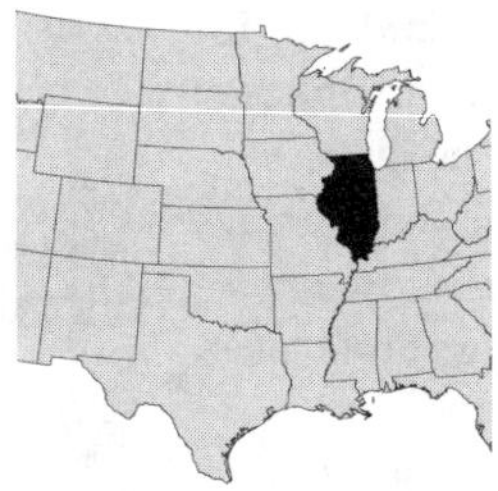

★ State Capitol

Major Urban Area

—— Major Roadway

Demographic and Socioeconomic Profile

Demographics and Socioeconomic Figures			
Population and Households	**2000**	**2005**	**2006**
Total Population	12,419,293	12,440,351	12,831,970
Number of Households	4,591,779	4,691,020	4,724,252
Average Household Size	2.6	2.7	2.7
Age and Ethnicity			
Median Age	34.7	35.6	35.7
Population 18 Years of Age and Older	9,180,064	9,208,765	9,615,583
Population 65 Years of Age and Older	1,498,929	1,436,153	1,532,373
Caucasian Population	9,123,564	8,986,032	9,074,653
African-American Population	1,864,619	1,803,613	1,898,346
Hispanic Population	1,529,141	1,804,619	1,888,439
Asian Population	423,440	507,687	536,992
Foreign-Born Population (%)	12.3	13.6	13.8
Income			
Per Capita Personal Income (USD)	$32,185	$36,361	$38,297
Median Household Income (USD)	$46,590	$50,260	$52,006
Individuals Below Poverty Level	10.7%	12.0%	12.3%

Data: U.S. Census, American Community Survey; U.S. Department of Commerce, Bureau of Economic Analysis

28.9% hold a bachelor degree or higher compared to 21.2% in Illinois. Nationally, 9.9% hold professional or graduate degrees compared to 10.8% in Illinois.

In fiscal year 2004–5, Illinois had total tax revenues of $49.1 billion. The largest share was generated from property taxes, followed by sales and gross receipts taxes. The per capita tax burden in Illinois was $3,863 for 2004–5, some $185 above the national average. In terms of business taxes, the state ranked thirty-fourth in a study from Anderson Economic Group. Forbes Magazine and the Tax Foundation ranked the state's business climate fortieth and twenty-eighth, respectively, while ALEC ranked Illinois forty-second in its state competitiveness index. One is considered best for each ranking.

Population Projections

Year	2010	2015	2020	2025
Total Population	12,916,894	13,097,218	13,236,720	13,340,507
Median Age	36.0	36.3	37.0	37.4
Population 18 Years of Age and Older	9,719,988	9,882,541	9,980,950	10,075,188
Population 65 Years of Age and Older	1,600,863	1,777,487	1,988,764	2,226,431

Data: U.S. Census Bureau

Workforce and Industry Profile

Workforce

	2000	2005	2006
Civilian Labor Force	6,467,692	6,483,791	6,613,346
Labor Force Participation Rate	69.2%	66.7%	67.5%
Unemployment Rate	4.5%	5.7%	4.5%
Average Wage Per Job (USD)	$38,044	$39,290	$40,910
Education Attainment (Population 25 Years and Older)	**(%)**	**(%)**	**(%)**
High School Graduate or Higher	81.4	85.7	85.0
Bachelors Degree or Higher	26.1	29.2	28.9
Graduate or Professional Degree	9.5	10.9	10.8

Data: U.S. Census Bureau, American Community Survey; U.S. Department of Commerce, Bureau of Economic Analysis; U.S. Department of Labor, Bureau of Labor Statistics

Industry Overview

	1998	2004	2005
Total Employees	5,221,782	5,217,160	5,235,866
Total Payroll ($1,000s)	$175,703,556	$207,884,485	$217,221,786
Total Establishments	304,533	315,854	318,927
Establishments with 1–19 Employees	259,572	269,744	273,249
Establishments with 20–49 Employees	26,877	27,849	27,331
Establishments with 50–249 Employees	15,634	15,901	15,984
Establishments with 250–999 Employees	2,124	2,031	2,022
Establishments with 1,000+ Employees	326	329	341

Data: U.S. Census Bureau, County Business Patterns

Major Industries (Ranked by 2005 Employment; Payroll in $1,000s)				
Industry	1998 Employment	2005 Employment	1998 Payroll	2005 Payroll
Health Care and Social Assistance	612,855	677,927	17,914,037	25,360,320
Manufacturing	883,472	676,298	33,319,088	30,078,477
Retail Trade	632,626	629,286	11,503,179	14,365,019
Accommodation and Food Services	395,322	446,724	4,554,156	6,277,520
Admin., Support, Waste Mngt., Remediation Services	407,556	442,999	9,080,901	11,482,098
Professional, Scientific, Technical Services	311,731	350,082	16,023,793	22,464,307
Finance and Insurance	338,042	341,884	17,736,564	24,867,356
Wholesale Trade	330,787	322,342	15,093,685	17,770,519
Other Services (except Public Admin.)	247,420	257,238	5,247,616	6,657,706
Construction	225,301	250,157	10,004,410	13,615,634

Data: U.S. Census Bureau, County Business Patterns

Taxes and Business Climate

State and Local Taxes		
Combined Revenues ($1,000s)	**2003–4**	**2004–5**
Revenue from Property Taxes	17,888,828	18,690,132
Revenue from Sales and Gross Receipts Taxes	15,344,201	16,693,556
Revenue from Individual Income Taxes	7,218,428	7,936,884
Revenue from Corporate Income Taxes	1,278,538	2,183,126
Revenue from Other Taxes	3,460,734	3,634,797
Total Tax Revenue	45,190,729	49,138,495
Per Capita Taxes		
Property Tax Per Capita	1,407	1,469
Sales and Gross Receipts Tax Per Capita	1,207	1,312
Individual Income Tax Per Capita	568	624
Corporate Income Tax Per Capita	101	172
Other Taxes Per Capita	272	286
Total Taxes Per Capita	3,555	3,863

Data: U.S. Census Bureau; Anderson Economic Group, LLC

Business Climate Measures	
Anderson Economic Group: 2007 Business Tax Ranking (1 is Best)	34
Forbes Magazine: 2007 Best States for Business Ranking (1 is Best)	40
Tax Foundation: 2008 Business Tax Climate Ranking (1 is Best)	28
ALEC-Laffer 2007 Economic Competitiveness Ranking (1 is Best)	42
2003–4 Employer Firm Births	28,907
2003–4 Employer Firm Terminations	26,492

Data: Anderson Economic Group; Tax Foundation; Forbes Magazine; U.S. Census, Statistics of U.S. Businesses; American Legislative Exchange Council

Voting Behavior and Elected Officials

Voter Registration and Turnout (%)

	1992	1996	2000	2004
Registered Voters Who Voted	76.5	64.7	66.5	70.3
Citizens Age 18+ Who Voted	58.9	49.3	51.7	56.0

Data: Dave Leip's Atlas of U.S. Presidential Elections

Presidential Election Results (Nationwide Winner Listed First)

2004	Popular Vote (%)	Electoral Votes
George W. Bush (Republican, Incumbent)	44.5	0
John Kerry (Democrat)	54.8	21
Other	0.7	0
2000		
George W. Bush (Republican)	42.6	0
Albert Gore (Democrat)	54.6	22
Ralph Nader (Green)	2.2	0
Other	0.6	0
1996		
William Clinton (Democrat, Incumbent)	54.3	22
Robert Dole (Republican)	36.8	0
H. Ross Perot (Reformist)	8.0	0
Other	0.8	0
1992		
William Clinton (Democrat)	48.6	22
George H. W. Bush (Republican, Incumbent)	34.3	0
H. Ross Perot (Independent)	16.6	0
Other	0.4	0

Data: Dave Leip's Atlas of U.S. Presidential Elections

Governor and U.S. Congressional Seats				
Governor	**Party**	**Year Term Began**	**Term**	**Max. Consecutive Terms**
Rod Blagojevich	D	2007	Second	No limit
U.S. Senators	**Party**	**Year Elected**	**Term Expires**	
Richard Durbin	D	1996	2009	
Barack Obama	D	2004	2011	
U.S. Representatives		**Republican**	**Democrat**	**Other**
		8	10	0

Data: National Governors Association; U.S. Senate, Office of the Clerk; U.S. House of Representatives

Business and Economic Agencies

Agency	Website Address
Illinois State Chamber of Commerce	www.ilchamber.org
Department of Commerce and Economic Opportunity	www.commerce.state.il.us/dceo
Illinois Small Business Dev. Center	www.ilsbdc.biz
Illinois Secretary of State	www.sos.state.il.us

Data: Various agency websites

Indiana

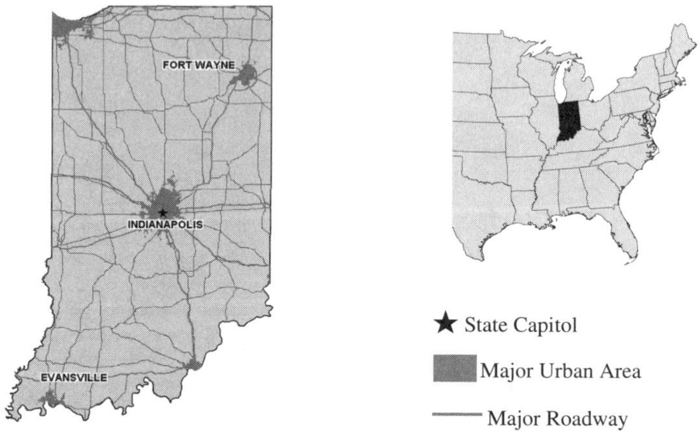

With a population of 6.3 million people, Indiana was the fifteenth most populous state in the United States in 2006. From 2000 to 2006 the state's population increased by 233,035 people, and is projected to increase to 6.7 million by 2025. This 0.3% projected annual growth rate compares to the projected national average of 0.8%. The state's 2006 per capita personal income of $32,226 was higher compared to $30,883 in 2005 and fifteenth lowest in the United States, some $4,403 below the national average. Per capita income in Indiana grew at an average annual rate of 2.9% from 2000 to 2006, compared to 3.5% nationally.

Indiana's largest industry in terms of 2005 employment was manufacturing. The fastest growing industry was professional, scientific, and technical services, with 4.3% annual employment growth from 1998 to 2005. The second fastest growing industry was administration, support, waste management, and remediation services. The state's workforce is generally less educated than other states—85.2% of the state's adult population has graduated from high school, compared to an 84.1% national average; 21.7% hold a bachelor degree or higher (national

Demographic and Socioeconomic Profile

Demographics and Socioeconomic Figures			
Population and Households	**2000**	**2005**	**2006**
Total Population	6,080,485	6,093,372	6,313,520
Number of Households	2,336,306	2,443,010	2,435,274
Average Household Size	2.5	2.5	2.5
Age and Ethnicity			
Median Age	35.2	36.1	36.3
Population 18 Years of Age and Older	4,507,679	4,500,356	4,733,923
Population 65 Years of Age and Older	752,885	727,171	780,992
Caucasian Population	5,317,334	5,247,604	5,427,561
African-American Population	504,449	522,377	551,864
Hispanic Population	210,538	277,558	299,398
Asian Population	57,193	72,494	81,054
Foreign-Born Population (%)	3.1	4.0	4.2
Income			
Per Capita Personal Income (USD)	$27,132	$30,883	$32,226
Median Household Income (USD)	$41,567	$43,993	$45,394
Individuals Below Poverty Level	9.5%	12.2%	12.7%

Data: U.S. Census, American Community Survey; U.S. Department of Commerce, Bureau of Economic Analysis

average is 27.0%); and 8.0% hold professional or graduate degrees compared to the national average of 9.9%.

Indiana's total tax revenue was $21.3 billion for fiscal year 2004–5, up from the 2003–4 total revenue of $18.7 billion. The largest share of tax revenue in 2004–5 was generated from property taxes, followed by sales and gross receipts taxes. On a per capita basis, residents of Indiana paid taxes of $3,410, compared to the national average of $3,705 for 2004–5. In terms of business taxes, the state ranked thirtieth in a study from Anderson Economic Group. Forbes Magazine and the Tax Foundation ranked the state's business climate twenty-seventh and twelfth, respectively, ALEC also ranked Indiana twelfth in its state competitiveness index. One is considered best for each ranking.

Population Projections

Year	2010	2015	2020	2025
Total Population	6,392,139	6,517,631	6,627,008	6,721,322
Median Age	36.5	36.8	37.4	37.5
Population 18 Years of Age and Older	4,795,954	4,903,401	4,992,020	5,055,039
Population 65 Years of Age and Older	811,290	906,361	1,019,707	1,140,690

Data: U.S. Census Bureau

Workforce and Industry Profile

Workforce

	2000	2005	2006
Civilian Labor Force	3,144,379	3,227,444	3,271,496
Labor Force Participation Rate	68.3%	67.5%	67.7%
Unemployment Rate	2.9%	5.3%	5.0%
Average Wage Per Job (USD)	$31,017	$34,080	$35,190
Education Attainment (Population 25 Years and Older)	**(%)**	**(%)**	**(%)**
High School Graduate or Higher	82.1	85.3	85.2
Bachelors Degree or Higher	19.4	21.3	21.7
Graduate or Professional Degree	7.2	7.7	8.0

Data: U.S. Census Bureau, American Community Survey; U.S. Department of Commerce, Bureau of Economic Analysis; U.S. Department of Labor, Bureau of Labor Statistics

Industry Overview

	1998	2004	2005
Total Employees	2,510,866	2,586,799	2,610,899
Total Payroll ($1,000s)	$71,435,864	$85,098,401	$88,145,224
Total Establishments	146,197	149,381	149,871
Establishments with 1–19 Employees	123,653	126,069	126,655
Establishments with 20–49 Employees	13,836	14,306	14,106
Establishments with 50–249 Employees	7,559	7,817	7,882
Establishments with 250–999 Employees	987	1,014	1,056
Establishments with 1,000+ Employees	162	175	172

Data: U.S. Census Bureau, County Business Patterns

Major Industries (Ranked by 2005 Employment; Payroll in $1,000s)				
Industry	1998 Employment	2005 Employment	1998 Payroll	2005 Payroll
Manufacturing	635,658	554,273	23,729,035	24,191,908
Health Care and Social Assistance	313,865	354,481	8,403,195	12,213,877
Retail Trade	344,444	346,073	5,719,109	6,912,064
Accommodation and Food Services	216,578	245,467	2,066,860	2,934,176
Admin., Support, Waste Mngt., Remediation Services	136,135	165,704	2,782,884	4,151,772
Construction	138,326	139,661	4,770,384	5,963,039
Other Services (except Public Admin.)	124,828	132,061	2,097,725	2,750,929
Wholesale Trade	115,519	117,305	4,082,819	5,206,097
Professional, Scientific, Technical Services	81,704	110,046	2,789,896	5,022,670
Finance and Insurance	110,993	107,628	4,202,678	5,324,071

Data: U.S. Census Bureau, County Business Patterns

Taxes and Business Climate

State and Local Taxes		
Combined Revenues ($1,000s)	**2003–4**	**2004–5**
Revenue from Property Taxes	6,073,538	7,638,992
Revenue from Sales and Gross Receipts Taxes	6,992,455	7,279,831
Revenue from Individual Income Taxes	4,231,727	4,811,592
Revenue from Corporate Income Taxes	644,787	824,803
Revenue from Other Taxes	732,517	781,859
Total Tax Revenue	18,675,024	21,337,077
Per Capita Taxes		
Property Tax Per Capita	975	1,221
Sales and Gross Receipts Tax Per Capita	1,123	1,163
Individual Income Tax Per Capita	680	769
Corporate Income Tax Per Capita	104	132
Other Taxes Per Capita	118	125
Total Taxes Per Capita	2,999	3,410

Data: U.S. Census Bureau; Anderson Economic Group, LLC

Business Climate Measures	
Anderson Economic Group: 2007 Business Tax Ranking (1 is Best)	30
Forbes Magazine: 2007 Best States for Business Ranking (1 is Best)	27
Tax Foundation: 2008 Business Tax Climate Ranking (1 is Best)	12
ALEC-Laffer 2007 Economic Competitiveness Ranking (1 is Best)	12
2003–4 Employer Firm Births	13,321
2003–4 Employer Firm Terminations	11,988

Data: Anderson Economic Group; Tax Foundation; Forbes Magazine; U.S. Census, Statistics of U.S. Businesses; American Legislative Exchange Council

Voting Behavior and Elected Officials

Voter Registration and Turnout (%)

	1992	1996	2000	2004
Registered Voters Who Voted	72.5	61.2	55.1	57.4
Citizens Age 18+ Who Voted	55.2	48.8	48.8	53.7

Data: Dave Leip's Atlas of U.S. Presidential Elections

Presidential Election Results (Nationwide Winner Listed First)

2004	Popular Vote (%)	Electoral Votes
George W. Bush (Republican, Incumbent)	59.9	11
John Kerry (Democrat)	39.3	0
Other	0.8	0
2000		
George W. Bush (Republican)	56.7	12
Albert Gore (Democrat)	41.0	0
Ralph Nader (Green)	0.8	0
Other	1.5	0
1996		
William Clinton (Democrat, Incumbent)	41.6	0
Robert Dole (Republican)	47.1	12
H. Ross Perot (Reformist)	10.5	0
Other	0.8	0
1992		
William Clinton (Democrat)	36.8	0
George H. W. Bush (Republican, Incumbent)	42.9	12
H. Ross Perot (Independent)	19.8	0
Other	0.5	0

Data: Dave Leip's Atlas of U.S. Presidential Elections

Governor and U.S. Congressional Seats				
Governor	**Party**	**Year Term Began**	**Term**	**Max. Consecutive Terms**
Mitch Daniels	R	2005	First	2
U.S. Senators	**Party**	**Year Elected**	**Term Expires**	
Evan Bayh	D	1998	2011	
Richard G. Lugar	R	1976	2013	
U.S. Representatives		**Republican**	**Democrat**	**Other**
		4	4	0

Data: National Governors Association; U.S. Senate, Office of the Clerk; U.S. House of Representatives

Business and Economic Agencies

Agency	Website Address
Indiana Chamber of Commerce	www.indianachamber.com
Indiana Economic Development Corporation	www.in.gov/iedc
Indiana Small Business Dev. Center	www.isbdc.org
Indiana Secretary of State	www.state.in.us/sos/business

Data: Various agency websites

Iowa

Iowa is located in the Middle West region of the United Stats and had a population of 3.0 million people in 2006, making it the twenty-first least populous state. The state's population increased by 55,761 people from 2000 to 2006, and is projected to increase slightly by 2025. The projected annual growth rate of less than 0.1% compares to the national average of 0.8%. Per capita personal income in Iowa was $33,017 in 2006, up from $31,473 in 2005. For 2006, this was $3,612 below the national average and the twenty-first lowest in the country. The state's per capita income grew at an average annual rate of 3.7% from 2000 to 2006, compared to 3.5% nationally.

The state's workforce generally has less education than other states—88.9% of the state's adult population has graduated from high school, compared to an 84.1% national average; 24.0% hold a bachelor degree or higher (national average is 27.0%); and 7.4% hold professional or graduate degrees (national average is 9.9%). In 2005, the state's largest industry in terms of employment was manufacturing, followed by health care and

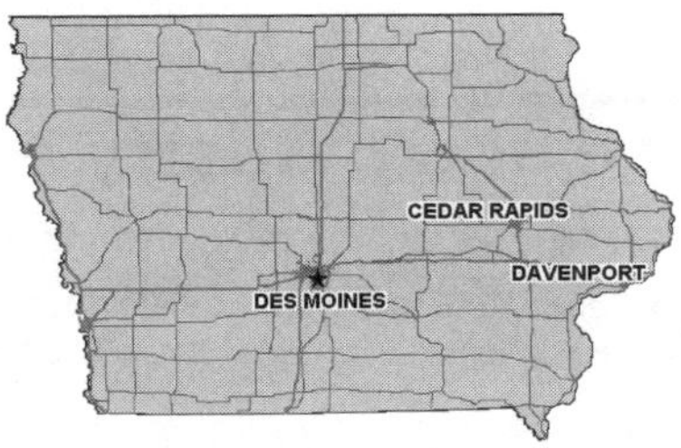

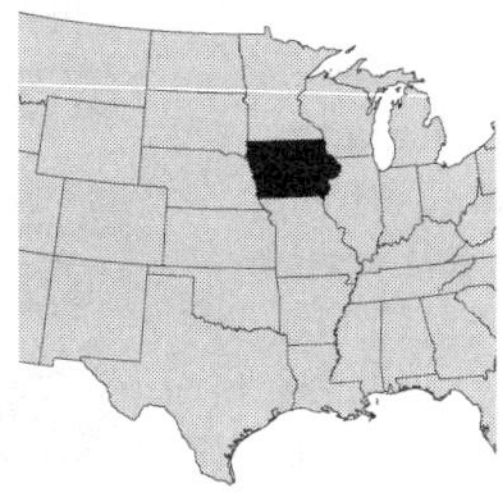

★ State Capitol
Major Urban Area
Major Roadway

Demographic and Socioeconomic Profile

Demographics and Socioeconomic Figures			
Population and Households	**2000**	**2005**	**2006**
Total Population	2,926,324	2,862,541	2,982,085
Number of Households	1,149,276	1,200,833	1,208,765
Average Household Size	2.5	2.4	2.4
Age and Ethnicity			
Median Age	36.6	38.6	37.8
Population 18 Years of Age and Older	2,193,990	2,194,615	2,267,565
Population 65 Years of Age and Older	436,377	402,167	435,373
Caucasian Population	2,749,737	2,675,878	2,772,535
African-American Population	59,758	62,827	67,297
Hispanic Population	81,501	106,052	112,987
Asian Population	35,023	41,510	45,647
Foreign-Born Population (%)	3.1	3.6	3.8
Income			
Per Capita Personal Income (USD)	$26,554	$31,473	$33,017
Median Household Income (USD)	$39,469	$43,609	$44,491
Individuals Below Poverty Level	9.1%	10.9%	11.0%

Data: U.S. Census, American Community Survey; U.S. Department of Commerce, Bureau of Economic Analysis

social assistance. The fastest growing industry was transportation and warehousing, with 4.2% annual employment growth from 1998 to 2005.

In fiscal year 2004–5, Iowa had total tax revenues of $9.7 billion. The largest share was generated from property taxes, followed by sales and gross receipts taxes. The per capita tax burden in Iowa was $3,284 for 2004–5, some $421 below the national average, but a $230 increase from 2003–4. In terms of business taxes, Iowa ranked twenty-seventh in a study from Anderson Economic Group. The state's business climate was ranked twenty-fourth by Forbes Magazine and forty-fifth by the Tax Foundation. Iowa was ranked ranked twenty-seventh by ALEC in its state competitiveness index. One is considered best for each ranking.

Population Projections

Year	2010	2015	2020	2025
Total Population	3,009,907	3,026,380	3,020,496	2,993,222
Median Age	38.3	38.9	40.1	41.3
Population 18 Years of Age and Older	2,298,851	2,319,340	2,323,127	2,311,474
Population 65 Years of Age and Older	449,887	494,565	556,540	619,227

Data: U.S. Census Bureau

Workforce and Industry Profile

Workforce

	2000	2005	2006
Civilian Labor Force	1,601,920	1,639,703	1,664,339
Labor Force Participation Rate	71.7%	71.5%	72.1%
Unemployment Rate	2.8%	4.3%	3.7%
Average Wage Per Job (USD)	$27,929	$32,340	$33,250
Education Attainment (Population 25 Years and Older)	**(%)**	**(%)**	**(%)**
High School Graduate or Higher	86.1	89.6	88.9
Bachelors Degree or Higher	21.2	23.8	24.0
Graduate or Professional Degree	6.5	7.3	7.4

Data: U.S. Census Bureau, American Community Survey; U.S. Department of Commerce, Bureau of Economic Analysis; U.S. Department of Labor, Bureau of Labor Statistics

Industry Overview

	1998	2004	2005
Total Employees	1,213,285	1,241,864	1,261,108
Total Payroll ($1,000s)	$30,409,574	$37,643,817	$39,420,961
Total Establishments	80,838	81,565	82,087
Establishments with 1–19 Employees	70,187	70,485	70,958
Establishments with 20–49 Employees	6,524	6,839	6,877
Establishments with 50–249 Employees	3,598	3,674	3,688
Establishments with 250–999 Employees	462	491	487
Establishments with 1,000+ Employees	67	76	77

Data: U.S. Census Bureau, County Business Patterns

Major Industries (Ranked by 2005 Employment; Payroll in $1,000s)				
Industry	1998 Employment	2005 Employment	1998 Payroll	2005 Payroll
Manufacturing	245,282	225,567	8,193,004	9,025,961
Health Care and Social Assistance	172,793	188,242	4,111,821	5,921,736
Retail Trade	177,723	178,216	2,846,480	3,494,449
Accommodation and Food Services	103,641	108,439	907,513	1,105,219
Finance and Insurance	73,746	91,727	2,715,795	4,380,754
Wholesale Trade	64,101	63,176	1,991,922	2,558,534
Construction	58,557	62,855	1,947,744	2,573,372
Admin., Support, Waste Mngt., Remediation Services	58,306	62,829	993,597	1,386,775
Other Services (except Public Admin.)	52,875	54,175	790,560	1,018,514
Transportation and Warehousing	37,379	49,876	1,050,574	1,698,170

Data: U.S. Census Bureau, County Business Patterns

Taxes and Business Climate

State and Local Taxes		
Combined Revenues ($1,000s)	**2003–4**	**2004–5**
Revenue from Property Taxes	3,188,869	3,302,265
Revenue from Sales and Gross Receipts Taxes	3,011,578	3,155,247
Revenue from Individual Income Taxes	2,010,610	2,312,898
Revenue from Corporate Income Taxes	89,826	186,169
Revenue from Other Taxes	717,865	747,982
Total Tax Revenue	9,018,748	9,704,861
Per Capita Taxes		
Property Tax Per Capita	1,080	1,117
Sales and Gross Receipts Tax Per Capita	1,020	1,068
Individual Income Tax Per Capita	681	783
Corporate Income Tax Per Capita	30	63
Other Taxes Per Capita	243	253
Total Taxes Per Capita	3,054	3,284

Data: U.S. Census Bureau; Anderson Economic Group, LLC

Business Climate Measures

Anderson Economic Group: 2007 Business Tax Ranking (1 is Best)	27
Forbes Magazine: 2007 Best States for Business Ranking (1 is Best)	24
Tax Foundation: 2008 Business Tax Climate Ranking (1 is Best)	45
ALEC-Laffer 2007 Economic Competitiveness Ranking (1 is Best)	27
2003–4 Employer Firm Births	6,495
2003–4 Employer Firm Terminations	6,217

Data: Anderson Economic Group; Tax Foundation; Forbes Magazine; U.S. Census, Statistics of U.S. Businesses; American Legislative Exchange Council

Voting Behavior and Elected Officials

Voter Registration and Turnout (%)

	1992	1996	2000	2004
Registered Voters Who Voted	79.5	69.5	71.4	75.9
Citizens Age 18+ Who Voted	65.3	57.7	60.0	66.9

Data: Dave Leip's Atlas of U.S. Presidential Elections

Presidential Election Results (Nationwide Winner Listed First)

2004	Popular Vote (%)	Electoral Votes
George W. Bush (Republican, Incumbent)	49.9	7
John Kerry (Democrat)	49.2	0
Other	0.9	0
2000		
George W. Bush (Republican)	48.2	0
Albert Gore (Democrat)	48.5	7
Ralph Nader (Green)	2.2	0
Other	1.0	0
1996		
William Clinton (Democrat, Incumbent)	50.3	7
Robert Dole (Republican)	39.9	0
H. Ross Perot (Reformist)	8.5	0
Other	1.3	0
1992		
William Clinton (Democrat)	43.3	7
George H. W. Bush (Republican, Incumbent)	37.3	0
H. Ross Perot (Independent)	18.7	0
Other	0.7	0

Data: Dave Leip's Atlas of U.S. Presidential Elections

Governor and U.S. Congressional Seats				
Governor	**Party**	**Year Term Began**	**Term**	**Max. Consecutive Terms**
Chet Culver	D	2007	First	No limit
U.S. Senators	**Party**	**Year Elected**	**Term Expires**	
Chuck Grassley	R	1980	2011	
Tom Harkin	D	1984	2009	
U.S. Representatives		**Republican**	**Democrat**	**Other**
		2	3	0

Data: National Governors Association; U.S. Senate, Office of the Clerk; U.S. House of Representatives

Business and Economic Agencies

Agency	Website Address
Iowa Chamber Alliance	www.iowachamberalliance.org
Iowa Department of Economic Development	www.iowalifechanging.com
Iowa Small Business Dev. Center	www.iowasbdc.org
Iowa Secretary of State	www.sos.state.ia.us

Data: Various agency websites

Kansas

Kansas, located in the Middle West region of the United States, had a population of 2.8 million people in 2006, making it the eighteenth least populous state. The state's population increased by 75,657 people from 2000 to 2006, and is projected to increase to 2.9 million by 2025. This 0.3% projected annual growth rate compares to the projected national average of 0.8%. Per capita personal income in Kansas was $34,744 in 2006, up from $32,666 in 2005. For 2006, this was twenty-ninth lowest in the country and $1,885 below the national average. From 2000 to 2006 per capita income in Kansas grew at an average annual rate of 3.9%, compared to 3.5% nationally.

In 2005, the state's largest industry in terms of employment was manufacturing, followed by health care and social assistance. The fastest growing industry was administration, support, waste management, and remediation services, with 2.9% annual employment growth from 1998 to 2005. The state's workforce is generally more educated than other states—88.5% of the state's adult population has graduated from high school, compared to an 84.1% national average. Nationally, an average of

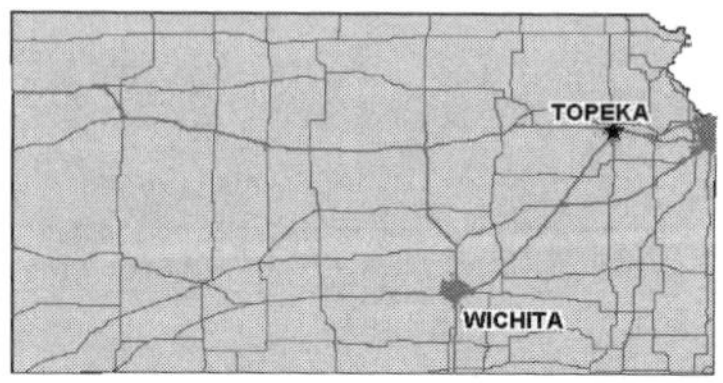

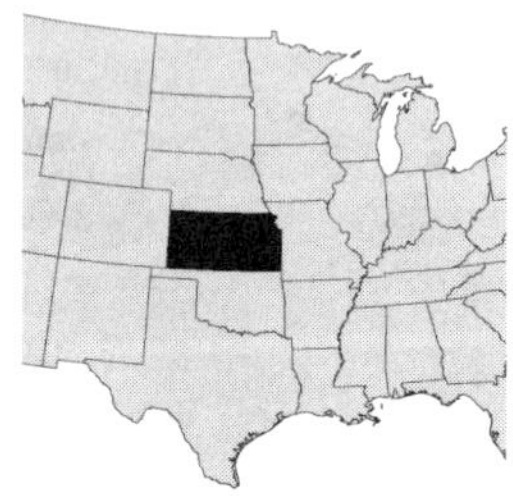

★ State Capitol

Major Urban Area

Major Roadway

Demographic and Socioeconomic Profile

Demographics and Socioeconomic Figures			
Population and Households	**2000**	**2005**	**2006**
Total Population	2,688,418	2,662,616	2,764,075
Number of Households	1,037,891	1,071,938	1,088,288
Average Household Size	2.5	2.5	2.5
Age and Ethnicity			
Median Age	35.2	36.1	36.3
Population 18 Years of Age and Older	1,977,198	1,991,169	2,069,408
Population 65 Years of Age and Older	355,681	330,128	355,664
Caucasian Population	2,312,119	2,269,482	2,361,047
African-American Population	150,584	147,455	153,560
Hispanic Population	186,299	224,152	236,351
Asian Population	44,772	53,129	60,646
Foreign-Born Population (%)	5.0	5.8	6.3
Income			
Per Capita Personal Income (USD)	$27,694	$32,666	$34,744
Median Household Income (USD)	$40,624	$42,920	$45,478
Individuals Below Poverty Level	9.9%	11.7%	12.4%

Data: U.S. Census, American Community Survey; U.S. Department of Commerce, Bureau of Economic Analysis

28.6% hold a bachelor degree or higher compared to 20.0% in Kansas. Nationally, 9.9% hold professional or graduate degrees compared to 9.8% in Kansas.

In fiscal year 2004–5, Kansas had total tax revenues of $9.4 billion. The largest share was generated from sales and gross receipts taxes, followed by property taxes. The per capita tax burden in Kansas was $3,423 for 2004–5, some $282 below the national average. In terms of business taxes, the state ranked thirty-fifth in a study from Anderson Economic Group. Forbes Magazine and the Tax Foundation ranked the state's business climate twentieth and thirty-third, respectively, while ALEC ranked Kansas at twenty-ninth in its state competitiveness index. One is considered best for each ranking.

Population Projections

Year	2010	2015	2020	2025
Total Population	2,805,470	2,852,690	2,890,566	2,919,002
Median Age	36.4	36.9	37.8	38.5
Population 18 Years of Age and Older	2,106,474	2,144,722	2,176,667	2,205,455
Population 65 Years of Age and Older	375,315	419,748	479,919	544,756

Data: U.S. Census Bureau

Workforce and Industry Profile

Workforce

	2000	2005	2006
Civilian Labor Force	1,405,104	1,464,151	1,466,004
Labor Force Participation Rate	70.2%	70.6%	70.2%
Unemployment Rate	3.8%	5.1%	4.5%
Average Wage Per Job (USD)	$29,360	$33,960	$34,960
Education Attainment (Population 25 Years and Older)	**(%)**	**(%)**	**(%)**
High School Graduate or Higher	86.0	88.7	88.5
Bachelors Degree or Higher	25.8	28.2	28.6
Graduate or Professional Degree	8.7	9.6	9.8

Data: U.S. Census Bureau, American Community Survey; U.S. Department of Commerce, Bureau of Economic Analysis; U.S. Department of Labor, Bureau of Labor Statistics

Industry Overview

	1998	2004	2005
Total Employees	1,081,941	1,116,277	1,116,216
Total Payroll ($1,000s)	$28,747,577	$35,725,813	$36,646,065
Total Establishments	74,019	75,827	76,173
Establishments with 1–19 Employees	64,030	65,554	65,796
Establishments with 20–49 Employees	6,304	6,499	6,512
Establishments with 50–249 Employees	3,263	3,325	3,409
Establishments with 250–999 Employees	373	402	407
Establishments with 1,000+ Employees	49	47	49

Data: U.S. Census Bureau, County Business Patterns

Major Industries (Ranked by 2005 Employment; Payroll in $1,000s)				
Industry	1998 Employment	2005 Employment	1998 Payroll	2005 Payroll
Manufacturing	196,519	177,170	6,666,326	7,221,614
Health Care and Social Assistance	154,002	169,777	3,801,133	5,487,089
Retail Trade	149,270	148,988	2,476,930	2,952,169
Accommodation and Food Services	90,431	101,824	842,346	1,101,854
Admin., Support, Waste Mngt., Remediation Services	54,086	65,957	1,076,557	1,694,687
Construction	60,896	62,331	1,947,778	2,465,977
Finance and Insurance	52,839	58,675	1,875,213	2,786,136
Professional, Scientific, Technical Services	49,417	56,793	1,762,448	2,418,500
Wholesale Trade	63,953	54,461	2,370,432	2,345,990
Other Services (except Public Admin.)	51,825	52,010	870,742	1,005,537

Data: U.S. Census Bureau, County Business Patterns

Taxes and Business Climate

State and Local Taxes		
Combined Revenues ($1,000s)	2003–4	2004–5
Revenue from Property Taxes	3,246,616	3,090,403
Revenue from Sales and Gross Receipts Taxes	3,427,052	3,470,022
Revenue from Individual Income Taxes	1,915,530	2,050,562
Revenue from Corporate Income Taxes	166,609	248,135
Revenue from Other Taxes	486,166	526,374
Total Tax Revenue	9,241,973	9,385,496
Per Capita Taxes		
Property Tax Per Capita	1,187	1,127
Sales and Gross Receipts Tax Per Capita	1,253	1,266
Individual Income Tax Per Capita	701	748
Corporate Income Tax Per Capita	61	91
Other Taxes Per Capita	178	192
Total Taxes Per Capita	3,380	3,423

Data: U.S. Census Bureau; Anderson Economic Group, LLC

Business Climate Measures

Anderson Economic Group: 2007 Business Tax Ranking (1 is Best)	35
Forbes Magazine: 2007 Best States for Business Ranking (1 is Best)	20
Tax Foundation: 2008 Business Tax Climate Ranking (1 is Best)	33
ALEC-Laffer 2007 Economic Competitiveness Ranking (1 is Best)	29
2003–4 Employer Firm Births	6,854
2003–4 Employer Firm Terminations	6,307

Data: Anderson Economic Group; Tax Foundation; Forbes Magazine; U.S. Census, Statistics of U.S. Businesses; American Legislative Exchange Council

Voting Behavior and Elected Officials

Voter Registration and Turnout (%)

	1992	1996	2000	2004
Registered Voters Who Voted	84.7	74.6	66.0	70.1
Citizens Age 18+ Who Voted	63.0	56.6	54.2	58.6

Data: Dave Leip's Atlas of U.S. Presidential Elections

Presidential Election Results (Nationwide Winner Listed First)

2004	Popular Vote (%)	Electoral Votes
George W. Bush (Republican, Incumbent)	62.0	6
John Kerry (Democrat)	36.6	0
Other	1.4	0
2000		
George W. Bush (Republican)	58.0	6
Albert Gore (Democrat)	37.2	0
Ralph Nader (Green)	3.4	0
Other	1.4	0
1996		
William Clinton (Democrat, Incumbent)	36.1	0
Robert Dole (Republican)	54.3	6
H. Ross Perot (Reformist)	8.6	0
Other	1.0	0
1992		
William Clinton (Democrat)	33.7	0
George H. W. Bush (Republican, Incumbent)	38.9	6
H. Ross Perot (Independent)	27.0	0
Other	0.4	0

Data: Dave Leip's Atlas of U.S. Presidential Elections

Governor and U.S. Congressional Seats				
Governor	**Party**	**Year Term Began**	**Term**	**Max. Consecutive Terms**
Kathleen Sebelius	D	2007	Second	2
U.S. Senators	**Party**	**Year Elected**	**Term Expires**	
Sam Brownback	R	1996	2011	
Pat Roberts	R	1996	2009	
U.S. Representatives		**Republican**	**Democrat**	**Other**
		2	2	0

Data: National Governors Association; U.S. Senate, Office of the Clerk; U.S. House of Representatives

Business and Economic Agencies

Agency	Website Address
Kansas Chamber of Commerce and Industry	www.kansaschamber.org
Kansas Department of Commerce	www.kansascommerce.com
Kansas Small Business Dev. Center	www.fhsu.edu/ksbdc
Kansas Secretary of State, Business Services	www.kssos.org/business/business.html

Data: Various agency websites

Kentucky

With a population of 4.2 million people, Kentucky was the eighteenth least populous state in the United States in 2006. From 2000 to 2006 the state's population increased by 164,305 people, and is projected to increase to 4.5 million by 2025. This 0.3% projected annual growth rate compares to the projected national average of 0.8%. The state's 2006 per capita personal income of $29,719 was higher compared to $28,352 in 2005 but twenty-ninth lowest in the United States, some $6,910 below the national average. Per capita income in Kentucky grew at an average annual rate of 3.3% from 2000 to 2006, compared to 3.5% nationally.

Kentucky's largest industry in terms of 2005 employment was manufacturing. The fastest growing industry was administration, support, waste management, and remediation services, with 3.5% annual employment growth from 1998 to 2005. The second fastest growing industry was transportation and warehousing. The state's workforce is generally less educated than other states—79.6% of the state's adult population has graduated from high school, compared to an 84.1% national average;

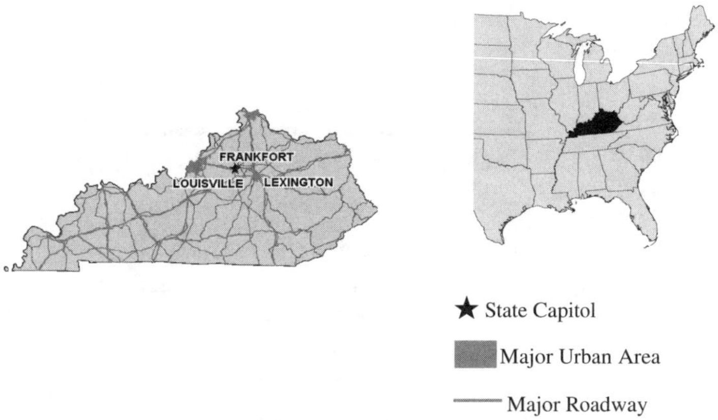

Demographic and Socioeconomic Profile

Demographics and Socioeconomic Figures			
Population and Households	**2000**	**2005**	**2006**
Total Population	4,041,769	4,058,633	4,206,074
Number of Households	1,590,647	1,653,898	1,651,911
Average Household Size	2.5	2.5	2.5
Age and Ethnicity			
Median Age	35.9	37.5	37.3
Population 18 Years of Age and Older	3,047,928	3,082,522	3,205,733
Population 65 Years of Age and Older	503,668	495,885	535,303
Caucasian Population	3,639,168	3,646,690	3,762,571
African-American Population	293,915	292,012	310,146
Hispanic Population	56,414	69,702	83,015
Asian Population	28,994	35,561	38,835
Foreign-Born Population (%)	2.0	2.4	2.7
Income			
Per Capita Personal Income (USD)	$24,412	$28,352	$29,719
Median Household Income (USD)	$33,672	$37,369	$39,372
Individuals Below Poverty Level	15.8%	16.8%	17.0%

Data: U.S. Census, American Community Survey; U.S. Department of Commerce, Bureau of Economic Analysis

20.0% hold a bachelor degree or higher (national average is 27.0%); and 8.2% hold professional or graduate degrees compared to the national average of 9.9%.

Kentucky's total tax revenue was $12.3 billion for fiscal year 2004–5, up from the 2003–4 total revenue of $11.5 billion. The largest share of tax revenue in 2004–5 was generated from sales and gross receipts taxes, followed by individual income taxes. On a per capita basis, residents of Kentucky paid taxes of $2,940, compared to the national average of $3,705 for 2004–5. In terms of business taxes, the state ranked eighteenth in a study from Anderson Economic Group. Forbes Magazine and the Tax Foundation ranked the state's business climate forty-first and thirty-sixth, respectively, while ALEC ranked Kentucky forty-sixth in its state competitiveness index. One is considered best for each ranking.

Population Projections

Year	2010	2015	2020	2025
Total Population	4,265,117	4,351,188	4,424,431	4,489,662
Median Age	38.0	38.6	39.4	39.8
Population 18 Years of Age and Older	3,262,810	3,344,209	3,417,155	3,480,547
Population 65 Years of Age and Older	557,471	637,351	729,741	826,659

Data: U.S. Census Bureau

Workforce and Industry Profile

Workforce

	2000	2005	2006
Civilian Labor Force	1,949,013	1,999,118	2,038,971
Labor Force Participation Rate	63.2%	62.3%	62.9%
Unemployment Rate	4.2%	6.0%	5.7%
Average Wage Per Job (USD)	$28,801	$32,550	$33,490
Education Attainment (Population 25 Years and Older)	**(%)**	**(%)**	**(%)**
High School Graduate or Higher	74.1	79.0	79.6
Bachelors Degree or Higher	17.1	19.3	20.0
Graduate or Professional Degree	6.9	7.8	8.2

Data: U.S. Census Bureau, American Community Survey; U.S. Department of Commerce, Bureau of Economic Analysis; U.S. Department of Labor, Bureau of Labor Statistics

Industry Overview

	1998	2004	2005
Total Employees	1,443,015	1,489,497	1,514,199
Total Payroll ($1,000s)	$36,889,001	$46,163,189	$47,983,162
Total Establishments	89,593	91,797	92,176
Establishments with 1–19 Employees	76,564	78,015	78,359
Establishments with 20–49 Employees	8,100	8,581	8,550
Establishments with 50–249 Employees	4,227	4,513	4,533
Establishments with 250–999 Employees	638	621	664
Establishments with 1,000+ Employees	64	67	70

Data: U.S. Census Bureau, County Business Patterns

Major Industries (Ranked by 2005 Employment; Payroll in $1,000s)				
Industry	1998 Employment	2005 Employment	1998 Payroll	2005 Payroll
Manufacturing	290,665	253,804	9,829,745	10,625,628
Health Care and Social Assistance	194,305	224,193	5,052,060	7,623,152
Retail Trade	221,580	223,666	3,385,861	4,340,765
Accommodation and Food Services	127,561	147,371	1,245,296	1,676,868
Admin., Support, Waste Mngt., Remediation Services	70,020	89,259	1,103,006	1,742,196
Construction	77,191	82,815	2,263,487	2,974,769
Transportation and Warehousing	60,183	75,975	2,054,206	3,071,746
Other Services (except Public Admin.)	62,968	69,897	1,042,453	1,447,977
Wholesale Trade	69,862	69,769	2,214,967	2,992,997
Finance and Insurance	61,079	66,124	1,989,927	2,940,416

Data: U.S. Census Bureau, County Business Patterns

Taxes and Business Climate

State and Local Taxes		
Combined Revenues ($1,000s)	**2003–4**	**2004–5**
Revenue from Property Taxes	2,136,455	2,246,867
Revenue from Sales and Gross Receipts Taxes	4,313,337	4,649,379
Revenue from Individual Income Taxes	3,629,392	3,792,231
Revenue from Corporate Income Taxes	381,538	478,505
Revenue from Other Taxes	999,772	1,094,830
Total Tax Revenue	11,460,494	12,261,812
Per Capita Taxes		
Property Tax Per Capita	516	539
Sales and Gross Receipts Tax Per Capita	1,041	1,115
Individual Income Tax Per Capita	876	909
Corporate Income Tax Per Capita	92	115
Other Taxes Per Capita	241	262
Total Taxes Per Capita	2,767	2,940

Data: U.S. Census Bureau; Anderson Economic Group, LLC

Business Climate Measures	
Anderson Economic Group: 2007 Business Tax Ranking (1 is Best)	18
Forbes Magazine: 2007 Best States for Business Ranking (1 is Best)	41
Tax Foundation: 2008 Business Tax Climate Ranking (1 is Best)	36
ALEC-Laffer 2007 Economic Competitiveness Ranking (1 is Best)	46
2003–4 Employer Firm Births	8,232
2003–4 Employer Firm Terminations	7,645

Data: Anderson Economic Group; Tax Foundation; Forbes Magazine; U.S. Census, Statistics of U.S. Businesses; American Legislative Exchange Council

Voting Behavior and Elected Officials

Voter Registration and Turnout (%)

	1992	1996	2000	2004
Registered Voters Who Voted	71.9	58.1	60.4	64.3
Citizens Age 18+ Who Voted	53.7	47.4	50.7	57.5

Data: Dave Leip's Atlas of U.S. Presidential Elections

Presidential Election Results (Nationwide Winner Listed First)

2004	Popular Vote (%)	Electoral Votes
George W. Bush (Republican, Incumbent)	59.6	8
John Kerry (Democrat)	39.7	0
Other	0.8	0
2000		
George W. Bush (Republican)	56.5	8
Albert Gore (Democrat)	41.4	0
Ralph Nader (Green)	1.5	0
Other	0.6	0
1996		
William Clinton (Democrat, Incumbent)	45.8	8
Robert Dole (Republican)	44.9	0
H. Ross Perot (Reformist)	8.7	0
Other	0.6	0
1992		
William Clinton (Democrat)	44.6	8
George H. W. Bush (Republican, Incumbent)	41.3	0
H. Ross Perot (Independent)	13.7	0
Other	0.5	0

Data: Dave Leip's Atlas of U.S. Presidential Elections

Governor and U.S. Congressional Seats				
Governor	Party	Year Term Began	Term	Max. Consecutive Terms
Steven Beshear	D	2007	First	2
U.S. Senators	Party	Year Elected	Term Expires	
Mitch McConnell	R	1984	2009	
Jim Bunning	R	1998	2011	
U.S. Representatives		Republican	Democrat	Other
		4	2	0

Data: National Governors Association; U.S. Senate, Office of the Clerk; U.S. House of Representatives

Business and Economic Agencies

Agency	Website Address
Kentucky Chamber of Commerce	www.kychamber.com
Kentucky Cabinet for Economic Development	www.thinkkentucky.com
Kentucky Small Business Dev. Center	www.ksbdc.org
Kentucky Secretary of State, Business Services	www.sos.ky.gov/business

Data: Various agency websites

Louisiana

Louisiana is located in the West South Central region of the United States and had a population of 4.3 million people in 2006, making it the twenty-sixth least populous state. The state's population decreased by 181,208 people from 2000 to 2006. From 2005 to 2006 the state's population declined by 2.3%. Louisiana's population is projected to increase, however, to 4.8 million by 2025. This 0.6% projected annual growth rate compares to the national average of 0.8%. Per capita personal income in Louisiana was $31,369 in 2006, up significantly from $24,781 in 2005. For 2006, this was $5,260 below the national average and the eleventh lowest in the country. Louisiana's per capita income grew at an average annual rate of 5.2% from 2000 to 2006, compared to 3.5% nationally.

The state's workforce generally has less education than other states—79.4% of the state's adult population has graduated from high school, compared to an 84.1% national average; 20.3% hold a bachelor degree or higher (national average is 27.0%); and 6.8% hold professional or graduate degrees (national average is 9.9%). In 2005, the state's largest industry in terms of employment

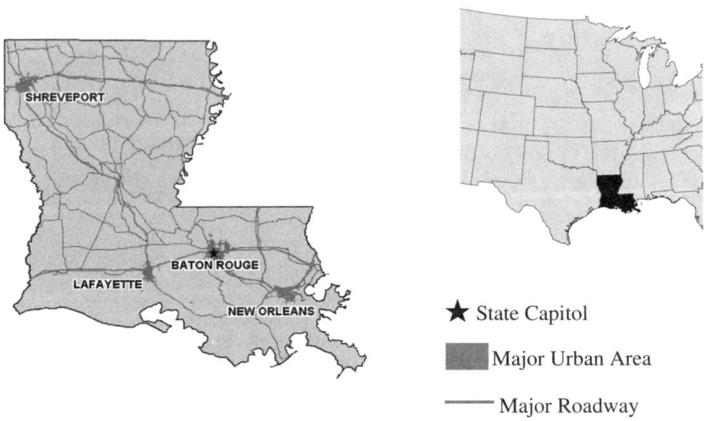

Demographic and Socioeconomic Profile

Demographics and Socioeconomic Figures			
Population and Households	**2000**	**2005**	**2006**
Total Population	4,468,976	4,389,747	4,287,768
Number of Households	1,656,053	1,676,599	1,564,978
Average Household Size	2.6	2.6	2.7
Age and Ethnicity			
Median Age	34.0	35.4	35.6
Population 18 Years of Age and Older	3,250,523	3,249,119	3,198,771
Population 65 Years of Age and Older	518,097	498,883	522,874
Caucasian Population	2,855,964	2,795,263	2,760,233
African-American Population	1,444,566	1,425,685	1,356,981
Hispanic Population	107,854	123,066	123,281
Asian Population	55,492	58,392	57,084
Foreign-Born Population (%)	2.6	2.8	2.9
Income			
Per Capita Personal Income (USD)	$23,078	$24,781	$31,369
Median Household Income (USD)	$32,566	$36,729	$39,337
Individuals Below Poverty Level	19.6%	19.8%	19.0%

Data: U.S. Census, American Community Survey; U.S. Department of Commerce, Bureau of Economic Analysis

was health care and social assistance, followed by retail trade. The fastest growing industry was administration, support, waste management, and remediation services, with 2.5% annual employment growth from 1998 to 2005.

In fiscal year 2004–5, Louisiana had total tax revenues of $14.3 billion. The largest share was generated from sales and gross receipts taxes, followed by property taxes. The per capita tax burden in Louisiana was $3,181 for 2004–5, some $524 below the national average, but a $282 increase from 2003–4. In terms of business taxes, Louisiana ranked eleventh in a study from Anderson Economic Group. The state's business climate was ranked forty-ninth by Forbes Magazine and thirty-second by the Tax Foundation. Louisiana was ranked twenty-first by ALEC in its state competitiveness index. One is considered best for each ranking.

Note that in 2005 Louisiana's largest city, New Orleans, was significantly impacted by Hurricane Katrina, forcing many to leave the state. This at least partially explains the population decline in recent years, as well as the variation in per capita personal incomes.

Population Projections

Year	2010	2015	2020	2025
Total Population	4,612,679	4,673,721	4,719,160	4,762,398
Median Age	35.7	36.4	37.5	38.3
Population 18 Years of Age and Older	3,441,177	3,497,533	3,546,384	3,609,162
Population 65 Years of Age and Older	582,340	663,788	763,468	868,502

Data: U.S. Census Bureau

Workforce and Industry Profile

Workforce

	2000	2005	2006
Civilian Labor Force	2,031,292	2,077,123	1,990,120
Labor Force Participation Rate	61.7%	62.7%	61.6%
Unemployment Rate	5.0%	6.7%	4.0%
Average Wage Per Job (USD)	$27,889	$31,430	$32,900
Education Attainment (Population 25 Years and Older)	**(%)**	**(%)**	**(%)**
High School Graduate or Higher	74.8	80.5	79.4
Bachelors Degree or Higher	18.7	20.6	20.3
Graduate or Professional Degree	6.5	7.1	6.8

Data: U.S. Census Bureau, American Community Survey; U.S. Department of Commerce, Bureau of Economic Analysis; U.S. Department of Labor, Bureau of Labor Statistics

Industry Overview

	1998	2004	2005
Total Employees	1,577,220	1,623,680	1,617,507
Total Payroll ($1,000s)	$40,802,387	$49,047,249	$50,657,624
Total Establishments	100,667	103,067	102,790
Establishments with 1–19 Employees	85,803	87,549	87,638
Establishments with 20–49 Employees	9,421	9,841	9,535
Establishments with 50–249 Employees	4,775	5,032	4,986
Establishments with 250–999 Employees	580	549	537
Establishments with 1,000+ Employees	88	96	94

Data: U.S. Census Bureau, County Business Patterns

Major Industries (Ranked by 2005 Employment; Payroll in $1,000s)				
Industry	1998 Employment	2005 Employment	1998 Payroll	2005 Payroll
Health Care and Social Assistance	234,869	264,664	5,910,937	7,940,735
Retail Trade	226,586	227,856	3,610,877	4,572,205
Accommodation and Food Services	157,120	180,353	1,724,134	2,194,457
Manufacturing	171,549	145,173	6,373,959	7,074,264
Construction	124,838	117,564	3,622,058	4,080,813
Admin., Support, Waste Mngt., Remediation Services	90,251	107,110	1,688,891	2,408,681
Professional, Scientific, Technical Services	74,826	85,308	2,580,019	3,535,206
Other Services (except Public Admin.)	78,090	77,819	1,330,511	1,524,548
Wholesale Trade	79,877	72,586	2,592,307	2,990,452
Finance and Insurance	68,110	67,802	2,391,798	3,054,677

Data: U.S. Census Bureau, County Business Patterns

Taxes and Business Climate

State and Local Taxes		
Combined Revenues ($1,000s)	2003–4	2004–5
Revenue from Property Taxes	2,263,204	2,429,386
Revenue from Sales and Gross Receipts Taxes	7,239,436	7,676,704
Revenue from Individual Income Taxes	2,192,038	2,392,727
Revenue from Corporate Income Taxes	236,745	352,136
Revenue from Other Taxes	1,134,007	1,451,042
Total Tax Revenue	13,065,430	14,301,995
Per Capita Taxes		
Property Tax Per Capita	502	540
Sales and Gross Receipts Tax Per Capita	1,606	1,708
Individual Income Tax Per Capita	486	532
Corporate Income Tax Per Capita	53	78
Other Taxes Per Capita	252	323
Total Taxes Per Capita	2,899	3,181

Data: U.S. Census Bureau; Anderson Economic Group, LLC

Business Climate Measures	
Anderson Economic Group: 2007 Business Tax Ranking (1 is Best)	11
Forbes Magazine: 2007 Best States for Business Ranking (1 is Best)	49
Tax Foundation: 2008 Business Tax Climate Ranking (1 is Best)	32
ALEC-Laffer 2007 Economic Competitiveness Ranking (1 is Best)	21
2003–4 Employer Firm Births	9,340
2003–4 Employer Firm Terminations	8,556

Data: Anderson Economic Group; Tax Foundation; Forbes Magazine; U.S. Census, Statistics of U.S. Businesses; American Legislative Exchange Council

Voting Behavior and Elected Officials

Voter Registration and Turnout (%)

	1992	1996	2000	2004
Registered Voters Who Voted	78.1	69.7	63.1	66.5
Citizens Age 18+ Who Voted	59.8	57.0	54.3	58.5

Data: Dave Leip's Atlas of U.S. Presidential Elections

Presidential Election Results (Nationwide Winner Listed First)

2004	Popular Vote (%)	Electoral Votes
George W. Bush (Republican, Incumbent)	56.7	9
John Kerry (Democrat)	42.2	0
Other	1.1	0
2000		
George W. Bush (Republican)	52.6	9
Albert Gore (Democrat)	44.9	0
Ralph Nader (Green)	1.2	0
Other	1.4	0
1996		
William Clinton (Democrat, Incumbent)	52.0	9
Robert Dole (Republican)	39.9	0
H. Ross Perot (Reformist)	6.9	0
Other	1.1	0
1992		
William Clinton (Democrat)	45.6	9
George H. W. Bush (Republican, Incumbent)	41.0	0
H. Ross Perot (Independent)	11.8	0
Other	1.6	0

Data: Dave Leip's Atlas of U.S. Presidential Elections

Governor and U.S. Congressional Seats				
Governor	**Party**	**Year Term Began**	**Term**	**Max. Consecutive Terms**
Bobby Jindal	R	2008	First	2
U.S. Senators	**Party**	**Year Elected**	**Term Expires**	
Mary L. Landrieu	D	1996	2009	
David Vitter	R	2004	2011	
U.S. Representatives		**Republican**	**Democrat**	**Other**
		4	2	0

Data: National Governors Association; U.S. Senate, Office of the Clerk; U.S. House of Representatives

Business and Economic Agencies

Agency	Website Address
Louisiana Association of Business and Industry	www.labi.org
Louisiana Economic Development	www.lded.state.la.us
Louisiana Small Business Dev. Center	www.lsbdc.org
Louisiana Secretary of State Commercial Division	www.sos.louisiana.gov/tabid/66/Default.aspx

Data: Various agency websites

Maine

Maine, located in the New England region of the United States, had a population of 1.3 million people in 2006, making it the eleventh least populous state. The state's population increased by 46,651 people from 2000 to 2006, and is projected to increase to 1.4 million by 2025. This 0.4% projected annual growth rate compares to the projected national average of 0.8%. Per capita personal income in Maine was $31,931 in 2006, up from $30,825 in 2005. For 2006, this was twelfth lowest in the country and $4,698 below the national average. From 2000 to 2006 per capita income in Maine grew at an average annual rate of 3.5%, equal to the national rate.

In 2005, the state's largest industry in terms of employment was health care and social assistance, followed by retail trade. The fastest growing industry was finance and insurance, with 4.7% annual employment growth from 1998 to 2005. The state's workforce is generally less educated than other states—88.7% of the state's adult population has graduated from high school, compared to an 84.1% national average. Nationally, an average of 27.0% hold a bachelor degree

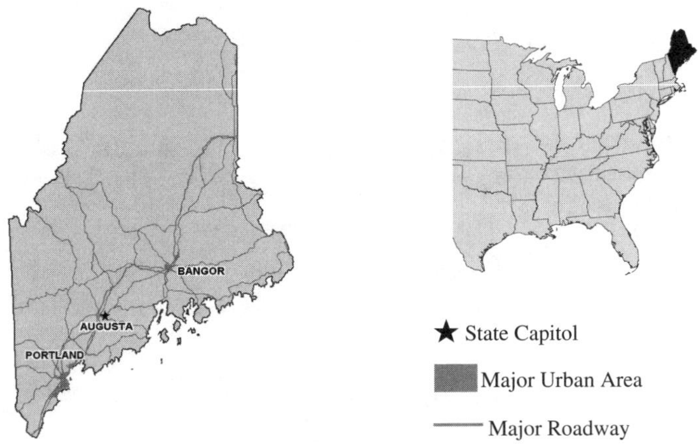

Demographic and Socioeconomic Profile

Demographics and Socioeconomic Figures			
Population and Households	**2000**	**2005**	**2006**
Total Population	1,274,923	1,283,673	1,321,574
Number of Households	518,200	542,158	548,247
Average Household Size	2.4	2.4	2.3
Age and Ethnicity			
Median Age	38.6	41.2	41.0
Population 18 Years of Age and Older	973,945	1,007,454	1,039,702
Population 65 Years of Age and Older	183,642	181,315	192,434
Caucasian Population	1,236,422	1,239,525	1,265,541
African-American Population	6,047	8,788	13,669
Hispanic Population	9,226	12,059	12,622
Asian Population	8,259	10,907	12,004
Foreign-Born Population (%)	2.9	3.0	3.2
Income			
Per Capita Personal Income (USD)	$25,969	$30,825	$31,931
Median Household Income (USD)	$37,240	$42,801	$43,439
Individuals Below Poverty Level	10.9%	12.6%	12.9%

Data: U.S. Census, American Community Survey; U.S. Department of Commerce, Bureau of Economic Analysis

or higher compared to 25.8% in Maine. Nationally, 9.9% hold professional or graduate degrees compared to 8.9% in Maine.

In fiscal year 2004–5, Maine had total tax revenues of $5.2 billion. The largest share was generated from property taxes, followed by sales and gross receipts taxes. The per capita tax burden in Maine was $3,978 for 2004–5, some $273 above the national average. In terms of business taxes, the state ranked forty-ninth in a study from Anderson Economic Group. Forbes Magazine and the Tax Foundation ranked the state's business climate forty-eighth and forty-first, respectively, while ALEC ranked Maine at forty-fourth in its state competitiveness index. One is considered best for each ranking.

Population Projections

Year	2010	2015	2020	2025
Total Population	1,357,134	1,388,878	1,408,665	1,414,402
Median Age	42.2	43.4	44.1	45.3
Population 18 Years of Age and Older	1,087,902	1,120,280	1,140,230	1,149,909
Population 65 Years of Age and Older	212,278	250,195	293,990	339,038

Data: U.S. Census Bureau

Workforce and Industry Profile

Workforce

	2000	2005	2006
Civilian Labor Force	672,440	703,085	711,376
Labor Force Participation Rate	67.5%	66.8%	67.0%
Unemployment Rate	3.3%	4.8%	4.6%
Average Wage Per Job (USD)	$27,664	$33,920	$35,160
Education Attainment (Population 25 Years and Older)	**(%)**	**(%)**	**(%)**
High School Graduate or Higher	85.4	89.0	88.7
Bachelors Degree or Higher	22.9	25.6	25.8
Graduate or Professional Degree	7.9	8.6	8.9

Data: U.S. Census Bureau, American Community Survey; U.S. Department of Commerce, Bureau of Economic Analysis; U.S. Department of Labor, Bureau of Labor Statistics

Industry Overview

	1998	2004	2005
Total Employees	456,715	494,256	497,387
Total Payroll ($1,000s)	$11,559,136	$15,439,092	$15,873,419
Total Establishments	38,334	41,269	41,933
Establishments with 1–19 Employees	34,326	36,717	74,273
Establishments with 20–49 Employees	2,516	2,955	3,030
Establishments with 50–249 Employees	1,312	1,404	1,398
Establishments with 250–999 Employees	162	173	171
Establishments with 1,000+ Employees	18	20	18

Data: U.S. Census Bureau, County Business Patterns

Major Industries (Ranked by 2005 Employment; Payroll in $1,000s)				
Industry	1998 Employment	2005 Employment	1998 Payroll	2005 Payroll
Health Care and Social Assistance	79,828	97,973	2,029,109	3,260,097
Retail Trade	74,220	85,352	1,263,051	1,850,083
Manufacturing	80,640	60,995	2,630,781	2,496,875
Accommodation and Food Services	41,273	45,484	512,859	717,503
Finance and Insurance	21,374	29,421	839,098	1,293,728
Construction	23,766	27,065	729,676	1,060,191
Admin., Support, Waste Mngt., Remediation Services	23,318	25,282	445,008	696,562
Professional, Scientific, Technical Services	16,708	22,199	584,864	1,028,862
Other Services (except Public Admin.)	17,445	19,968	294,070	409,546
Wholesale Trade	20,932	19,456	658,579	809,605

Data: U.S. Census Bureau, County Business Patterns

Taxes and Business Climate

State and Local Taxes		
Combined Revenues ($1,000s)	**2003–4**	**2004–5**
Revenue from Property Taxes	2,099,394	2,151,968
Revenue from Sales and Gross Receipts Taxes	1,336,680	1,363,266
Revenue from Individual Income Taxes	1,160,389	1,299,252
Revenue from Corporate Income Taxes	111,616	135,863
Revenue from Other Taxes	274,462	269,359
Total Tax Revenue	4,982,541	5,219,708
Per Capita Taxes		
Property Tax Per Capita	1,596	1,640
Sales and Gross Receipts Tax Per Capita	1,016	1,039
Individual Income Tax Per Capita	882	990
Corporate Income Tax Per Capita	85	104
Other Taxes Per Capita	209	205
Total Taxes Per Capita	3,789	3,978

Data: U.S. Census Bureau; Anderson Economic Group, LLC

Business Climate Measures	
Anderson Economic Group: 2007 Business Tax Ranking (1 is Best)	49
Forbes Magazine: 2007 Best States for Business Ranking (1 is Best)	48
Tax Foundation: 2008 Business Tax Climate Ranking (1 is Best)	41
ALEC-Laffer 2007 Economic Competitiveness Ranking (1 is Best)	44
2003–4 Employer Firm Births	3,651
2003–4 Employer Firm Terminations	3,289

Data: Anderson Economic Group; Tax Foundation; Forbes Magazine; U.S. Census, Statistics of U.S. Businesses; American Legislative Exchange Council

Voting Behavior and Elected Officials

Voter Registration and Turnout (%)

	1992	1996	2000	2004
Registered Voters Who Voted	69.7	60.5	68.8	72.3
Citizens Age 18+ Who Voted	72.0	64.1	66.9	72.7

Data: Dave Leip's Atlas of U.S. Presidential Elections

Presidential Election Results (Nationwide Winner Listed First)

2004	Popular Vote (%)	Electoral Votes
George W. Bush (Republican, Incumbent)	44.6	0
John Kerry (Democrat)	53.6	4
Other	1.9	0
2000		
George W. Bush (Republican)	44.0	0
Albert Gore (Democrat)	49.1	4
Ralph Nader (Green)	5.7	0
Other	1.2	0
1996		
William Clinton (Democrat, Incumbent)	51.6	4
Robert Dole (Republican)	30.8	0
H. Ross Perot (Reformist)	14.2	0
Other	3.4	0
1992		
William Clinton (Democrat)	38.8	4
George H. W. Bush (Republican, Incumbent)	30.4	0
H. Ross Perot (Independent)	30.4	0
Other	0.4	0

Data: Dave Leip's Atlas of U.S. Presidential Elections

Governor and U.S. Congressional Seats				
Governor	Party	Year Term Began	Term	Max. Consecutive Terms
John Baldacci	D	2007	Second	2
U.S. Senators	Party	Year Elected	Term Expires	
Susan M. Collins	R	1996	2009	
Olympia J. Snowe	R	1994	2013	
U.S. Representatives		Republican	Democrat	Other
		0	2	0

Data: National Governors Association; U.S. Senate, Office of the Clerk; U.S. House of Representatives

Business and Economic Agencies

Agency	Website Address
Maine State Chamber of Commerce	www.mainechamber.org
The Maine Department of Economic and Community Development	www.econdevmaine.com
Maine Small Business Dev. Center	www.mainesbdc.org
Maine Bureau of Corporations	www.state.me.us/sos/cec/index.html

Data: Various agency websites

Maryland

With a population of 5.6 million people, Maryland was the nineteenth most populous state in the United States in 2006. From 2000 to 2006 the state's population increased by 319,241 people, and is projected to increase to 6.7 million by 2025. This 1.0% projected annual growth rate compares to the projected national average of 0.8%. The state's 2006 per capita personal income of $43,447 was higher compared to $41,587 in 2005 and fifth highest in the United States, some $7,145 above the national average. Per capita income in Maryland grew at an average annual rate of 4.2% from 2000 to 2006, compared to 3.5% nationally.

Maryland's largest industry in terms of 2005 employment was health care and social assistance. The fastest growing industry was professional, scientific, and technical services, with 3.6% annual employment growth from 1998 to 2005. The second fastest growing industry was construction. The state's workforce is generally more educated than other states—87.1% of the state's adult population has graduated from high school, compared to an 84.1% national average; 35.1% hold a bachelor degree or higher (national average is 27.0%); and 15.7% hold

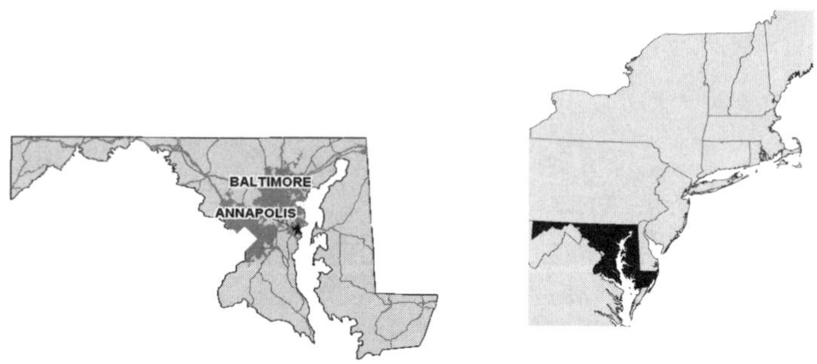

★ State Capitol

Major Urban Area

Major Roadway

Demographic and Socioeconomic Profile

Demographics and Socioeconomic Figures			
Population and Households	**2000**	**2005**	**2006**
Total Population	5,296,486	5,461,318	5,615,727
Number of Households	1,980,859	2,085,647	2,089,031
Average Household Size	2.6	2.6	2.6
Age and Ethnicity			
Median Age	36.0	37.1	37.3
Population 18 Years of Age and Older	3,943,067	4,063,655	4,253,595
Population 65 Years of Age and Older	598,004	609,450	647,332
Caucasian Population	3,391,021	3,356,489	3,441,497
African-American Population	1,468,243	1,564,914	1,624,858
Hispanic Population	227,105	316,257	336,390
Asian Population	209,713	258,529	276,362
Foreign-Born Population (%)	9.8	11.7	12.2
Income			
Per Capita Personal Income (USD)	$34,257	$41,587	$43,774
Median Household Income (USD)	$52,868	$61,592	$65,144
Individuals Below Poverty Level	8.5%	8.2%	7.8%

Data: U.S. Census, American Community Survey; U.S. Department of Commerce, Bureau of Economic Analysis

professional or graduate degrees compared to the national average of 9.9%.

Maryland's total tax revenue was $23.9 billion for fiscal year 2004–5, up from the 2003–4 total revenue of $22.3 billion. The largest share of tax revenue in 2004–5 was generated from individual income taxes, followed by sales and gross receipts taxes. On a per capita basis, residents of Maryland paid taxes of $4,288, compared to the national average of $3,705 for 2004–5. In terms of business taxes, the state ranked twenty-third in a study from Anderson Economic Group. Forbes Magazine and the Tax Foundation ranked the state's business climate twelfth and twenty-fourth, respectively, while ALEC ranked Maryland thirty-second in its state competitiveness index. One is considered best for each ranking.

Population Projections

Year	2010	2015	2020	2025
Total Population	5,904,970	6,208,392	6,497,626	6,762,732
Median Age	36.8	36.1	36.4	36.9
Population 18 Years of Age and Older	4,498,676	4,721,718	4,911,565	5,098,221
Population 65 Years of Age and Older	717,987	837,124	962,160	1,104,757

Data: U.S. Census Bureau

Workforce and Industry Profile

Workforce

	2000	2005	2006
Civilian Labor Force	2,811,657	2,942,960	3,009,143
Labor Force Participation Rate	70.4%	68.8%	69.7%
Unemployment Rate	3.6%	4.2%	3.9%
Average Wage Per Job (USD)	$36,395	$42,080	$44,030
Education Attainment (Population 25 Years and Older)	**(%)**	**(%)**	**(%)**
High School Graduate or Higher	83.8	87.0	87.1
Bachelors Degree or Higher	31.4	34.5	35.1
Graduate or Professional Degree	13.4	15.2	15.7

Data: U.S. Census Bureau, American Community Survey; U.S. Department of Commerce, Bureau of Economic Analysis; U.S. Department of Labor, Bureau of Labor Statistics

Industry Overview

	1998	2004	2005
Total Employees	1,938,727	2,151,474	2,167,999
Total Payroll ($1,000s)	$59,817,673	$84,346,365	$88,964,728
Total Establishments	126,577	136,062	138,481
Establishments with 1–19 Employees	108,830	115,881	118,182
Establishments with 20–49 Employees	10,961	12,322	12,375
Establishments with 50–249 Employees	5,980	6,980	7,034
Establishments with 250–999 Employees	702	770	777
Establishments with 1,000+ Employees	104	109	113

Data: U.S. Census Bureau, County Business Patterns

Major Industries (Ranked by 2005 Employment; Payroll in $1,000s)				
Industry	1998 Employment	2005 Employment	1998 Payroll	2005 Payroll
Health Care and Social Assistance	258,901	300,272	7,607,050	11,855,818
Retail Trade	273,016	299,658	5,245,293	7,225,671
Professional, Scientific, Technical Services	172,671	221,269	8,145,127	13,706,692
Accommodation and Food Services	160,294	188,835	1,838,370	2,710,753
Construction	142,650	181,735	4,851,310	8,298,193
Admin., Support, Waste Mngt., Remediation Services	160,362	164,841	3,665,695	4,778,658
Manufacturing	163,123	135,120	6,191,401	6,717,027
Finance and Insurance	104,336	121,374	4,556,298	8,071,435
Other Services (except Public Admin.)	105,452	114,255	2,288,378	3,168,978
Wholesale Trade	91,987	97,350	3,925,037	5,215,987

Data: U.S. Census Bureau, County Business Patterns

Taxes and Business Climate

State and Local Taxes		
Combined Revenues ($1,000s)	**2003–4**	**2004–5**
Revenue from Property Taxes	6,018,629	5,594,371
Revenue from Sales and Gross Receipts Taxes	5,455,744	5,758,944
Revenue from Individual Income Taxes	8,286,551	9,153,415
Revenue from Corporate Income Taxes	569,700	807,054
Revenue from Other Taxes	2,000,503	2,585,271
Total Tax Revenue	22,331,127	23,899,055
Per Capita Taxes		
Property Tax Per Capita	1,082	1,004
Sales and Gross Receipts Tax Per Capita	981	1,033
Individual Income Tax Per Capita	1,490	1,642
Corporate Income Tax Per Capita	102	145
Other Taxes Per Capita	360	464
Total Taxes Per Capita	4,016	4,288

Data: U.S. Census Bureau; Anderson Economic Group, LLC

Business Climate Measures	
Anderson Economic Group: 2007 Business Tax Ranking (1 is Best)	23
Forbes Magazine: 2007 Best States for Business Ranking (1 is Best)	12
Tax Foundation: 2008 Business Tax Climate Ranking (1 is Best)	24
ALEC-Laffer 2007 Economic Competitiveness Ranking (1 is Best)	32
2003–4 Employer Firm Births	13,302
2003–4 Employer Firm Terminations	11,154

Data: Anderson Economic Group; Tax Foundation; Forbes Magazine; U.S. Census, Statistics of U.S. Businesses; American Legislative Exchange Council

Voting Behavior and Elected Officials

Voter Registration and Turnout (%)

	1992	1996	2000	2004
Registered Voters Who Voted	80.6	69.1	74.5	77.7
Citizens Age 18+ Who Voted	53.4	46.6	51.4	57.8

Data: Dave Leip's Atlas of U.S. Presidential Elections

Presidential Election Results (Nationwide Winner Listed First)

2004	Popular Vote (%)	Electoral Votes
George W. Bush (Republican, Incumbent)	42.9	0
John Kerry (Democrat)	55.9	10
Other	1.2	0
2000		
George W. Bush (Republican)	40.2	0
Albert Gore (Democrat)	56.6	10
Ralph Nader (Green)	2.7	0
Other	0.6	0
1996		
William Clinton (Democrat, Incumbent)	54.3	10
Robert Dole (Republican)	38.3	0
H. Ross Perot (Reformist)	6.5	0
Other	1.0	0
1992		
William Clinton (Democrat)	49.8	10
George H. W. Bush (Republican, Incumbent)	35.6	0
H. Ross Perot (Independent)	14.2	0
Other	0.4	0

Data: Dave Leip's Atlas of U.S. Presidential Elections

Governor and U.S. Congressional Seats				
Governor	**Party**	**Year Term Began**	**Term**	**Max. Consecutive Terms**
Martin O'Malley	D	2007	First	2
U.S. Senators	**Party**	**Year Elected**	**Term Expires**	
Barbara A. Mikulski	D	1986	2011	
Ben Cardin	D	2006	2013	
U.S. Representatives		**Republican**	**Democrat**	**Other**
		2	6	0

Data: National Governors Association; U.S. Senate, Office of the Clerk; U.S. House of Representatives

Business and Economic Agencies

Agency	Website Address
Maryland Chamber of Commerce	www.mdchamber.org
Maryland Department of Business and Economic Development	www.dbed.state.md.us
Maryland Small Business Dev. Center	www.mdsbdc.umd.edu
Maryland Department of Assessments & Taxation	www.dat.state.md.us/sdatweb/charter.html

Data: Various agency websites

Massachusetts

Massachusetts is located in the New England region of the United States and had a population of 6.4 million people in 2006, making it the thirteenth most populous state. The state's population increased by 88,096 people from 2000 to 2006, and is projected to increase to 6.9 million by 2025. This 0.4% projected annual growth rate is above the national average of 0.8%. Per capita personal income in Massachusetts was $46,255 in 2006, up from $43,601 in 2005. For 2006, this was $9,626 above the national average and the third highest in the country. The state's per capita income grew at an average annual rate of 3.4%, just under the national average of 3.5%.

The state's workforce generally has less education than other states—87.9% of the state's adult population has graduated from high school, compared to an 84.1% national average; 37.0% hold a bachelor degree or higher (national average is 27.0%); and 15.6% hold professional or graduate degrees (national average is 9.9%). In 2005, the state's largest industry in terms of employment was health care and social assistance, followed by retail trade. The fastest growing

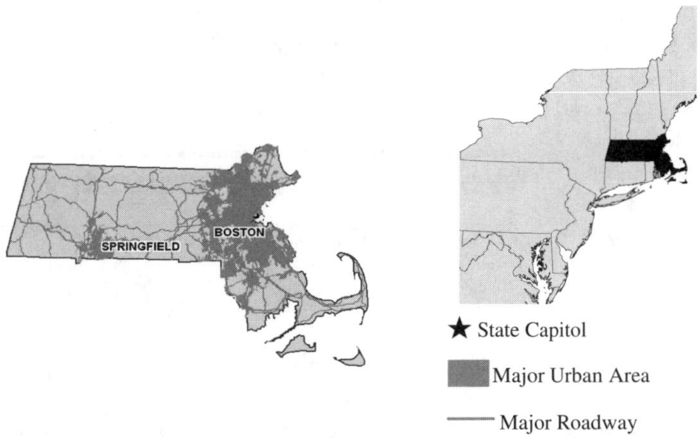

Demographic and Socioeconomic Profile

Demographics and Socioeconomic Figures			
Population and Households	**2000**	**2005**	**2006**
Total Population	6,349,097	6,182,860	6,437,193
Number of Households	2,443,580	2,448,032	2,446,485
Average Household Size	2.5	2.5	2.5
Age and Ethnicity			
Median Age	36.5	38.2	38.3
Population 18 Years of Age and Older	4,853,130	4,732,189	4,988,716
Population 65 Years of Age and Older	859,601	796,788	856,886
Caucasian Population	5,365,139	5,156,426	5,329,576
African-American Population	337,157	363,095	393,207
Hispanic Population	427,340	490,839	510,482
Asian Population	238,246	292,537	310,441
Foreign-Born Population (%)	12.2	14.4	14.1
Income			
Per Capita Personal Income (USD)	$37,756	$43,601	$46,255
Median Household Income (USD)	$50,502	$57,184	$59,963
Individuals Below Poverty Level	9.3%	10.3%	9.9%

Data: U.S. Census, American Community Survey; U.S. Department of Commerce, Bureau of Economic Analysis

industry was educational services, with 2.8% annual employment growth from 1998 to 2005.

In fiscal year 2004–5, Massachusetts had total tax revenues of $28.8 billion. The largest share was generated from property taxes, followed by individual taxes. The per capita tax burden in Massachusetts was $4,473 for 2004–5, some $768 above the national average, and an increase from 2003–4. In terms of business taxes, Massachusetts ranked sixteenth in a study from Anderson Economic Group. The state's business climate was ranked thirty-sixth by Forbes Magazine and thirty-fourth by the Tax Foundation. Massachusetts was ranked twenty-sixth by ALEC in its state competitiveness index. One is considered best for each ranking.

Population Projections

Year	2010	2015	2020	2025
Total Population	6,649,441	6,758,580	6,855,546	6,938,636
Median Age	38.8	39.2	39.5	39.7
Population 18 Years of Age and Older	5,165,588	5,284,629	5,362,379	5,419,996
Population 65 Years of Age and Older	908,565	1,025,448	1,159,817	1,317,940

Data: U.S. Census Bureau

Workforce and Industry Profile

Workforce

	2000	2005	2006
Civilian Labor Force	3,365,573	3,374,188	3,404,394
Labor Force Participation Rate	68.3%	66.7%	67.0%
Unemployment Rate	2.7%	4.8%	5.0%
Average Wage Per Job (USD)	$44,329	$45,970	$47,340
Education Attainment (Population 25 Years and Older)	**(%)**	**(%)**	**(%)**
High School Graduate or Higher	84.8	88.0	87.9
Bachelors Degree or Higher	33.2	36.9	37.0
Graduate or Professional Degree	13.7	15.7	15.6

Data: U.S. Census Bureau, American Community Survey; U.S. Department of Commerce, Bureau of Economic Analysis; U.S. Department of Labor, Bureau of Labor Statistics

Industry Overview

	1998	2004	2005
Total Employees	2,924,913	2,979,690	2,996,347
Total Payroll ($1,000s)	$105,871,311	$135,244,829	$140,580,627
Total Establishments	167,929	175,933	175,291
Establishments with 1–19 Employees	143,459	150,563	150,120
Establishments with 20–49 Employees	14,454	15,276	15,068
Establishments with 50–249 Employees	8,658	8,851	8,838
Establishments with 250–999 Employees	1,148	1,043	1,062
Establishments with 1,000+ Employees	210	200	203

Data: U.S. Census Bureau, County Business Patterns

Major Industries (Ranked by 2005 Employment; Payroll in $1,000s)				
Industry	1998 Employment	2005 Employment	1998 Payroll	2005 Payroll
Health Care and Social Assistance	452,465	485,617	13,494,246	19,545,348
Retail Trade	340,548	369,290	6,558,993	8,908,761
Manufacturing	409,938	285,916	17,170,367	15,570,158
Professional, Scientific, Technical Services	201,084	243,889	11,773,454	18,513,912
Accommodation and Food Services	232,603	241,077	2,994,758	4,045,039
Finance and Insurance	214,807	206,327	13,055,694	19,344,901
Admin., Support, Waste Mngt., Remediation Services	179,590	186,902	4,639,257	6,409,268
Educational Services	152,797	185,539	4,016,307	5,922,084
Wholesale Trade	147,661	149,283	7,145,803	9,591,832
Construction	106,184	126,481	4,591,611	7,118,084

Data: U.S. Census Bureau, County Business Patterns

Taxes and Business Climate

State and Local Taxes		
Combined Revenues ($1,000s)	**2003–4**	**2004–5**
Revenue from Property Taxes	9,814,315	10,341,126
Revenue from Sales and Gross Receipts Taxes	5,740,153	5,932,045
Revenue from Individual Income Taxes	8,830,334	9,690,270
Revenue from Corporate Income Taxes	1,301,076	1,332,796
Revenue from Other Taxes	1,329,269	1,460,725
Total Tax Revenue	27,015,147	28,756,962
Per Capita Taxes		
Property Tax Per Capita	1,532	1,608
Sales and Gross Receipts Tax Per Capita	896	923
Individual Income Tax Per Capita	1,378	1,507
Corporate Income Tax Per Capita	203	207
Other Taxes Per Capita	207	227
Total Taxes Per Capita	4,217	4,473

Data: U.S. Census Bureau; Anderson Economic Group, LLC

Business Climate Measures	
Anderson Economic Group: 2007 Business Tax Ranking (1 is Best)	16
Forbes Magazine: 2007 Best States for Business Ranking (1 is Best)	36
Tax Foundation: 2008 Business Tax Climate Ranking (1 is Best)	34
ALEC-Laffer 2007 Economic Competitiveness Ranking (1 is Best)	26
2003–4 Employer Firm Births	15,512
2003–4 Employer Firm Terminations	16,819

Data: Anderson Economic Group; Tax Foundation; Forbes Magazine; U.S. Census, Statistics of U.S. Businesses; American Legislative Exchange Council

Voting Behavior and Elected Officials

Voter Registration and Turnout (%)

	1992	1996	2000	2004
Registered Voters Who Voted	82.7	73.8	67.4	71.1
Citizens Age 18+ Who Voted	60.2	55.0	55.7	58.9

Data: Dave Leip's Atlas of U.S. Presidential Elections

Presidential Election Results (Nationwide Winner Listed First)

2004	Popular Vote (%)	Electoral Votes
George W. Bush (Republican, Incumbent)	36.8	0
John Kerry (Democrat)	61.9	12
Other	1.3	0
2000		
George W. Bush (Republican)	32.5	0
Albert Gore (Democrat)	59.8	12
Ralph Nader (Green)	6.4	0
Other	1.3	0
1996		
William Clinton (Democrat, Incumbent)	61.5	12
Robert Dole (Republican)	28.1	0
H. Ross Perot (Reformist)	8.9	0
Other	1.6	0
1992		
William Clinton (Democrat)	47.5	12
George H. W. Bush (Republican, Incumbent)	29.0	0
H. Ross Perot (Independent)	22.7	0
Other	0.7	0

Data: Dave Leip's Atlas of U.S. Presidential Elections

Governor and U.S. Congressional Seats				
Governor	**Party**	**Year Term Began**	**Term**	**Max. Consecutive Terms**
Deveal Patrick	D	2007	First	No limit
U.S. Senators	**Party**	**Year Elected**	**Term Expires**	
John Kerry	D	1984	2009	
Edward Kennedy	D	1962	2013	
U.S. Representatives		**Republican**	**Democrat**	**Other**
		0	10	0

Data: National Governors Association; U.S. Senate, Office of the Clerk; U.S. House of Representatives

Business and Economic Agencies

Agency	Website Address
Massachusetts Economic Development	www.mass.gov
Massachusetts Small Business Dev. Center	www.msbdc.org
Massachusetts Corporations Division	www.sec.state.ma.us/cor/coridx.htm

Data: Various agency websites

Michigan

Michigan, located in the East North Central region of the United States, had a population of 10.1 million people in 2006, making it the eighth most populous state. The state's population increased by 157,199 people from 2000 to 2006, and is projected to increase to 10.7 million by 2025. This 0.3% projected annual growth rate compares to the projected national average of 0.8%. Per capita personal income in Michigan was $3,784 in 2006, up from $32,719 in 2005. For 2006, this was twenty-seventh lowest in the country and $2,845 below the national average. From 2000 to 2006 per capita income in Michigan grew at an average annual rate of 2.3%, compared to 3.5% nationally.

In 2005, the state's largest industry in terms of employment was manufacturing, followed by health care and social assistance. The fastest growing industry was professional, scientific, and technical services, with 6.1% annual employment growth from 1998 to 2005. The state's workforce is generally less educated than other states—87.2% of the state's adult population has graduated from high school, compared to an 84.1% national average. Nationally, an average of 24.5% hold a bachelor

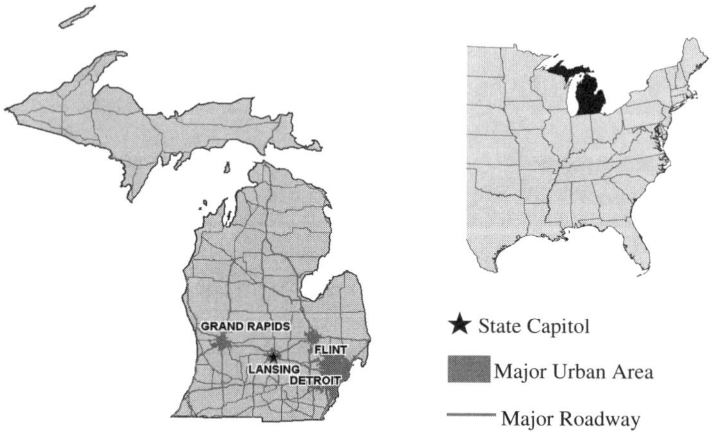

Demographic and Socioeconomic Profile

Demographics and Socioeconomic Figures			
Population and Households	**2000**	**2005**	**2006**
Total Population	9,938,444	9,865,583	10,095,643
Number of Households	3,785,661	3,887,994	3,869,117
Average Household Size	2.6	2.5	2.5
Age and Ethnicity			
Median Age	35.5	36.9	37.3
Population 18 Years of Age and Older	7,345,849	7,352,920	7,618,222
Population 65 Years of Age and Older	1,219,232	1,194,502	1,260,367
Caucasian Population	7,960,342	7,890,608	8,026,545
African-American Population	1,401,723	1,379,010	1,426,809
Hispanic Population	322,160	371,627	392,770
Asian Population	174,824	227,585	236,972
Foreign-Born Population (%)	5.3	6.1	5.9
Income			
Per Capita Personal Income (USD)	$29,552	$32,719	$33,784
Median Household Income (USD)	$44,667	$46,039	$47,182
Individuals Below Poverty Level	10.5%	13.2%	13.5%

Data: U.S. Census, American Community Survey; U.S. Department of Commerce, Bureau of Economic Analysis

degree or higher compared to 30.4% in Michigan. Nationally, 9.9% hold professional or graduate degrees compared to 9.2% in Michigan.

In fiscal year 2004–5, Michigan had total tax revenues of $35.3 billion. The largest share was generated from property taxes, followed by sales and gross receipts taxes. The per capita tax burden in Michigan was $3,492 for 2004–5, some $213 below the national average. In terms of business taxes, the state ranked twenty-sixth in a study from Anderson Economic Group. Forbes Magazine and the Tax Foundation ranked the state's business climate forty-sixth and twenty-ninth, respectively, while ALEC ranked Michigan sixteenth in its state competitiveness index. One is considered best for each ranking.

Population Projections

Year	2010	2015	2020	2025
Total Population	10,428,683	10,599,122	10,695,993	10,713,730
Median Age	37.4	37.8	38.6	39.4
Population 18 Years of Age and Older	7,941,625	8,120,199	8,216,729	8,241,856
Population 65 Years of Age and Older	1,334,491	1,506,856	1,711,476	1,926,396

Data: U.S. Census Bureau

Workforce and Industry Profile

Workforce

	2000	2005	2006
Civilian Labor Force	5,143,916	5,072,054	5,081,336
Labor Force Participation Rate	68.4%	65.4%	65.2%
Unemployment Rate	3.7%	6.8%	6.9%
Average Wage Per Job (USD)	$37,011	$40,040	$41,230
Education Attainment (Population 25 Years and Older)	**(%)**	**(%)**	**(%)**
High School Graduate or Higher	83.4	87.0	87.2
Bachelors Degree or Higher	21.8	24.7	24.5
Graduate or Professional Degree	8.1	9.5	9.2

Data: U.S. Census Bureau, American Community Survey; U.S. Department of Commerce, Bureau of Economic Analysis; U.S. Department of Labor, Bureau of Labor Statistics

Industry Overview

	1998	2004	2005
Total Employees	3,919,567	3,895,914	3,796,876
Total Payroll ($1,000s)	$128,649,484	$147,721,534	$148,456,286
Total Establishments	235,403	237,984	237,523
Establishments with 1–19 Employees	201,308	203,298	204,045
Establishments with 20–49 Employees	21,230	21,638	20,492
Establishments with 50–249 Employees	11,163	11,417	11,338
Establishments with 250–999 Employees	1,456	1,405	1,432
Establishments with 1,000+ Employees	246	226	216

Data: U.S. Census Bureau, County Business Patterns

Major Industries (Ranked by 2005 Employment; Payroll in $1,000s)				
Industry	1998 Employment	2005 Employment	1998 Payroll	2005 Payroll
Manufacturing	828,751	635,234	35,615,528	31,631,273
Health Care and Social Assistance	486,987	528,673	14,340,634	19,567,164
Retail Trade	537,895	499,121	9,629,527	10,364,568
Accommodation and Food Services	320,768	331,065	3,167,701	3,861,399
Admin., Support, Waste Mngt., Remediation Services	271,928	319,299	6,276,011	9,169,536
Professional, Scientific, Technical Services	192,200	291,171	8,926,124	18,336,119
Other Services (except Public Admin.)	178,300	173,470	3,419,688	3,894,591
Wholesale Trade	191,469	172,853	8,163,387	9,277,616
Finance and Insurance	164,990	163,807	6,929,849	8,744,903
Construction	179,122	160,493	7,147,499	7,589,911

Data: U.S. Census Bureau, County Business Patterns

Taxes and Business Climate

State and Local Taxes		
Combined Revenues ($1,000s)	**2003–4**	**2004–5**
Revenue from Property Taxes	11,978,654	12,918,887
Revenue from Sales and Gross Receipts Taxes	11,065,649	11,784,107
Revenue from Individual Income Taxes	6,361,981	6,565,176
Revenue from Corporate Income Taxes	1,841,010	1,907,190
Revenue from Other Taxes	2,230,888	2,119,798
Total Tax Revenue	33,478,182	35,295,158
Per Capita Taxes		
Property Tax Per Capita	1,186	1,278
Sales and Gross Receipts Tax Per Capita	1,095	1,166
Individual Income Tax Per Capita	630	650
Corporate Income Tax Per Capita	182	189
Other Taxes Per Capita	221	210
Total Taxes Per Capita	3,313	3,492

Data: U.S. Census Bureau; Anderson Economic Group, LLC

Business Climate Measures	
Anderson Economic Group: 2007 Business Tax Ranking (1 is Best)	26
Forbes Magazine: 2007 Best States for Business Ranking (1 is Best)	46
Tax Foundation: 2008 Business Tax Climate Ranking (1 is Best)	29
ALEC-Laffer 2007 Economic Competitiveness Ranking (1 is Best)	16
2003–4 Employer Firm Births	20,758
2003–4 Employer Firm Terminations	20,836

Data: Anderson Economic Group; Tax Foundation; Forbes Magazine; U.S. Census, Statistics of U.S. Businesses; American Legislative Exchange Council

Voting Behavior and Elected Officials

Voter Registration and Turnout (%)

	1992	1996	2000	2004
Registered Voters Who Voted	69.5	57.6	61.7	67.5
Citizens Age 18+ Who Voted	61.7	54.4	57.6	64.2

Data: Dave Leip's Atlas of U.S. Presidential Elections

Presidential Election Results (Nationwide Winner Listed First)

2004	Popular Vote (%)	Electoral Votes
George W. Bush (Republican, Incumbent)	47.8	0
John Kerry (Democrat)	51.2	17
Other	1.0	0
2000		
George W. Bush (Republican)	46.1	0
Albert Gore (Democrat)	51.3	18
Ralph Nader (Green)	2.0	0
Other	0.6	0
1996		
William Clinton (Democrat, Incumbent)	51.7	18
Robert Dole (Republican)	38.5	0
H. Ross Perot (Reformist)	8.8	0
Other	1.1	0
1992		
William Clinton (Democrat)	43.8	18
George H. W. Bush (Republican, Incumbent)	36.4	0
H. Ross Perot (Independent)	19.3	0
Other	0.6	0

Data: Dave Leip's Atlas of U.S. Presidential Elections

Governor and U.S. Congressional Seats				
Governor	**Party**	**Year Term Began**	**Term**	**Max. Consecutive Terms**
Jennifer Granholm	D	2007	Second	2
U.S. Senators	**Party**	**Year Elected**	**Term Expires**	
Carl Levin	D	1978	2009	
Debbie Stabenow	D	2000	2013	
U.S. Representatives		**Republican**	**Democrat**	**Other**
		9	6	0

Data: National Governors Association; U.S. Senate, Office of the Clerk; U.S. House of Representatives

Business and Economic Agencies

Agency	Website Address
Michigan Chamber of Commerce	www.michamber.com
Michigan Economic Development Corporation	www.themedc.org
Michigan Small Business & Tech Dev. Center	www.misbtdc.org
Michigan Department of Labor and Economic Growth	www.michigan.gov/dleg

Data: Various agency websites

Minnesota

With a population of 5.2 million people, Minnesota was the twenty-first most populous state in the United States in 2006. From 2000 to 2006 the state's population increased by 247,622 people, and is projected to increase to 6.1 million by 2025. This 0.9% projected annual growth rate compares to the projected national average of 0.8%. The state's 2006 per capita personal income of $38,751 was higher compared to $37,164 in 2005 and thirteenth highest in the United States, some $2,122 above the national average. Per capita income in Minnesota grew at an average annual rate of 3.2% from 2000 to 2006, compared to 3.5% nationally.

Minnesota's largest industry in terms of 2005 employment was health care and social assistance. The fastest growing industry was construction, with 3.3% annual employment growth from 1998 to 2005. The second fastest growing industry was health care and social assistance. The state's workforce is generally more educated than other states—90.7 of the state's adult population has graduated from high school, compared to an 84.1% national average; 30.4% hold

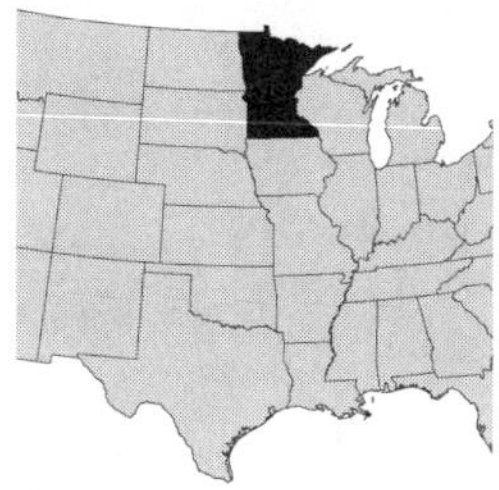

★ State Capitol

Major Urban Area

Major Roadway

Demographic and Socioeconomic Profile

Demographics and Socioeconomic Figures			
Population and Households	**2000**	**2005**	**2006**
Total Population	4,919,479	4,989,848	5,167,101
Number of Households	1,895,127	2,020,144	2,042,297
Average Household Size	2.5	2.5	2.5
Age and Ethnicity			
Median Age	35.4	36.7	36.8
Population 18 Years of Age and Older	3,632,940	3,763,129	3,909,171
Population 65 Years of Age and Older	593,415	577,318	628,105
Caucasian Population	4,402,124	4,390,040	4,538,957
African-American Population	167,857	205,160	228,354
Hispanic Population	141,786	181,959	195,138
Asian Population	139,245	177,645	179,295
Foreign-Born Population (%)	5.3	6.3	6.6
Income			
Per Capita Personal Income (USD)	$32,017	$37,164	$38,751
Median Household Income (USD)	$47,111	$52,024	$54,023
Individuals Below Poverty Level	7.9%	9.2%	9.8%

Data: U.S. Census, American Community Survey; U.S. Department of Commerce, Bureau of Economic Analysis

a bachelor degree or higher (national average is 27.0%); and 9.6% hold professional or graduate degrees compared to the national average of 9.9%.

Minnesota's total tax revenue was $21.0 billion for fiscal year 2004–5, up from the 2003–4 total revenue of $19.4 billion. The largest share of tax revenue in 2004–5 was generated from sales and gross receipts taxes, followed by individual income taxes. On a per capita basis, residents of Minnesota paid taxes of $4,098, compared to the national average of $3,705 for 2004–5. In terms of business taxes, the state ranked fourth in a study from Anderson Economic Group. Forbes Magazine and the Tax Foundation ranked the state's business climate tenth and forty-second, respectively. ALEC ranked Minnesota thirty-fifth in its state competitiveness index. One is considered best for each ranking.

Population Projections

Year	2010	2015	2020	2025
Total Population	5,420,636	5,668,211	5,900,769	6,108,787
Median Age	36.5	36.7	37.5	38.4
Population 18 Years of Age and Older	4,130,673	4,318,787	4,484,545	4,636,987
Population 65 Years of Age and Older	670,429	774,390	909,950	1,063,116

Data: U.S. Census Bureau

Workforce and Industry Profile

Workforce

	2000	2005	2006
Civilian Labor Force	2,807,668	2,915,949	2,939,304
Labor Force Participation Rate	75.2%	73.8%	73.6%
Unemployment Rate	3.1%	4.1%	4.0%
Average Wage Per Job (USD)	$35,413	$40,340	$41,510
Education Attainment (Population 25 Years and Older)	**(%)**	**(%)**	**(%)**
High School Graduate or Higher	87.9	90.9	90.7
Bachelors Degree or Higher	27.4	30.7	30.4
Graduate or Professional Degree	8.3	9.7	9.6

Data: U.S. Census Bureau, American Community Survey; U.S. Department of Commerce, Bureau of Economic Analysis; U.S. Department of Labor, Bureau of Labor Statistics

Industry Overview

	1998	2004	2005
Total Employees	2,271,671	2,393,126	2,430,853
Total Payroll ($1,000s)	$70,094,975	$92,395,099	$96,992,711
Total Establishments	134,981	148,626	150,231
Establishments with 1–19 Employees	115,369	127,350	128,700
Establishments with 20–49 Employees	11,910	13,050	13,126
Establishments with 50–249 Employees	6,637	7,144	7,293
Establishments with 250–999 Employees	918	935	964
Establishments with 1,000+ Employees	147	147	148

Data: U.S. Census Bureau, County Business Patterns

Major Industries (Ranked by 2005 Employment; Payroll in $1,000s)				
Industry	1998 Employment	2005 Employment	1998 Payroll	2005 Payroll
Health Care and Social Assistance	304,550	377,267	8,290,432	13,297,478
Manufacturing	378,392	336,311	13,760,626	15,434,841
Retail Trade	295,669	308,231	5,089,588	7,063,822
Accommodation and Food Services	181,104	214,543	1,923,350	2,768,082
Finance and Insurance	129,833	150,673	6,191,235	10,175,833
Wholesale Trade	133,590	141,320	5,616,725	8,262,854
Admin., Support, Waste Mngt., Remediation Services	140,086	137,410	2,847,993	4,103,389
Professional, Scientific, Technical Services	110,695	127,953	4,944,905	7,495,145
Construction	98,539	123,782	4,227,371	6,555,958
Other Services (except Public Admin.)	115,687	116,696	2,015,766	2,392,418

Data: U.S. Census Bureau, County Business Patterns

Taxes and Business Climate

State and Local Taxes		
Combined Revenues ($1,000s)	**2003–4**	**2004–5**
Revenue from Property Taxes	4,920,174	5,250,869
Revenue from Sales and Gross Receipts Taxes	6,564,330	6,832,316
Revenue from Individual Income Taxes	5,709,584	6,341,164
Revenue from Corporate Income Taxes	637,183	933,981
Revenue from Other Taxes	1,592,366	1,598,309
Total Tax Revenue	19,423,637	20,956,639
Per Capita Taxes		
Property Tax Per Capita	965	1,027
Sales and Gross Receipts Tax Per Capita	1,288	1,336
Individual Income Tax Per Capita	1,120	1,240
Corporate Income Tax Per Capita	125	183
Other Taxes Per Capita	312	313
Total Taxes Per Capita	3,811	4,098

Data: U.S. Census Bureau; Anderson Economic Group, LLC

Business Climate Measures	
Anderson Economic Group: 2007 Business Tax Ranking (1 is Best)	4
Forbes Magazine: 2007 Best States for Business Ranking (1 is Best)	10
Tax Foundation: 2008 Business Tax Climate Ranking (1 is Best)	42
ALEC-Laffer 2007 Economic Competitiveness Ranking (1 is Best)	35
2003–4 Employer Firm Births	13,967
2003–4 Employer Firm Terminations	11,915

Data: Anderson Economic Group; Tax Foundation; Forbes Magazine; U.S. Census, Statistics of U.S. Businesses; American Legislative Exchange Council

Voting Behavior and Elected Officials

Voter Registration and Turnout (%)

	1992	1996	2000	2004
Registered Voters Who Voted	74.8	71.5	74.7	79.5
Citizens Age 18+ Who Voted	71.6	64.3	67.1	74.2

Data: Dave Leip's Atlas of U.S. Presidential Elections

Presidential Election Results (Nationwide Winner Listed First)

2004	Popular Vote	Electoral Votes
George W. Bush (Republican, Incumbent)	47.6	0
John Kerry (Democrat)	51.1	9
Other	1.3	0
2000		
George W. Bush (Republican)	45.5	0
Albert Gore (Democrat)	47.9	10
Ralph Nader (Green)	5.2	0
Other	1.4	0
1996		
William Clinton (Democrat, Incumbent)	51.1	10
Robert Dole (Republican)	35.0	0
H. Ross Perot (Reformist)	11.8	0
Other	2.2	0
1992		
William Clinton (Democrat)	43.5	10
George H. W. Bush (Republican, Incumbent)	31.9	0
H. Ross Perot (Independent)	24.0	0
Other	0.7	0

Data: Dave Leip's Atlas of U.S. Presidential Elections

Governor and U.S. Congressional Seats				
Governor	**Party**	**Year Term Began**	**Term**	**Max. Consecutive Terms**
Tim Pawlenty	R	2007	Second	No limit
U.S. Senators	**Party**	**Year Elected**	**Term Expires**	
Norm Coleman	R	2002	2009	
Amy Klobuchar	D	2007	2013	
U.S. Representatives		**Republican**	**Democrat**	**Other**
		3	5	0

Data: National Governors Association; U.S. Senate, Office of the Clerk; U.S. House of Representatives

Business and Economic Agencies

Agency	Website Address
Minnesota Chamber of Commerce	www.mnchamber.com
Minnesota Department of Commerce	www.commerce.state.mn.us
Minnesota Small Business Dev. Center	www.mnsbdc.com
Minnesota Secretary of State	www.sos.state.mn.us/home

Data: Various agency websites

Mississippi

With a population of 2.9 million people, Mississippi is the thirty-first most populous state in 2006. The state's population increased by 65,882 people from 2000 to 2006, and is projected to increase to 3.1 million by 2025. This 0.3% projected annual growth rate is below the national average of 0.8%. Per capita personal income in Mississippi was $26,908 in 2006, up from $25,454 in 2005. For 2006, this was $9,721 below the national average and the lowest in the country. The state's per capita income grew at an average annual rate of 4.2% from 2000 to 2006, compared to 3.5% nationally.

The state's workforce generally has less education than other states—77.9% of the state's adult population has graduated from high school, compared to an 84.1% national average; 18.8% hold a bachelor degree or higher (national average is 27.0%); and 6.1% hold professional or graduate degrees (national average is 9.9%). In 2005, the state's largest industry in terms of employment was manufacturing, followed by health care and social assistance. The fastest growing industry was transportation and warehousing, with 3.8% annual employment growth from 1998 to 2005.

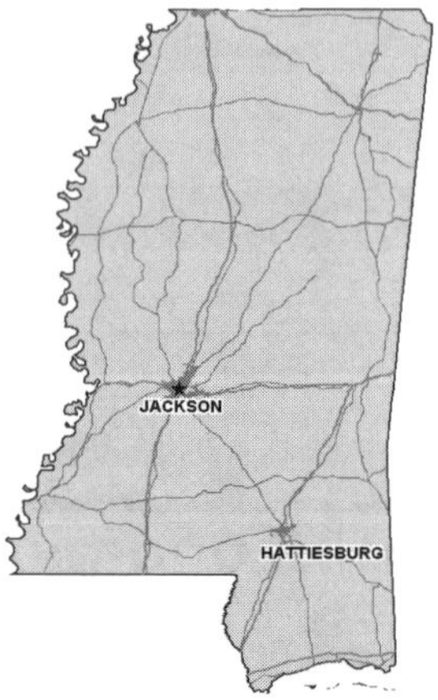

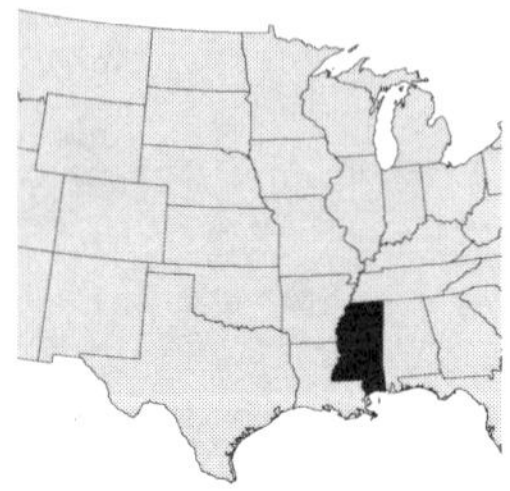

★ State Capitol

Major Urban Area

Major Roadway

Demographic and Socioeconomic Profile

Demographics and Socioeconomic Figures			
Population and Households	**2000**	**2005**	**2006**
Total Population	2,844,658	2,824,156	2,910,540
Number of Households	1,046,434	1,084,034	1,075,521
Average Household Size	2.6	2.6	2.6
Age and Ethnicity			
Median Age	33.8	35.5	35.4
Population 18 Years of Age and Older	2,070,254	2,080,210	2,151,613
Population 65 Years of Age and Older	344,288	337,462	360,693
Caucasian Population	1,745,353	1,716,444	1,749,296
African-American Population	1,033,437	1,030,075	1,087,114
Hispanic Population	37,790	43,275	46,348
Asian Population	17,709	21,523	22,116
Foreign-Born Population (%)	1.4	1.5	1.8
Income			
Per Capita Personal Income (USD)	$21,005	$25,454	$26,908
Median Household Income (USD)	$31,330	$32,938	$34,473
Individuals Below Poverty Level	19.9%	21.3%	21.1%

Data: U.S. Census, American Community Survey; U.S. Department of Commerce, Bureau of Economic Analysis

In fiscal year 2004–5, Mississippi had total tax revenues of $7.5 billion. The largest share was generated from sales and gross receipts taxes, followed by property taxes. The per capita tax burden in Mississippi was $2,583 for 2004–5, some $1,122 below the national average, and a $139 increase from 2003–4. In terms of business taxes, Mississippi ranked forty-third in a 2007 report by Anderson Economic Group. The state's business climate was also ranked forty-third by Forbes Magazine and eighteenth by the Tax Foundation. Mississippi was ranked twenty-third by ALEC in its state competitiveness index. One is considered best for each ranking.

Population Projections

Year	2010	2015	2020	2025
Total Population	2,971,412	3,014,409	3,044,812	3,069,420
Median Age	36.5	37.8	39.4	40.6
Population 18 Years of Age and Older	2,211,962	2,261,862	2,307,758	2,351,380
Population 65 Years of Age and Older	379,025	433,428	499,190	573,543

Data: U.S. Census Bureau

Workforce and Industry Profile

Workforce

	2000	2005	2006
Civilian Labor Force	1,314,154	1,329,629	1,307,347
Labor Force Participation Rate	62.6%	61.5%	60.1%
Unemployment Rate	5.7%	7.8%	6.8%
Average Wage Per Job (USD)	$25,205	$29,100	$30,460
Education Attainment (Population 25 Years and Older)	**(%)**	**(%)**	**(%)**
High School Graduate or Higher	72.9	78.5	77.9
Bachelors Degree or Higher	16.9	18.7	18.8
Graduate or Professional Degree	5.8	6.5	6.1

Data: U.S. Census Bureau, American Community Survey; U.S. Department of Commerce, Bureau of Economic Analysis; U.S. Department of Labor, Bureau of Labor Statistics

Industry Overview

	1998	2004	2005
Total Employees	937,023	928,313	926,952
Total Payroll ($1,000s)	$21,066,790	$24,817,597	$25,796,066
Total Establishments	59,771	60,534	60,542
Establishments with 1–19 Employees	51,949	52,201	52,370
Establishments with 20–49 Employees	4,921	5,377	5,236
Establishments with 50–249 Employees	2,430	2,561	2,533
Establishments with 250–999 Employees	405	335	344
Establishments with 1,000+ Employees	66	60	59

Data: U.S. Census Bureau, County Business Patterns

Major Industries (Ranked by 2005 Employment; Payroll in $1,000s)				
Industry	1998 Employment	2005 Employment	1998 Payroll	2005 Payroll
Manufacturing	230,175	176,767	5,882,128	5,792,877
Health Care and Social Assistance	126,613	141,936	3,309,588	4,674,594
Retail Trade	138,422	140,119	2,156,337	2,692,884
Accommodation and Food Services	93,376	114,571	1,163,591	1,598,053
Construction	49,854	49,735	1,291,418	1,665,301
Admin., Support, Waste Mngt., Remediation Services	43,815	44,528	703,619	891,257
Other Services (except Public Admin.)	39,511	40,534	585,933	742,731
Finance and Insurance	34,047	35,616	1,049,663	1,388,034
Wholesale Trade	39,464	35,256	1,123,409	1,307,500
Transportation and Warehousing	25,871	33,548	693,395	1,067,633

Data: U.S. Census Bureau, County Business Patterns

Taxes and Business Climate

State and Local Taxes		
Combined Revenues ($1,000s)	2003–4	2004–5
Revenue from Property Taxes	1,859,756	1,967,447
Revenue from Sales and Gross Receipts Taxes	3,458,788	3,584,852
Revenue from Individual Income Taxes	1,061,704	1,174,065
Revenue from Corporate Income Taxes	243,846	283,242
Revenue from Other Taxes	464,625	481,075
Total Tax Revenue	7,088,719	7,490,681
Per Capita Taxes		
Property Tax Per Capita	641	678
Sales and Gross Receipts Tax Per Capita	1,192	1,236
Individual Income Tax Per Capita	366	405
Corporate Income Tax Per Capita	84	98
Other Taxes Per Capita	160	166
Total Taxes Per Capita	2,444	2,583

Data: U.S. Census Bureau; Anderson Economic Group, LLC

Business Climate Measures

Anderson Economic Group: 2007 Business Tax Ranking (1 is Best)	43
Forbes Magazine: 2007 Best States for Business Ranking (1 is Best)	43
Tax Foundation: 2008 Business Tax Climate Ranking (1 is Best)	18
ALEC-Laffer 2007 Economic Competitiveness Ranking (1 is Best)	23
2003–4 Employer Firm Births	5,668
2003–4 Employer Firm Terminations	5,202

Data: Anderson Economic Group; Tax Foundation; Forbes Magazine; U.S. Census, Statistics of U.S. Businesses; American Legislative Exchange Council

Voting Behavior and Elected Officials

Voter Registration and Turnout (%)

	1992	1996	2000	2004
Registered Voters Who Voted	59.9	52.1	57.2	63.9
Citizens Age 18+ Who Voted	52.8	45.4	48.1	54.4

Data: Dave Leip's Atlas of U.S. Presidential Elections

Presidential Election Results (Nationwide Winner Listed First)

2004	Popular Vote (%)	Electoral Votes
George W. Bush (Republican, Incumbent)	59.4	6
John Kerry (Democrat)	39.7	0
Other	0.8	0
2000		
George W. Bush (Republican)	57.6	7
Albert Gore (Democrat)	40.7	0
Ralph Nader (Green)	0.8	0
Other	0.9	0
1996		
William Clinton (Democrat, Incumbent)	44.1	0
Robert Dole (Republican)	49.2	7
H. Ross Perot (Reformist)	5.8	0
Other	0.9	0
1992		
William Clinton (Democrat)	40.8	0
George H. W. Bush (Republican, Incumbent)	49.7	7
H. Ross Perot (Independent)	8.7	0
Other	0.8	0

Data: Dave Leip's Atlas of U.S. Presidential Elections

Governor and U.S. Congressional Seats				
Governor	**Party**	**Year Term Began**	**Term**	**Max. Consecutive Terms**
Haley Barbour	R	2004	First	2
U.S. Senators	**Party**	**Year Elected**	**Term Expires**	
Thad Cochran	R	1978	2009	
Roger Wicker	R	2007	2013	
U.S. Representatives		**Republican**	**Democrat**	**Other**
		1	2	0

Data: National Governors Association; U.S. Senate, Office of the Clerk; U.S. House of Representatives

Business and Economic Agencies

Agency	Website Address
Mississippi Economic Council	www.msmec.com
Mississippi Development Authority	www.mississippi.org
Mississippi Small Business Dev. Center	www.olemiss.edu/depts/mssbdc
Mississippi Secretary of State, Business Services	www.sos.state.ms.us/busserv

Data: Various agency websites

Missouri

Missouri, located in the West North Central region of the United States, had a population of 5.8 million people in 2006, making it the eighteenth most populous state. The state's population increased by 247,502 people from 2000 to 2006, and is projected to increase to 6.3 million by 2025. This 0.4% projected annual growth rate compares to the projected national average of 0.8%. Per capita personal income in Missouri was $32,793 in 2006, up from $31,380 in 2005. For 2006, this was the twentieth lowest in the country and $3,836 below the national average. From 2000 to 2006 per capita income in Missouri grew at an average annual rate of 3.1%, compared to 3.5% nationally.

In 2005, the state's largest industry in terms of employment was health care and social assistance, followed by retail trade. The fastest growing industry was construction, with 3.0% annual employment growth from 1998 to 2005. The state's workforce is generally more educated than other states—84.8% of the state's adult population has graduated from high school, compared to an 84.1% national average. Nationally, an average of

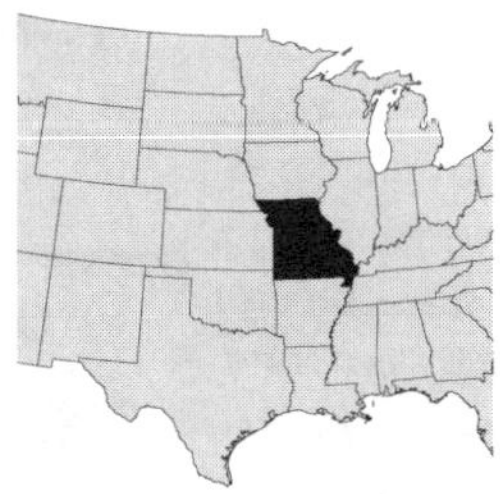

★ State Capitol

Major Urban Area

Major Roadway

Demographic and Socioeconomic Profile

Demographics and Socioeconomic Figures			
Population and Households	**2000**	**2005**	**2006**
Total Population	5,595,211	5,631,910	5,842,713
Number of Households	2,194,594	2,285,280	2,305,027
Average Household Size	2.5	2.5	2.5
Age and Ethnicity			
Median Age	36.1	37.4	37.2
Population 18 Years of Age and Older	4,169,109	4,260,766	4,420,284
Population 65 Years of Age and Older	756,038	721,138	779,605
Caucasian Population	4,746,952	4,760,327	4,905,832
African-American Population	622,087	627,978	661,535
Hispanic Population	116,373	148,994	160,898
Asian Population	60,429	78,554	86,010
Foreign-Born Population (%)	2.7	3.4	3.3
Income			
Per Capita Personal Income (USD)	$27,241	$31,380	$32,793
Median Household Income (USD)	$37,934	$41,974	$42,841
Individuals Below Poverty Level	11.7%	13.3%	13.6%

Data: U.S. Census, American Community Survey; U.S. Department of Commerce, Bureau of Economic Analysis

24.3% hold a bachelor degree or higher compared to 27.4% in Missouri. Nationally, 9.9% hold professional or graduate degrees compared to 8.7% in Missouri.

In fiscal year 2004–5, Missouri had total tax revenues of $17.4 billion. The largest share was generated from sales and gross receipts taxes, followed by property taxes. The per capita tax burden in Missouri was $3,002 for 2004–5, some $703 below the national average. In terms of business taxes, the state ranked second in a study from Anderson Economic Group. Forbes Magazine and the Tax Foundation ranked the state's business climate sixteenth and fifteenth, respectively, while ALEC ranked Missouri seventeen in its state competitiveness index. One is considered best for each ranking.

Population Projections

Year	2010	2015	2020	2025
Total Population	5,922,078	6,069,556	6,199,882	6,315,366
Median Age	37.6	37.9	38.6	39.2
Population 18 Years of Age and Older	4,510,684	4,633,827	4,739,310	4,839,119
Population 65 Years of Age and Older	821,645	922,418	1,047,071	1,189,605

Data: U.S. Census Bureau

Workforce and Industry Profile

Workforce

	2000	2005	2006
Civilian Labor Force	2,973,092	3,008,146	3,032,434
Labor Force Participation Rate	70.2%	67.7%	67.5%
Unemployment Rate	3.3%	5.3%	4.8%
Average Wage Per Job (USD)	$31,385	$34,660	$35,670
Education Attainment (Population 25 Years and Older)	**(%)**	**(%)**	**(%)**
High School Graduate or Higher	81.3	85.0	84.8
Bachelors Degree or Higher	21.6	24.0	24.3
Graduate or Professional Degree	7.6	8.6	8.7

Data: U.S. Census Bureau, American Community Survey; U.S. Department of Commerce, Bureau of Economic Analysis; U.S. Department of Labor, Bureau of Labor Statistics

Industry Overview

	1998	2004	2005
Total Employees	2,310,122	2,421,450	2,425,403
Total Payroll ($1,000s)	$64,669,474	$79,157,172	$82,340,359
Total Establishments	143,912	153,985	154,306
Establishments with 1–19 Employees	123,828	132,554	132,741
Establishments with 20–49 Employees	12,250	13,216	16,654
Establishments with 50–249 Employees	6,801	7,182	7,157
Establishments with 250–999 Employees	885	879	906
Establishments with 1,000+ Employees	148	154	148

Data: U.S. Census Bureau, County Business Patterns

Major Industries (Ranked by 2005 Employment; Payroll in $1,000s)				
Industry	1998 Employment	2005 Employment	1998 Payroll	2005 Payroll
Health Care and Social Assistance	320,300	355,301	8,508,854	11,730,526
Retail Trade	304,009	321,615	5,452,695	6,780,597
Manufacturing	382,003	298,117	12,487,544	11,640,421
Accommodation and Food Services	203,301	234,662	2,165,787	2,867,580
Construction	120,864	148,881	4,279,334	6,218,667
Admin., Support, Waste Mngt., Remediation Services	126,561	145,378	2,345,691	3,568,454
Finance and Insurance	123,925	136,316	4,878,339	7,067,143
Professional, Scientific, Technical Services	108,911	133,171	4,351,928	6,968,986
Wholesale Trade	126,722	130,004	4,638,609	5,291,381
Other Services (except Public Admin.)	112,331	120,543	1,957,301	2,568,413

Data: U.S. Census Bureau, County Business Patterns

Taxes and Business Climate

State and Local Taxes		
Combined Revenues ($1,000s)	2003–4	2004–5
Revenue from Property Taxes	4,304,387	4,695,477
Revenue from Sales and Gross Receipts Taxes	6,694,944	7,031,545
Revenue from Individual Income Taxes	4,033,495	4,318,505
Revenue from Corporate Income Taxes	224,366	237,476
Revenue from Other Taxes	998,186	1,091,261
Total Tax Revenue	16,255,378	17,374,264
Per Capita Taxes		
Property Tax Per Capita	747	811
Sales and Gross Receipts Tax Per Capita	1,162	1,215
Individual Income Tax Per Capita	700	746
Corporate Income Tax Per Capita	39	41
Other Taxes Per Capita	173	189
Total Taxes Per Capita	2,822	3,002

Data: U.S. Census Bureau; Anderson Economic Group, LLC

Business Climate Measures	
Anderson Economic Group: 2007 Business Tax Ranking (1 is Best)	2
Forbes Magazine: 2007 Best States for Business Ranking (1 is Best)	16
Tax Foundation: 2008 Business Tax Climate Ranking (1 is Best)	15
ALEC-Laffer 2007 Economic Competitiveness Ranking (1 is Best)	17
2003–4 Employer Firm Births	16,421
2003–4 Employer Firm Terminations	13,503

Data: Anderson Economic Group; Tax Foundation; Forbes Magazine; U.S. Census, Statistics of U.S. Businesses; American Legislative Exchange Council

Voting Behavior and Elected Officials

Voter Registration and Turnout (%)

	1992	1996	2000	2004
Registered Voters Who Voted	77.9	64.6	61.1	65.1
Citizens Age 18+ Who Voted	62.0	54.0	56.6	63.6

Data: Dave Leip's Atlas of U.S. Presidential Elections

Presidential Election Results (Nationwide Winner Listed First)

2004	Popular Vote (%)	Electoral Votes
George W. Bush (Republican, Incumbent)	53.3	11
John Kerry (Democrat)	46.1	0
Other	0.6	0
2000		
George W. Bush (Republican)	50.4	11
Albert Gore (Democrat)	47.1	0
Ralph Nader (Green)	1.6	0
Other	0.9	0
1996		
William Clinton (Democrat, Incumbent)	47.5	11
Robert Dole (Republican)	41.2	0
H. Ross Perot (Reformist)	10.1	0
Other	1.2	0
1992		
William Clinton (Democrat)	44.1	11
George H. W. Bush (Republican, Incumbent)	33.9	0
H. Ross Perot (Independent)	21.7	0
Other	0.3	0

Data: Dave Leip's Atlas of U.S. Presidential Elections

Governor and U.S. Congressional Seats				
Governor	**Party**	**Year Term Began**	**Term**	**Max. Consecutive Terms**
Matt Blunt	D	2005	First	2
U.S. Senators	**Party**	**Year Elected**	**Term Expires**	
Claire McCaskill	D	2006	2013	
Christopher Bond	R	1986	2011	
U.S. Representatives		**Republican**	**Democrat**	**Other**
		5	4	0

Data: National Governors Association; U.S. Senate, Office of the Clerk; U.S. House of Representatives

Business and Economic Agencies

Agency	Website Address
Missouri Chamber of Commerce & Industry	www.mochamber.org
Missouri Department of Economic Development	www.ded.mo.gov
Missouri Small Business Dev. Center	www.missouribusiness.net/sbdc
Missouri Secretary of State, Corporations Division	www.sos.mo.gov/business/corporations

Data: Various agency websites

Montana

With a population of 944,632 people, Montana was the seventh least populous state in the United States in 2006. From 2000 to 2006 the state's population increased by 42,437 people, and is projected to increase to 1.0 million by 2025. This 0.5% projected annual growth rate compares to the projected national average of 0.8%. The state's 2006 per capita personal income of $30,886 was higher compared to $29,220 in 2005 and tenth lowest in the United States, some $5,743 below the national average. Per capita income in Montana grew at an average annual rate of 5.1% from 2000 to 2006, compared to 3.5% nationally.

Montana's largest industry in terms of 2005 employment was retail trade. The fastest growing industry was professional, scientific, and technical services, with 8.3% annual employment growth from 1998 to 2005. The second fastest growing industry was construction. The state's workforce is generally more educated than other states—90.1% of the state's adult population has graduated from high school, compared to an 84.1% national average; 27.4% hold a bachelor degree or higher (national average is 27.0%); and 8.5% hold professional or graduate degrees

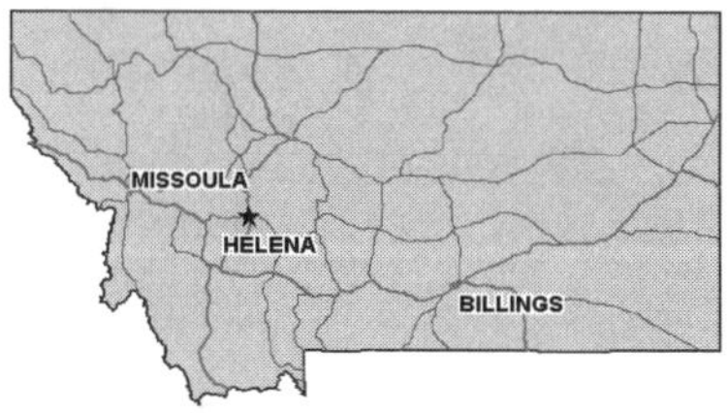

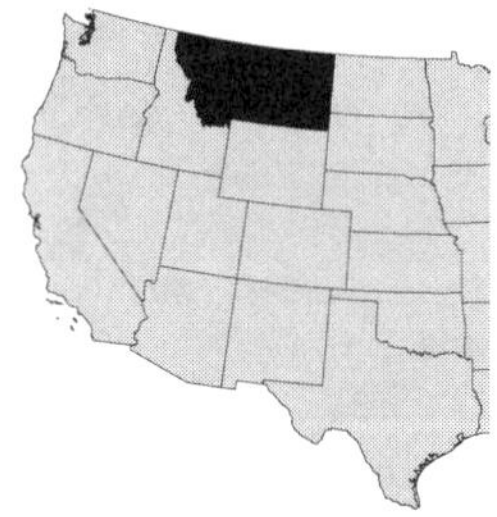

★ State Capitol

Major Urban Area

Major Roadway

Demographic and Socioeconomic Profile

Demographics and Socioeconomic Figures			
Population and Households	**2000**	**2005**	**2006**
Total Population	902,195	910,651	944,632
Number of Households	358,667	368,268	372,190
Average Household Size	2.4	2.5	2.5
Age and Ethnicity			
Median Age	37.5	40.2	39.5
Population 18 Years of Age and Older	672,251	706,921	726,534
Population 65 Years of Age and Older	120,931	121,064	131,318
Caucasian Population	817,604	824,721	847,192
African-American Population	2,359	4,135	4,470
Hispanic Population	18,490	20,232	20,513
Asian Population	4,363	5,508	5,525
Foreign-Born Population (%)	1.8	1.8	1.9
Income			
Per Capita Personal Income (USD)	$22,929	$29,220	$30,886
Median Household Income (USD)	$33,024	$39,301	$40,627
Individuals Below Poverty Level	14.6%	14.4%	13.6%

Data: U.S. Census, American Community Survey; U.S. Department of Commerce, Bureau of Economic Analysis

compared to the national average of 9.9%.

Montana's total tax revenue was $2.7 billion for fiscal year 2004–5, up from the 2003–4 total revenue of $2.4 billion. The largest share of tax revenue in 2004–5 was generated from property taxes, followed by individual income taxes. On a per capita basis, residents of Montana paid taxes of $2,910, compared to the national average of $3,705 for 2004–5. In terms of business taxes, the state ranked fifty-first in a study from Anderson Economic Group. Forbes Magazine and the Tax Foundation ranked the state's business climate forty-second and sixth, respectively, while ALEC ranked Montana thirty-third in its state competitiveness index. One is considered best for each ranking.

Population Projections

Year	2010	2015	2020	2025
Total Population	968,598	999,489	1,022,735	1,037,387
Median Age	40.4	41.5	42.7	44.3
Population 18 Years of Age and Older	756,286	783,498	804,685	821,871
Population 65 Years of Age and Older	144,961	173,778	211,783	247,769

Data: U.S. Census Bureau

Workforce and Industry Profile

Workforce

	2000	2005	2006
Civilian Labor Force	468,865	482,611	493,842
Labor Force Participation Rate	68.2%	66.3%	66.8%
Unemployment Rate	4.8%	3.9%	3.2%
Average Wage Per Job (USD)	$24,274	$30,220	$31,290
Education Attainment (Population 25 Years and Older)	**(%)**	**(%)**	**(%)**
High School Graduate or Higher	87.2	90.7	90.1
Bachelors Degree or Higher	24.4	26.5	27.4
Graduate or Professional Degree	7.2	8.0	8.5

Data: U.S. Census Bureau, American Community Survey; U.S. Department of Commerce, Bureau of Economic Analysis; U.S. Department of Labor, Bureau of Labor Statistics

Industry Overview

	1998	2004	2005
Total Employees	277,144	314,865	326,887
Total Payroll ($1,000s)	$5,960,687	$8,277,084	$8,950,520
Total Establishments	30,957	34,686	35,736
Establishments with 1–19 Employees	28,134	31,433	32,411
Establishments with 20–49 Employees	2,000	2,307	2,376
Establishments with 50–249 Employees	767	876	872
Establishments with 250–999 Employees	51	64	70
Establishments with 1,000+ Employees	5	6	7

Data: U.S. Census Bureau, County Business Patterns

Major Industries (Ranked by 2005 Employment; Payroll in $1,000s)				
Industry	1998 Employment	2005 Employment	1998 Payroll	2005 Payroll
Retail Trade	48,285	56,287	771,476	1,165,388
Health Care and Social Assistance	45,242	54,114	1,067,519	1,665,581
Accommodation and Food Services	37,393	42,447	347,915	474,679
Construction	16,767	23,795	500,826	876,686
Professional, Scientific, Technical Services	12,362	21,555	352,733	727,538
Manufacturing	20,686	19,470	599,839	739,644
Finance and Insurance	12,780	16,096	403,122	618,821
Other Services (except Public Admin.)	13,315	14,560	201,904	277,776
Wholesale Trade	15,025	13,931	398,273	488,131
Admin., Support, Waste Mngt., Remediation Services	11,000	12,884	178,935	262,120

Data: U.S. Census Bureau, County Business Patterns

Taxes and Business Climate

State and Local Taxes		
Combined Revenues ($1,000s)	**2003–4**	**2004–5**
Revenue from Property Taxes	958,779	997,447
Revenue from Sales and Gross Receipts Taxes	440,453	459,614
Revenue from Individual Income Taxes	605,582	713,390
Revenue from Corporate Income Taxes	67,723	98,214
Revenue from Other Taxes	358,798	454,037
Total Tax Revenue	2,431,335	2,722,702
Per Capita Taxes		
Property Tax Per Capita	1,034	1,066
Sales and Gross Receipts Tax Per Capita	475	491
Individual Income Tax Per Capita	653	762
Corporate Income Tax Per Capita	73	105
Other Taxes Per Capita	387	485
Total Taxes Per Capita	2,623	2,910

Data: U.S. Census Bureau; Anderson Economic Group, LLC

Business Climate Measures	
Anderson Economic Group: 2007 Business Tax Ranking (1 is Best)	51
Forbes Magazine: 2007 Best States for Business Ranking (1 is Best)	42
Tax Foundation: 2008 Business Tax Climate Ranking (1 is Best)	6
ALEC-Laffer 2007 Economic Competitiveness Ranking (1 is Best)	33
2003–4 Employer Firm Births	3,648
2003–4 Employer Firm Terminations	2,860

Data: Anderson Economic Group; Tax Foundation; Forbes Magazine; U.S. Census, Statistics of U.S. Businesses; American Legislative Exchange Council

Voting Behavior and Elected Officials

Voter Registration and Turnout (%)

	1992	1996	2000	2004
Registered Voters Who Voted	77.5	68.9	58.9	70.6
Citizens Age 18+ Who Voted	70.1	62.1	61.1	64.2

Data: Dave Leip's Atlas of U.S. Presidential Elections

Presidential Election Results (Nationwide Winner Listed First)

2004	Popular Vote (%)	Electoral Votes
George W. Bush (Republican, Incumbent)	59.1	3
John Kerry (Democrat)	38.6	0
Other	2.4	0
2000		
George W. Bush (Republican)	58.4	3
Albert Gore (Democrat)	33.4	0
Ralph Nader (Green)	6.0	0
Other	2.3	0
1996		
William Clinton (Democrat, Incumbent)	41.2	0
Robert Dole (Republican)	44.1	3
H. Ross Perot (Reformist)	13.6	0
Other	1.1	0
1992		
William Clinton (Democrat)	37.6	3
George H. W. Bush (Republican, Incumbent)	35.1	0
H. Ross Perot (Independent)	26.1	0
Other	1.1	0

Data: Dave Leip's Atlas of U.S. Presidential Elections

Governor and U.S. Congressional Seats				
Governor	**Party**	**Year Term Began**	**Term**	**Max. Consecutive Terms**
Brian Schweitzer	D	2005	First	2
U.S. Senators	**Party**	**Year Elected**	**Term Expires**	
Max Baucus	D	1978	2009	
Jon Tester	D	2006	2013	
U.S. Representatives		**Republican**	**Democrat**	**Other**
		1	0	0

Data: National Governors Association; U.S. Senate, Office of the Clerk; U.S. House of Representatives

Business and Economic Agencies

Agency	Website Address
Montana Chamber of Commerce	www.montanachamber.com
Montana Department of Commerce	www.commerce.state.mt.us
Montana Small Business Dev. Center	sbdc.mt.gov
Montana Secretary of State, Business Services Bureau	www.sos.state.mt.us/BSB

Data: Various agency websites

Nebraska

Nebraska is located in the West North Central region of the United States and had a population of 1.8 million people in 2006, making it the thirteenth least populous state. The state's population increased by 57,068 people from 2000 to 2006, and is projected to increase only slightly by 2025. The 0.1% projected annual growth rate is below the national average of 0.8%. Per capita personal income in Nebraska was $34,383 in 2006, up from $32,833 in 2005. For 2006, this was $2,246 below the national average and the twenty-sixth lowest in the country. The state's per capita income grew at an average annual rate of 3.7% from 2000 to 2006, compared to 3.5% nationally.

The state's workforce generally has less education than other states—89.5% of the state's adult population has graduated from high school, compared to an 84.1% national average; 26.9% hold a bachelor degree or higher (national average is 27.0%); and 8.4% hold professional or graduate degrees (national average is 9.9%). In 2005, the state's largest industry in terms of employment was health care and social assistance, followed by

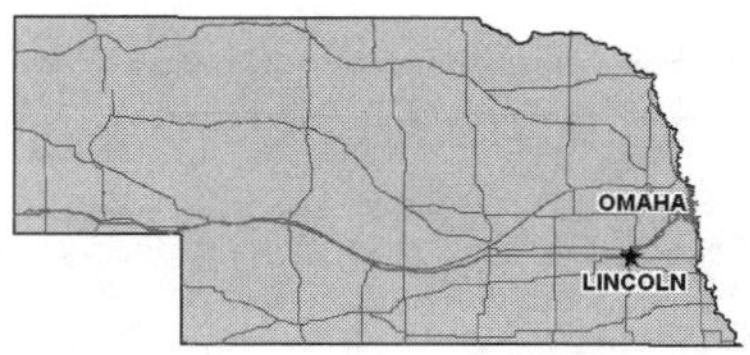

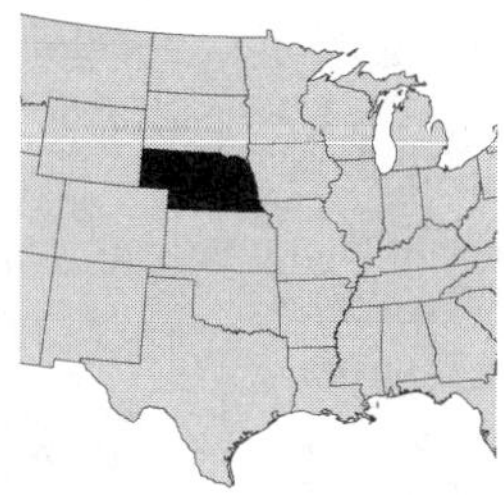

★ State Capitol

Major Urban Area

Major Roadway

Demographic and Socioeconomic Profile

Demographics and Socioeconomic Figures			
Population and Households	**2000**	**2005**	**2006**
Total Population	1,711,263	1,706,976	1,768,331
Number of Households	666,184	695,592	700,888
Average Household Size	2.5	2.5	2.5
Age and Ethnicity			
Median Age	35.3	36.2	36.0
Population 18 Years of Age and Older	1,261,648	1,278,044	1,322,921
Population 65 Years of Age and Older	232,359	217,917	233,275
Caucasian Population	1,533,787	1,529,471	1,566,980
African-American Population	67,435	68,389	72,095
Hispanic Population	93,872	122,518	130,230
Asian Population	21,126	24,820	29,815
Foreign-Born Population (%)	4.4	5.6	5.6
Income			
Per Capita Personal Income (USD)	$27,625	$32,833	$34,383
Median Household Income (USD)	$39,250	$43,841	$45,474
Individuals Below Poverty Level	9.7%	10.9%	11.5%

Data: U.S. Census, American Community Survey; U.S. Department of Commerce, Bureau of Economic Analysis

retail trade. The fastest growing industry was professional, scientific, and technical services, with 5.7% annual growth from 1998 to 2005.

In fiscal year 2004–5, Nebraska had total tax revenues of $6.6 billion. The largest share was generated from sales and gross receipts taxes, followed by property taxes. The per capita tax burden in Nebraska was $3,755 for 2004–5, some $50 above the national average, and a $146 increase from 2003–4. In terms of business taxes, Nebraska ranked twenty-fifth in a study from Anderson Economic Group. The state's business climate was ranked seventeenth by Forbes Magazine and forty-third by the Tax Foundation. Nebraska was ranked thirty-fourth by ALEC in its state competitiveness index. One is considered best for each ranking.

Population Projections

Year	2010	2015	2020	2025
Total Population	1,768,997	1,788,508	1,802,678	1,812,787
Median Age	36.7	37.2	37.9	38.3
Population 18 Years of Age and Older	1,322,741	1,334,423	1,344,066	1,355,661
Population 65 Years of Age and Older	243,313	271,379	308,994	347,809

Data: U.S. Census Bureau

Workforce and Industry Profile

Workforce

	2000	2005	2006
Civilian Labor Force	949,762	977,723	974,476
Labor Force Participation Rate	74.0%	73.4%	72.5%
Unemployment Rate	2.8%	3.9%	3.0%
Average Wage Per Job (USD)	$27,692	$33,310	$34,300
Education Attainment (Population 25 Years and Older)	**(%)**	**(%)**	**(%)**
High School Graduate or Higher	86.6	89.5	89.5
Bachelors Degree or Higher	23.7	27.3	26.9
Graduate or Professional Degree	7.3	8.5	8.4

Data: U.S. Census Bureau, American Community Survey; U.S. Department of Commerce, Bureau of Economic Analysis; U.S. Department of Labor, Bureau of Labor Statistics

Industry Overview

	1998	2004	2005
Total Employees	720,252	774,311	773,082
Total Payroll ($1,000s)	$18,178,238	$23,681,558	$24,180,753
Total Establishments	48,655	50,928	51,440
Establishments with 1–19 Employees	42,487	44,202	44,698
Establishments with 20–49 Employees	3,813	4,231	4,237
Establishments with 50–249 Employees	2,050	2,173	2,170
Establishments with 250–999 Employees	258	268	284
Establishments with 1,000+ Employees	47	54	51

Data: U.S. Census Bureau, County Business Patterns

Major Industries (Ranked by 2005 Employment; Payroll in $1,000s)				
Industry	1998 Employment	2005 Employment	1998 Payroll	2005 Payroll
Health Care and Social Assistance	95,015	109,104	2,487,228	3,633,981
Retail Trade	104,866	107,366	1,675,637	2,134,208
Manufacturing	109,645	102,367	3,255,216	3,662,922
Accommodation and Food Services	60,088	66,768	535,911	696,713
Admin., Support, Waste Mngt., Remediation Services	52,512	61,663	1,088,358	1,454,960
Finance and Insurance	47,979	59,858	1,710,584	2,915,960
Professional, Scientific, Technical Services	30,406	44,813	1,143,609	1,997,798
Construction	38,297	43,088	1,258,732	1,576,751
Wholesale Trade	40,357	37,932	1,255,481	1,625,672
Other Services (except Public Admin.)	33,786	36,065	530,062	704,234

Data: U.S. Census Bureau, County Business Patterns

Taxes and Business Climate

State and Local Taxes		
Combined Revenues ($1,000s)	**2003–4**	**2004–5**
Revenue from Property Taxes	2,007,118	2,101,827
Revenue from Sales and Gross Receipts Taxes	2,333,889	2,314,321
Revenue from Individual Income Taxes	1,242,603	1,393,897
Revenue from Corporate Income Taxes	167,429	198,380
Revenue from Other Taxes	556,845	577,813
Total Tax Revenue	6,307,884	6,586,238
Per Capita Taxes		
Property Tax Per Capita	1,148	1,198
Sales and Gross Receipts Tax Per Capita	1,335	1,319
Individual Income Tax Per Capita	711	795
Corporate Income Tax Per Capita	96	113
Other Taxes Per Capita	319	329
Total Taxes Per Capita	3,609	3,755

Data: U.S. Census Bureau; Anderson Economic Group, LLC

Business Climate Measures	
Anderson Economic Group: 2007 Business Tax Ranking (1 is Best)	25
Forbes Magazine: 2007 Best States for Business Ranking (1 is Best)	17
Tax Foundation: 2008 Business Tax Climate Ranking (1 is Best)	43
ALEC-Laffer 2007 Economic Competitiveness Ranking (1 is Best)	34
2003–4 Employer Firm Births	4,235
2003–4 Employer Firm Terminations	3,978

Data: Anderson Economic Group; Tax Foundation; Forbes Magazine; U.S. Census, Statistics of U.S. Businesses; American Legislative Exchange Council

Voting Behavior and Elected Officials

Voter Registration and Turnout (%)

	1992	1996	2000	2004
Registered Voters Who Voted	77.7	66.7	64.2	67.1
Citizens Age 18+ Who Voted	63.3	55.9	55.2	60.0

Data: Dave Leip's Atlas of U.S. Presidential Elections

Presidential Election Results (Nationwide Winner Listed First)

2004	Popular Vote (%)	Electoral Votes
George W. Bush (Republican, Incumbent)	65.9	5
John Kerry (Democrat)	32.7	0
Other	1.4	0
2000		
George W. Bush (Republican)	62.3	5
Albert Gore (Democrat)	33.3	0
Ralph Nader (Green)	3.5	0
Other	1.0	0
1996		
William Clinton (Democrat, Incumbent)	35.0	0
Robert Dole (Republican)	53.7	5
H. Ross Perot (Reformist)	10.5	0
Other	0.9	0
1992		
William Clinton (Democrat)	29.4	0
George H. W. Bush (Republican, Incumbent)	46.6	5
H. Ross Perot (Independent)	23.6	0
Other	0.4	0

Data: Dave Leip's Atlas of U.S. Presidential Elections

Governor and U.S. Congressional Seats				
Governor	**Party**	**Year Term Began**	**Term**	**Max. Consecutive Terms**
Dave Heineman	R	2005	First	2
U.S. Senators	**Party**	**Year Elected**	**Term Expires**	
Charles Hagel	R	1996	2009	
Ben Nelson	D	2000	2013	
U.S. Representatives		**Republican**	**Democrat**	**Other**
		3	0	0

Data: National Governors Association; U.S. Senate, Office of the Clerk; U.S. House of Representatives

Business and Economic Agencies

Agency	Website Address
Nebraska Chamber of Commerce & Industry	www.nechamber.com
Nebraska Department of Economic Development	www.neded.org
Nebraska Small Business Dev. Center	nbdc.unomaha.edu
Nebraska Scretary of State, Corporations Division	www.sos.state.ne.us/business/corp_serv

Data: Various agency websites

Nevada

Nevada had a population of 2.5 million people in 2006, making it the sixteenth least populous state. The state's population increased by 497,272 people from 2000 to 2006, and is projected to increase to 3.9 million by 2025. This 2.3% projected annual growth rate compares to the projected national average of 0.8%. Per capita personal income in Nevada was $39,015 in 2006, up from $37,420 in 2005. For 2006, this was eleventh highest in the country and $2,386 above the national average. From 2000 to 2006 per capita income in Nevada grew at an average annual rate of 4.2%, compared to 3.5% nationally.

In 2005, the state's largest industry in terms of employment was accommodation and food services, followed by retail trade. The fastest growing industry was administration, support, waste management, and remediation services, with 9.0% annual employment growth from 1998 to 2005. The state's workforce is generally less educated than other states—83.9% of the state's adult population has graduated from high school, compared to an 84.1% national average. Nationally, an average of 27.0% hold a bachelor degree or higher compared to 20.8% in Nevada. Nationally, 9.9%

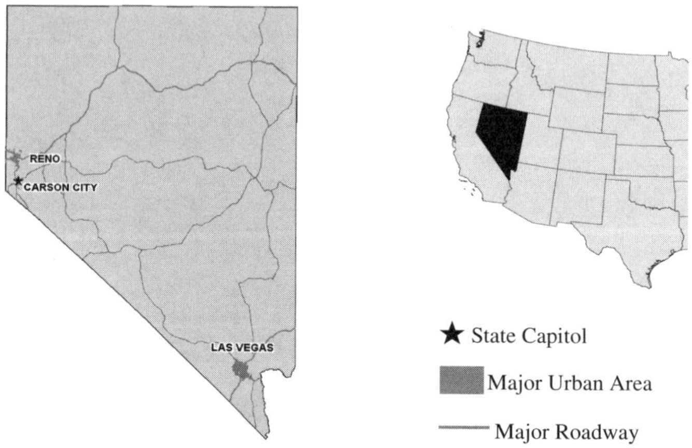

Demographic and Socioeconomic Profile

Demographics and Socioeconomic Figures			
Population and Households	**2000**	**2005**	**2006**
Total Population	1,998,257	2,381,281	2,495,529
Number of Households	751,165	906,719	936,828
Average Household Size	2.6	2.6	2.6
Age and Ethnicity			
Median Age	35.0	35.2	35.6
Population 18 Years of Age and Older	1,488,526	1,762,476	1,861,082
Population 65 Years of Age and Older	218,497	267,676	275,026
Caucasian Population	1,503,083	1,811,535	1,837,860
African-American Population	132,490	170,854	183,064
Hispanic Population	393,539	563,999	610,051
Asian Population	89,121	138,054	147,363
Foreign-Born Population (%)	15.8	17.4	19.1
Income			
Per Capita Personal Income (USD)	$30,437	$37,420	$39,015
Median Household Income (USD)	$44,581	$49,169	$52,998
Individuals Below Poverty Level	10.5%	11.1%	10.3%

Data: U.S. Census, American Community Survey; U.S. Department of Commerce, Bureau of Economic Analysis

hold professional or graduate degrees compared to 7.2% in Nevada.

In fiscal year 2004–5, Nevada had total tax revenues of $9.0 billion. The largest share was generated from sales and gross receipts taxes, followed by property taxes. The per capita tax burden in Nevada was $3,754 for 2004–5, just $49 above below the national average. In terms of business taxes, the state ranked thirty-eighth in a study from Anderson Economic Group. Forbes Magazine and the Tax Foundation ranked the state's business climate twenty-second and third, respectively, while ALEC ranked Nevada eleventh in its state competitiveness index. One is considered best for each ranking.

Population Projections

Year	2010	2015	2020	2025
Total Population	2,690,531	3,058,190	3,452,283	3,863,298
Median Age	37.8	38.7	39.0	39.1
Population 18 Years of Age and Older	2,025,446	2,306,302	2,595,522	2,895,136
Population 65 Years of Age and Older	329,621	421,719	531,120	659,700

Data: U.S. Census Bureau

Workforce and Industry Profile

Workforce

	2000	2005	2006
Civilian Labor Force	1,062,845	1,229,708	1,295,085
Labor Force Participation Rate	69.8%	67.2%	68.3%
Unemployment Rate	4.5%	4.2%	4.2%
Average Wage Per Job (USD)	$32,276	$34,750	$36,000
Education Attainment (Population 25 Years and Older)	**(%)**	**(%)**	**(%)**
High School Graduate or Higher	80.7	82.8	83.9
Bachelors Degree or Higher	18.2	20.6	20.8
Graduate or Professional Degree	6.1	11.6	7.2

Data: U.S. Census Bureau, American Community Survey; U.S. Department of Commerce, Bureau of Economic Analysis; U.S. Department of Labor, Bureau of Labor Statistics

Industry Overview

	1998	2004	2005
Total Employees	800,861	1,022,011	1,089,422
Total Payroll ($1,000s)	$21,847,334	$34,848,180	$39,261,902
Total Establishments	44,613	55,853	58,561
Establishments with 1–19 Employees	38,274	47,705	49,794
Establishments with 20–49 Employees	3,946	4,954	5,296
Establishments with 50–249 Employees	2,041	2,725	2,976
Establishments with 250–999 Employees	263	372	397
Establishments with 1,000+ Employees	89	97	98

Data: U.S. Census Bureau, County Business Patterns

Major Industries (Ranked by 2005 Employment; Payroll in $1,000s)				
Industry	1998 Employment	2005 Employment	1998 Payroll	2005 Payroll
Accommodation and Food Services	246,530	290,919	5,121,400	7,733,195
Retail Trade	95,507	135,522	2,038,341	3,583,275
Construction	77,682	122,231	2,705,048	5,267,935
Admin., Support, Waste Mngt., Remediation Services	53,102	97,088	1,172,519	3,157,541
Health Care and Social Assistance	60,524	88,200	1,938,561	3,649,668
Professional, Scientific, Technical Services	33,347	53,317	1,423,080	2,854,612
Manufacturing	39,029	45,068	1,298,552	1,897,233
Transportation and Warehousing	25,120	39,281	626,946	1,159,454
Finance and Insurance	27,360	38,672	1,012,252	1,946,376
Wholesale Trade	29,929	36,417	1,066,396	1,726,773

Data: U.S. Census Bureau, County Business Patterns

Taxes and Business Climate

State and Local Taxes		
Combined Revenues ($1,000s)	**2003–4**	**2004–5**
Revenue from Property Taxes	2,147,294	2,320,774
Revenue from Sales and Gross Receipts Taxes	4,568,096	5,333,746
Revenue from Individual Income Taxes	0	0
Revenue from Corporate Income Taxes	0	0
Revenue from Other Taxes	1,256,208	1,389,050
Total Tax Revenue	7,971,598	9,043,570
Per Capita Taxes		
Property Tax Per Capita	920	963
Sales and Gross Receipts Tax Per Capita	1,958	2,214
Individual Income Tax Per Capita	0	0
Corporate Income Tax Per Capita	0	0
Other Taxes Per Capita	538	577
Total Taxes Per Capita	3,417	3,754

Data: U.S. Census Bureau; Anderson Economic Group, LLC

Business Climate Measures	
Anderson Economic Group: 2007 Business Tax Ranking (1 is Best)	38
Forbes Magazine: 2007 Best States for Business Ranking (1 is Best)	22
Tax Foundation: 2008 Business Tax Climate Ranking (1 is Best)	3
ALEC-Laffer 2007 Economic Competitiveness Ranking (1 is Best)	11
2003–4 Employer Firm Births	7,852
2003–4 Employer Firm Terminations	5,971

Data: Anderson Economic Group; Tax Foundation; Forbes Magazine; U.S. Census, Statistics of U.S. Businesses; American Legislative Exchange Council

Voting Behavior and Elected Officials

Voter Registration and Turnout (%)

	1992	1996	2000	2004
Registered Voters Who Voted	77.9	59.7	69.7	77.5
Citizens Age 18+ Who Voted	50.0	38.3	40.9	50.0

Data: Dave Leip's Atlas of U.S. Presidential Elections

Presidential Election Results (Nationwide Winner Listed First)

2004	Popular Vote (%)	Electoral Votes
George W. Bush (Republican, Incumbent)	50.5	5
John Kerry (Democrat)	47.9	0
Other	1.7	0
2000		
George W. Bush (Republican)	49.5	4
Albert Gore (Democrat)	46.0	0
Ralph Nader (Green)	2.5	0
Other	2.0	0
1996		
William Clinton (Democrat, Incumbent)	43.9	4
Robert Dole (Republican)	42.9	0
H. Ross Perot (Reformist)	9.5	0
Other	3.7	0
1992		
William Clinton (Democrat)	37.4	4
George H. W. Bush (Republican, Incumbent)	34.7	0
H. Ross Perot (Independent)	26.2	0
Other	1.7	0

Data: Dave Leip's Atlas of U.S. Presidential Elections

Governor and U.S. Congressional Seats				
Governor	**Party**	**Year Term Began**	**Term**	**Max. Consecutive Terms**
Jim Gibbons	R	2007	First	2
U.S. Senators	**Party**	**Year Elected**	**Term Expires**	
John Ensign	R	2000	2013	
Harry Reid	D	1986	2011	
U.S. Representatives		**Republican**	**Democrat**	**Other**
		2	1	0

Data: National Governors Association; U.S. Senate, Office of the Clerk; U.S. House of Representatives

Business and Economic Agencies

Agency	Website Address
Las Vegas Chamber of Commerce	www.lvchamber.com
Nevada Comission on Economic Development	www.expand2nevada.com
Nevada Small Business Dev. Center	www.nsbdc.org
Nevada Secretary of State, Commercial Recordings Division	www.sos.state.nv.us/comm_rec

Data: Various agency websites

New Hampshire

With a population of 1.3 million people, New Hampshire was the tenth least populous state in the United States in 2006. From 2000 to 2006 the state's population increased by 79,109 people, and is projected to increase to 1.6 million by 2025. This 1.0% projected annual growth rate compares to the projected national average of 0.8%. The state's 2006 per capita personal income of $39,655 was higher compared to $37,480 in 2005 and seventh highest in the United States, some $3,026 above the national average. Per capita income in New Hampshire grew at an average annual rate of 2.9% from 2000 to 2006, compared to 3.5% nationally.

New Hampshire's largest industry in terms of 2005 employment was retail trade. The fastest growing industry was professional, scientific, and technical services, with 4.3% annual employment growth from 1998 to 2005. The second fastest growing industry was administration, support, waste management, and remediation services. The state's workforce is generally more educated than other states—89.9% of the state's adult population has graduated from high school,

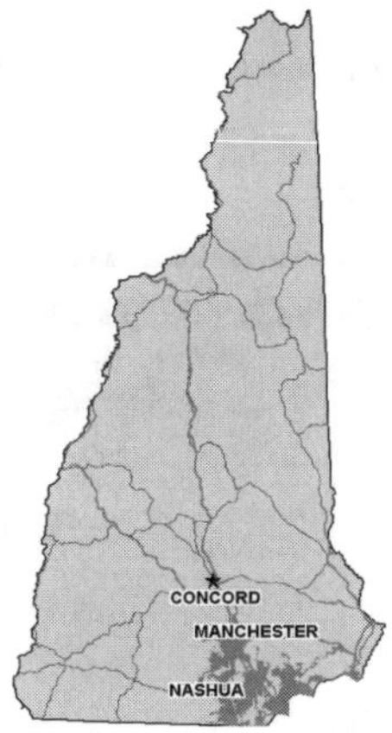

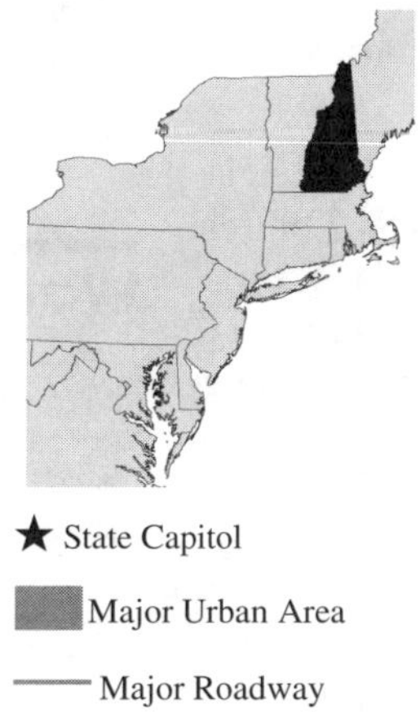

Demographic and Socioeconomic Profile

Demographics and Socioeconomic Figures			
Population and Households	**2000**	**2005**	**2006**
Total Population	1,235,786	1,272,486	1,314,895
Number of Households	474,606	497,054	504,503
Average Household Size	2.5	2.6	2.5
Age and Ethnicity			
Median Age	37.1	39.5	39.3
Population 18 Years of Age and Older	926,885	969,586	1,017,217
Population 65 Years of Age and Older	148,039	151,321	161,836
Caucasian Population	1,186,448	1,214,616	1,250,231
African-American Population	8,984	10,456	13,842
Hispanic Population	19,910	27,933	29,721
Asian Population	15,422	22,850	26,136
Foreign-Born Population (%)	4.4	5.7	5.4
Income			
Per Capita Personal Income (USD)	$33,396	$37,480	$39,655
Median Household Income (USD)	$49,467	$56,768	$59,683
Individuals Below Poverty Level	6.5%	7.5%	8.0%

Data: U.S. Census, American Community Survey; U.S. Department of Commerce, Bureau of Economic Analysis

compared to an 84.1% national average; 31.9% hold a bachelor degree or higher (national average is 27.0%); and 11.3% hold professional or graduate degrees compared to the national average of 9.9%.

New Hampshire's total tax revenue was $4.3 billion for fiscal year 2004–5, up from the 2003–4 total revenue of $4.1 billion. The largest share of tax revenue in 2004–5 was generated from property taxes, followed by sales and gross receipts taxes. On a per capita basis, residents of New Hampshire paid taxes of $3,315, compared to the national average of $3,705 for 2004–5. In terms of business taxes, the state ranked forty-eighth in a study from Anderson Economic Group. Forbes Magazine and the Tax Foundation ranked the state's business climate fourteenth and seventh, respectively, while ALEC ranked New Hampshire twentieth in its state competitiveness index. One is considered best for each ranking.

Population Projections

Year	2010	2015	2020	2025
Total Population	1,385,560	1,456,679	1,524,751	1,586,348
Median Age	39.6	39.8	40.3	41.3
Population 18 Years of Age and Older	1,081,396	1,143,197	1,194,887	1,241,954
Population 65 Years of Age and Older	178,823	217,498	261,856	311,456

Data: U.S. Census Bureau

Workforce and Industry Profile

Workforce

	2000	2005	2006
Civilian Labor Force	694,254	729,583	736,780
Labor Force Participation Rate	73.0%	71.0%	70.8%
Unemployment Rate	2.7%	3.6%	3.4%
Average Wage Per Job (USD)	$34,738	$37,990	$39,250
Education Attainment (Population 25 Years and Older)	**(%)**	**(%)**	**(%)**
High School Graduate or Higher	87.4	89.9	89.9
Bachelors Degree or Higher	28.7	31.8	31.9
Graduate or Professional Degree	10.0	11.7	11.3

Data: U.S. Census Bureau, American Community Survey; U.S. Department of Commerce, Bureau of Economic Analysis; U.S. Department of Labor, Bureau of Labor Statistics

Industry Overview

	1998	2004	2005
Total Employees	518,526	551,001	562,398
Total Payroll ($1,000s)	$14,863,829	$20,005,170	$21,026,773
Total Establishments	36,842	38,843	39,224
Establishments with 1–19 Employees	32,118	33,718	33,999
Establishments with 20–49 Employees	2,969	3,255	3,290
Establishments with 50–249 Employees	1,526	1,662	1,712
Establishments with 250–999 Employees	211	183	199
Establishments with 1,000+ Employees	18	25	24

Data: U.S. Census Bureau, County Business Patterns

Major Industries (Ranked by 2005 Employment; Payroll in $1,000s)				
Industry	1998 Employment	2005 Employment	1998 Payroll	2005 Payroll
Retail Trade	85,811	99,693	1,621,626	2,359,255
Health Care and Social Assistance	68,223	79,240	1,853,351	2,936,765
Manufacturing	101,513	75,837	3,540,699	3,549,995
Accommodation and Food Services	46,138	56,070	530,934	803,288
Admin., Support, Waste Mngt., Remediation Services	30,307	39,544	750,584	1,191,169
Professional, Scientific, Technical Services	22,048	29,619	904,628	1,715,627
Finance and Insurance	24,936	28,136	958,836	1,678,378
Construction	22,749	27,877	831,245	1,349,971
Wholesale Trade	22,912	24,728	946,987	1,383,024
Other Services (except Public Admin.)	19,520	22,272	384,469	540,641

Data: U.S. Census Bureau, County Business Patterns

Taxes and Business Climate

State and Local Taxes		
Combined Revenues ($1,000s)	2003–4	2004–5
Revenue from Property Taxes	2,519,714	2,650,326
Revenue from Sales and Gross Receipts Taxes	674,354	705,116
Revenue from Individual Income Taxes	54,769	67,686
Revenue from Corporate Income Taxes	407,603	476,489
Revenue from Other Taxes	413,231	420,160
Total Tax Revenue	4,069,671	4,319,777
Per Capita Taxes		
Property Tax Per Capita	1,940	2,034
Sales and Gross Receipts Tax Per Capita	519	541
Individual Income Tax Per Capita	42	52
Corporate Income Tax Per Capita	314	366
Other Taxes Per Capita	318	322
Total Taxes Per Capita	3,133	3,315

Data: U.S. Census Bureau; Anderson Economic Group, LLC

Business Climate Measures

Anderson Economic Group: 2007 Business Tax Ranking (1 is Best)	48
Forbes Magazine: 2007 Best States for Business Ranking (1 is Best)	14
Tax Foundation: 2008 Business Tax Climate Ranking (1 is Best)	7
ALEC-Laffer 2007 Economic Competitiveness Ranking (1 is Best)	20
2003–4 Employer Firm Births	3,685
2003–4 Employer Firm Terminations	3,161

Data: Anderson Economic Group; Tax Foundation; Forbes Magazine; U.S. Census, Statistics of U.S. Businesses; American Legislative Exchange Council

Voting Behavior and Elected Officials

Voter Registration and Turnout (%)

	1992	1996	2000	2004
Registered Voters Who Voted	81.3	66.1	66.6	79.2
Citizens Age 18+ Who Voted	63.1	57.3	61.4	69.1

Data: Dave Leip's Atlas of U.S. Presidential Elections

Presidential Election Results (Nationwide Winner Listed First)

2004	Popular Vote (%)	Electoral Votes
George W. Bush (Republican, Incumbent)	48.9	0
John Kerry (Democrat)	50.3	4
Other	0.9	0
2000		
George W. Bush (Republican)	48.1	4
Albert Gore (Democrat)	46.8	0
Ralph Nader (Green)	3.9	0
Other	1.2	0
1996		
William Clinton (Democrat, Incumbent)	49.3	4
Robert Dole (Republican)	39.4	0
H. Ross Perot (Reformist)	9.7	0
Other	1.6	0
1992		
William Clinton (Democrat)	38.9	4
George H. W. Bush (Republican, Incumbent)	37.6	0
H. Ross Perot (Independent)	22.6	0
Other	0.9	0

Data: Dave Leip's Atlas of U.S. Presidential Elections

Governor and U.S. Congressional Seats				
Governor	**Party**	**Year Term Began**	**Term**	**Max. Consecutive Terms**
John Lynch	D	2005	First	No limit
U.S. Senators	**Party**	**Year Elected**	**Term Expires**	
John E. Sununu	R	2002	2009	
Judd Gregg	R	1992	2011	
U.S. Representatives		**Republican**	**Democrat**	**Other**
		0	2	0

Data: National Governors Association; U.S. Senate, Office of the Clerk; U.S. House of Representatives

Business and Economic Agencies

Agency	Website Address
Business and Industry Association of New Hampshire	www.nhbia.org
State of New Hampshire Economic Development	www.nheconomy.com
New Hampshire Small Business Dev. Center	www.nhsbdc.org
New Hampshire Secretary of State, Corporate Division	www.sos.nh.gov/corporate

Data: Various agency websites

New Jersey

New Jersey is located in the New England region of the United States and had a population of 8.7 million people in 2006, making it the eleventh least populous state. The state's population increased by 310,210 people from 2000 to 2006, and is projected to increase to 9.6 million by 2025. This 0.5% projected annual growth rate is below the national average of 0.8%. Per capita personal income in New Jersey was $46,328 in 2006, up from $43,318 in 2005. For 2006, this was $9,699 above the national average and the second highest in the country. The state's per capita income grew at an average annual rate of 3.2% from 2000 to 2006, compared to 3.5% nationally.

The state's workforce generally has more education than other states—86.1% of the state's adult population has graduated from high school, compared to an 84.1% national average; 33.5% hold a bachelor degree or higher (national average is 27.0%); and 12.4% hold professional or graduate degrees (national average is 9.9%). In 2005, the state's largest industry in terms of employment was health care and social assistance, followed by retail trade. The fastest growing industry was professional,

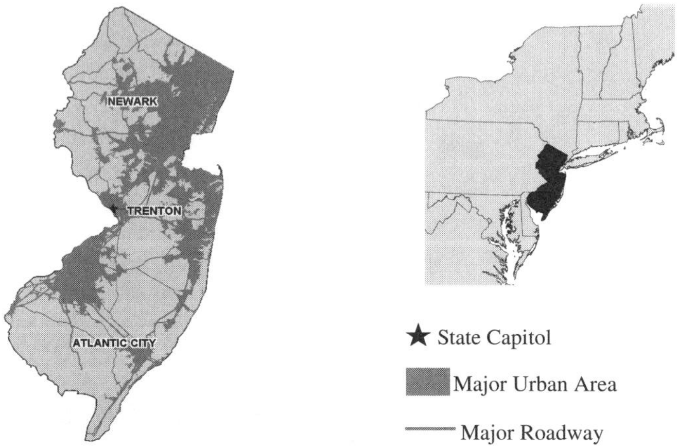

Demographic and Socioeconomic Profile

Demographics and Socioeconomic Figures			
Population and Households	**2000**	**2005**	**2006**
Total Population	8,414,350	8,521,427	8,724,560
Number of Households	3,064,645	3,141,956	3,135,490
Average Household Size	2.7	2.7	2.7
Age and Ethnicity			
Median Age	36.7	38.0	38.2
Population 18 Years of Age and Older	6,332,876	6,366,744	6,634,907
Population 65 Years of Age and Older	1,113,035	1,068,010	1,125,605
Caucasian Population	6,099,439	5,954,926	6,073,160
African-American Population	1,127,266	1,130,967	1,187,161
Hispanic Population	1,116,149	1,307,412	1,364,699
Asian Population	481,794	620,588	652,378
Foreign-Born Population (%)	17.5	19.5	20.1
Income			
Per Capita Personal Income (USD)	$38,364	$43,318	$46,328
Median Household Income (USD)	$55,146	$61,672	$64,470
Individuals Below Poverty Level	8.5%	8.7%	8.7%

Data: U.S. Census, American Community Survey; U.S. Department of Commerce, Bureau of Economic Analysis

scientific, and technical services, with 3.8% annual growth from 1998 to 2005.

In fiscal year 2004–5, New Jersey had total tax revenues of $42.6 billion. The largest share was generated from property taxes, followed by sales and gross receipts taxes. The per capita tax burden in New Jersey was $4,916 for 2004–5, some $1,211 above the national average, and a $361 increase from 2003–4. In terms of business taxes, New Jersey ranked thirty-seventh in a study from Anderson Economic Group. The state's business climate was ranked nineteenth by Forbes Magazine and forty-ninth by the Tax Foundation. New Jersey was ranked forty-third by ALEC in its state competitiveness index. One is considered best for each ranking.

Population Projections

Year	2010	2015	2020	2025
Total Population	9,018,231	9,255,769	9,461,635	9,636,644
Median Age	38.9	39.3	39.6	40.2
Population 18 Years of Age and Older	6,930,007	7,151,894	7,323,271	7,477,125
Population 65 Years of Age and Older	1,231,585	1,385,167	1,552,544	1,762,460

Data: U.S. Census Bureau

Workforce and Industry Profile

Workforce

	2000	2005	2006
Civilian Labor Force	4,287,783	4,455,086	4,518,035
Labor Force Participation Rate	66.5%	66.3%	66.8%
Unemployment Rate	3.7%	4.5%	4.6%
Average Wage Per Job (USD)	$43,676	$43,860	$45,450
Education Attainment (Population 25 Years and Older)	**(%)**	**(%)**	**(%)**
High School Graduate or Higher	82.1	86.3	86.1
Bachelors Degree or Higher	29.8	34.2	33.5
Graduate or Professional Degree	11.0	12.5	12.4

Data: U.S. Census Bureau, American Community Survey; U.S. Department of Commerce, Bureau of Economic Analysis; U.S. Department of Labor, Bureau of Labor Statistics

Industry Overview

	1998	2004	2005
Total Employees	3,368,365	3,609,640	3,594,862
Total Payroll ($1,000s)	$125,787,145	$160,237,399	$166,018,238
Total Establishments	230,860	237,842	242,128
Establishments with 1–19 Employees	202,389	209,777	211,588
Establishments with 20–49 Employees	17,103	18,782	18,585
Establishments with 50–249 Employees	9,826	10,361	10,365
Establishments with 250–999 Employees	1,318	1,369	1,345
Establishments with 1,000+ Employees	224	250	245

Data: U.S. Census Bureau, County Business Patterns

Major Industries (Ranked by 2005 Employment; Payroll in $1,000s)				
Industry	1998 Employment	2005 Employment	1998 Payroll	2005 Payroll
Health Care and Social Assistance	405,935	479,536	13,192,467	19,367,540
Retail Trade	417,791	454,878	8,693,222	11,303,325
Manufacturing	405,275	304,976	16,756,666	15,352,555
Professional, Scientific, Technical Services	234,816	304,803	12,782,239	20,504,746
Admin., Support, Waste Mngt., Remediation Services	247,799	293,105	5,702,383	8,771,190
Accommodation and Food Services	249,836	274,639	3,897,674	4,978,755
Wholesale Trade	275,717	274,063	13,355,315	17,375,975
Finance and Insurance	200,646	216,384	11,166,663	16,995,391
Construction	143,243	175,322	5,828,494	9,240,445
Transportation and Warehousing	151,493	169,118	4,941,082	6,443,091

Data: U.S. Census Bureau, County Business Patterns

Taxes and Business Climate

State and Local Taxes		
Combined Revenues ($1,000s)	**2003–4**	**2004–5**
Revenue from Property Taxes	18,229,254	19,196,599
Revenue from Sales and Gross Receipts Taxes	9,780,318	10,238,453
Revenue from Individual Income Taxes	7,400,733	8,224,290
Revenue from Corporate Income Taxes	1,896,998	2,224,633
Revenue from Other Taxes	2,250,974	2,673,379
Total Tax Revenue	39,558,277	42,557,354
Per Capita Taxes		
Property Tax Per Capita	2,099	2,217
Sales and Gross Receipts Tax Per Capita	1,126	1,183
Individual Income Tax Per Capita	852	950
Corporate Income Tax Per Capita	218	257
Other Taxes Per Capita	259	309
Total Taxes Per Capita	4,555	4,916

Data: U.S. Census Bureau; Anderson Economic Group, LLC

Business Climate Measures

Anderson Economic Group: 2007 Business Tax Ranking (1 is Best)	37
Forbes Magazine: 2007 Best States for Business Ranking (1 is Best)	19
Tax Foundation: 2008 Business Tax Climate Ranking (1 is Best)	49
ALEC-Laffer 2007 Economic Competitiveness Ranking (1 is Best)	43
2003–4 Employer Firm Births	24,099
2003–4 Employer Firm Terminations	23,111

Data: Anderson Economic Group; Tax Foundation; Forbes Magazine; U.S. Census, Statistics of U.S. Businesses; American Legislative Exchange Council

Voting Behavior and Elected Officials

Voter Registration and Turnout (%)

	1992	1996	2000	2004
Registered Voters Who Voted	82.3	71.4	67.7	72.1
Citizens Age 18+ Who Voted	56.3	51.0	50.3	55.5

Data: Dave Leip's Atlas of U.S. Presidential Elections

Presidential Election Results (Nationwide Winner Listed First)

2004	Popular Vote (%)	Electoral Votes
George W. Bush (Republican, Incumbent)	46.2	0
John Kerry (Democrat)	52.9	15
Other	0.8	0
2000		
George W. Bush (Republican)	40.3	0
Albert Gore (Democrat)	56.1	15
Ralph Nader (Green)	3.0	0
Other	0.6	0
1996		
William Clinton (Democrat, Incumbent)	53.7	15
Robert Dole (Republican)	35.9	0
H. Ross Perot (Reformist)	8.5	0
Other	1.9	0
1992		
William Clinton (Democrat)	43.0	15
George H. W. Bush (Republican, Incumbent)	40.6	0
H. Ross Perot (Independent)	15.6	0
Other	0.9	0

Data: Dave Leip's Atlas of U.S. Presidential Elections

Governor and U.S. Congressional Seats

Governor	Party	Year Term Began	Term	Max. Consecutive Terms
Jon Corzine	D	2006	First	2
U.S. Senators	**Party**	**Year Elected**	**Term Expires**	
Frank R. Lautenberg	D	1982	2009	
Robert Menendez	D	2006	2013	
U.S. Representatives		**Republican**	**Democrat**	**Other**
		6	7	0

Data: National Governors Association; U.S. Senate, Office of the Clerk; U.S. House of Representatives

Business and Economic Agencies

Agency	Website Address
New Jersey State Chamber of Commerce	www.njchamber.com
New Jersey Economic Development Authority	www.njeda.com
New Jersey Small Business Dev. Center	www.njsbdc.com
New Jersey Department of State, Business and Corporate Information	www.state.nj.us/state/business

Data: Various agency websites

New Mexico

New Mexico had a population of 2 million people in 2006, making it the fifteenth least populous state. The state's population increased by 135,553 people from 2000 to 2006, and is projected to increase to 2.1 million by 2025. This 0.4% projected annual growth rate compares to the projected national average of 0.8%. Per capita personal income in New Mexico was $29,725 in 2006, up from $28,042 in 2005. For 2006, this was sixth lowest in the country and $6,904 below the national average. From 2000 to 2006 per capita income in New Mexico grew at an average annual rate of 5.0%, compared to 3.5% nationally.

In 2005, the state's largest industry in terms of employment was health care and social assistance, followed by retail trade. The fastest growing industry was health care and social assistance, with 3.2% annual employment growth from 1998 to 2005. The state's workforce is generally less educated than other states—81.5% of the state's adult population has graduated from high school, compared to an 84.1% national average. Nationally, an average of 27.0% hold a bachelor degree or higher compared to 25.3% in New

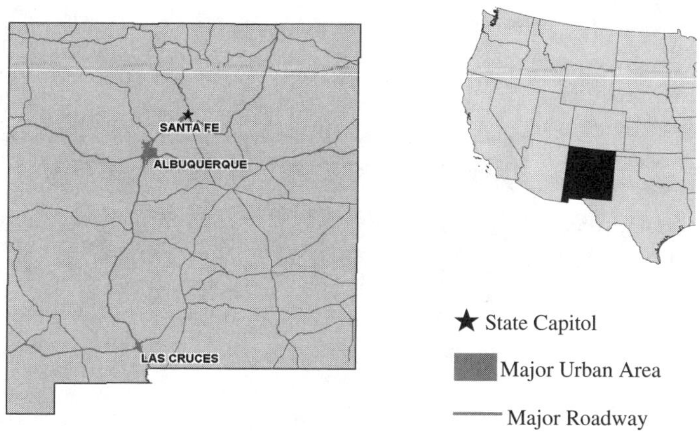

Demographic and Socioeconomic Profile

Demographics and Socioeconomic Figures			
Population and Households	**2000**	**2005**	**2006**
Total Population	1,819,046	1,887,200	1,954,599
Number of Households	677,971	727,820	726,033
Average Household Size	2.6	2.6	2.6
Age and Ethnicity			
Median Age	34.6	36.2	35.2
Population 18 Years of Age and Older	1,311,478	1,400,839	1,444,249
Population 65 Years of Age and Older	212,490	227,685	241,279
Caucasian Population	1,214,680	1,311,829	1,325,762
African-American Population	33,513	35,604	39,654
Hispanic Population	765,610	822,224	860,687
Asian Population	18,286	22,454	25,983
Foreign-Born Population (%)	8.2	8.9	10.1
Income			
Per Capita Personal Income (USD)	$22,135	$28,042	$29,725
Median Household Income (USD)	$34,133	$37,492	$40,629
Individuals Below Poverty Level	18.4%	18.5%	18.5%

Data: U.S. Census, American Community Survey; U.S. Department of Commerce, Bureau of Economic Analysis

Mexico. Nationally, 9.9% hold professional or graduate degrees compared to 10.9% in New Mexico.

In fiscal year 2004–5, New Mexico had total tax revenues of $6.1 billion. The largest share was generated from sales and gross receipts taxes, followed by individual income taxes. The per capita tax burden in New Mexico was $3,167 for 2004–5, some $538 below the national average. In terms of business taxes, the state ranked sixth in a study from Anderson Economic Group. Forbes Magazine and the Tax Foundation ranked the state's business climate twenty-sixth and twenty-third, respectively, while ALEC ranked New Mexico twenty-eighth in its state competitiveness index. One is considered best for each ranking.

Population Projections

Year	2010	2015	2020	2025
Total Population	1,980,225	2,041,539	2,084,341	2,106,584
Median Age	38.3	39.7	41.2	42.9
Population 18 Years of Age and Older	1,500,820	1,556,822	1,595,626	1,628,082
Population 65 Years of Age and Older	278,967	343,622	419,690	497,357

Data: U.S. Census Bureau

Workforce and Industry Profile

Workforce

	2000	2005	2006
Civilian Labor Force	852,293	915,489	935,350
Labor Force Participation Rate	63.5%	63.4%	63.5%
Unemployment Rate	5.0%	5.3%	4.2%
Average Wage Per Job (USD)	$27,497	$33,180	$33,980
Education Attainment (Population 25 Years and Older)	**(%)**	**(%)**	**(%)**
High School Graduate or Higher	78.9	82.0	81.5
Bachelors Degree or Higher	23.5	25.1	25.3
Graduate or Professional Degree	9.8	10.9	10.9

Data: U.S. Census Bureau, American Community Survey; U.S. Department of Commerce, Bureau of Economic Analysis; U.S. Department of Labor, Bureau of Labor Statistics

Industry Overview

	1998	2004	2005
Total Employees	540,186	580,576	595,249
Total Payroll ($1,000s)	$13,133,707	$16,811,505	$18,171,120
Total Establishments	42,608	44,205	45,006
Establishments with 1–19 Employees	37,254	38,295	39,033
Establishments with 20–49 Employees	3,544	3,953	3,906
Establishments with 50–249 Employees	1,618	1,739	1,847
Establishments with 250–999 Employees	173	200	204
Establishments with 1,000+ Employees	19	18	16

Data: U.S. Census Bureau, County Business Patterns

Major Industries (Ranked by 2005 Employment; Payroll in $1,000s)				
Industry	1998 Employment	2005 Employment	1998 Payroll	2005 Payroll
Health Care and Social Assistance	76,641	95,623	1,995,230	3,332,669
Retail Trade	89,883	95,043	1,569,283	2,132,370
Accommodation and Food Services	65,149	77,487	672,950	933,609
Construction	42,164	50,027	1,061,850	1,691,385
Admin., Support, Waste Mngt., Remediation Services	32,347	38,474	669,284	897,141
Professional, Scientific, Technical Services	35,771	35,769	1,514,635	1,719,953
Manufacturing	40,561	34,520	1,216,861	1,391,868
Other Services (except Public Admin.)	26,279	26,661	418,964	557,512
Finance and Insurance	21,847	24,666	679,563	1,022,546
Wholesale Trade	21,672	20,589	652,200	824,284

Data: U.S. Census Bureau, County Business Patterns

Taxes and Business Climate

State and Local Taxes		
Combined Revenues ($1,000s)	**2003–4**	**2004–5**
Revenue from Property Taxes	840,068	863,071
Revenue from Sales and Gross Receipts Taxes	2,627,794	2,854,345
Revenue from Individual Income Taxes	1,007,248	1,086,015
Revenue from Corporate Income Taxes	138,196	242,462
Revenue from Other Taxes	830,852	1,023,435
Total Tax Revenue	5,444,158	6,069,328
Per Capita Taxes		
Property Tax Per Capita	441	450
Sales and Gross Receipts Tax Per Capita	1,381	1,489
Individual Income Tax Per Capita	529	567
Corporate Income Tax Per Capita	73	127
Other Taxes Per Capita	437	534
Total Taxes Per Capita	2,861	3,167

Data: U.S. Census Bureau; Anderson Economic Group, LLC

Business Climate Measures

Anderson Economic Group: 2007 Business Tax Ranking (1 is Best)	6
Forbes Magazine: 2007 Best States for Business Ranking (1 is Best)	26
Tax Foundation: 2008 Business Tax Climate Ranking (1 is Best)	23
ALEC-Laffer 2007 Economic Competitiveness Ranking (1 is Best)	28
2003–4 Employer Firm Births	4,493
2003–4 Employer Firm Terminations	3,974

Data: Anderson Economic Group; Tax Foundation; Forbes Magazine; U.S. Census, Statistics of U.S. Businesses; American Legislative Exchange Council

Voting Behavior and Elected Officials

Voter Registration and Turnout (%)

	1992	1996	2000	2004
Registered Voters Who Voted	80.6	66.4	61.5	68.4
Citizens Age 18+ Who Voted	51.6	45.4	45.6	55.1

Data: Dave Leip's Atlas of U.S. Presidential Elections

Presidential Election Results (Nationwide Winner Listed First)

2004	Popular Vote (%)	Electoral Votes
George W. Bush (Republican, Incumbent)	49.8	5
John Kerry (Democrat)	49.1	0
Other	1.1	0
2000		
George W. Bush (Republican)	47.9	0
Albert Gore (Democrat)	47.9	5
Ralph Nader (Green)	3.6	0
Other	0.7	0
1996		
William Clinton (Democrat, Incumbent)	49.2	5
Robert Dole (Republican)	41.9	0
H. Ross Perot (Reformist)	5.8	0
Other	3.2	0
1992		
William Clinton (Democrat)	49.5	5
George H. W. Bush (Republican, Incumbent)	37.3	0
H. Ross Perot (Independent)	16.1	0
Other	0.6	0

Data: Dave Leip's Atlas of U.S. Presidential Elections

Governor and U.S. Congressional Seats				
Governor	Party	Year Term Began	Term	Max. Consecutive Terms
Bill Richardson	D	2007	Second	2
U.S. Senators	Party	Year Elected	Term Expires	
Pete V. Domenici	R	1972	2009	
Jeff Bingaman	D	1982	2013	
U.S. Representatives		Republican	Democrat	Other
		2	1	0

Data: National Governors Association; U.S. Senate, Office of the Clerk; U.S. House of Representatives

Business and Economic Agencies

Agency	Website Address
Association of Commerce and Industry of New Mexico	www.aci.nm.org
New Mexico Economic Development Department	www.edd.state.nm.us
New Mexico Small Business Dev. Center	www.nmsbdc.org
New Mexico, Public Regulation Commission	www.nmprc.state.nm.us/cb.htm

Data: Various agency websites

New York

With a population of 19.3 million people, New York was the third most populous state in the United States in 2006. From 2000 to 2006 the state's population increased by 329,726 people, and is projected to increase to 19.5 million by 2025. This 0.1% projected annual growth rate compares to the projected national average of 0.8%. The state's 2006 per capita personal income of $43,962 was higher compared to $40,916 in 2005 and fourth highest in the United States, some $7,333 above the national average. Per capita income in New York grew at an average annual rate of 3.9% from 2000 to 2006, compared to 3.5% nationally.

New York's largest industry in terms of 2005 employment was health care and social assistance. The fastest growing industry was educational services, with 2.7% annual employment growth from 1998 to 2005. The second fastest growing industry was professional, scientific, and technical services. The state's workforce is generally more educated than other states—84.1% of the state's adult population has graduated from high school, compared to an 84.1% national average; 31.2% hold a bachelor degree or higher (national average is 27.0%); and 13.3%

★ State Capitol

Major Urban Area

Major Roadway

Demographic and Socioeconomic Profile

Demographics and Socioeconomic Figures			
Population and Households	**2000**	**2005**	**2006**
Total Population	18,976,457	18,655,275	19,306,183
Number of Households	7,056,860	7,114,431	7,088,376
Average Household Size	2.6	2.6	2.6
Age and Ethnicity			
Median Age	35.9	37.5	37.4
Population 18 Years of Age and Older	14,302,266	14,135,504	14,792,694
Population 65 Years of Age and Older	2,450,697	2,370,873	2,520,888
Caucasian Population	12,891,118	12,508,643	12,816,272
African-American Population	2,986,242	2,858,062	2,990,260
Hispanic Population	2,865,016	3,028,658	3,139,590
Asian Population	1,044,423	1,246,567	1,322,971
Foreign-Born Population (%)	20.4	21.4	21.6
Income			
Per Capita Personal Income (USD)	$34,897	$40,916	$43,962
Median Household Income (USD)	$43,393	$49,480	$51,384
Individuals Below Poverty Level	14.6%	13.8%	14.2%

Data: U.S. Census, American Community Survey; U.S. Department of Commerce, Bureau of Economic Analysis

hold professional or graduate degrees compared to the national average of 9.9%.

New York's total tax revenue was $111.1 billion for fiscal year 2004–5, up from the 2003–4 total revenue of $101.4 billion. The largest share of tax revenue in 2004–5 was generated from individual income taxes, followed by property taxes. On a per capita basis, residents of New York paid taxes of $5,768, compared to the national average of $3,705 for 2004–5. In terms of business taxes, the state ranked twenty-second in a study from Anderson Economic Group. Forbes Magazine and the Tax Foundation ranked the state's business climate thirty-third and forty-eighth, respectively. ALEC ranked New York forty-ninth in its state competitiveness index. One is considered best for each ranking.

Population Projections

Year	2010	2015	2020	2025
Total Population	19,443,672	19,546,699	19,576,920	19,540,179
Median Age	37.9	38.1	38.6	39.1
Population 18 Years of Age and Older	15,022,796	15,193,695	15,201,880	15,171,558
Population 65 Years of Age and Older	2,651,655	2,943,496	3,250,020	3,606,687

Data: U.S. Census Bureau

Workforce and Industry Profile

Workforce

	2000	2005	2006
Civilian Labor Force	9,166,972	9,429,656	9,498,563
Labor Force Participation Rate	63.0%	62.8%	63.0%
Unemployment Rate	4.5%	5.0%	4.5%
Average Wage Per Job (USD)	$45,357	$44,060	$45,820
Education Attainment (Population 25 Years and Older)	**(%)**	**(%)**	**(%)**
High School Graduate or Higher	79.1	84.3	84.1
Bachelors Degree or Higher	27.4	31.3	31.2
Graduate or Professional Degree	11.8	13.4	13.3

Data: U.S. Census Bureau, American Community Survey; U.S. Department of Commerce, Bureau of Economic Analysis; U.S. Department of Labor, Bureau of Labor Statistics

Industry Overview

	1998	2004	2005
Total Employees	6,993,814	7,433,686	7,417,463
Total Payroll ($1,000s)	$274,634,982	$353,254,114	$370,842,630
Total Establishments	481,962	511,440	514,265
Establishments with 1–19 Employees	425,442	450,689	453,790
Establishments with 20–49 Employees	34,883	37,519	37,290
Establishments with 50–249 Employees	18,351	19,795	19,752
Establishments with 250–999 Employees	2,737	2,894	2,859
Establishments with 1,000+ Employees	549	543	574

Data: U.S. Census Bureau, County Business Patterns

Major Industries (Ranked by 2005 Employment; Payroll in $1,000s)				
Industry	1998 Employment	2005 Employment	1998 Payroll	2005 Payroll
Health Care and Social Assistance	1,134,481	1,297,637	35,796,990	50,393,418
Retail Trade	800,566	877,803	15,427,452	21,139,844
Finance and Insurance	587,464	579,827	56,877,864	83,556,622
Professional, Scientific, Technical Services	485,199	578,103	26,435,717	39,540,151
Manufacturing	752,511	571,986	27,017,165	24,908,069
Accommodation and Food Services	479,455	558,057	6,912,726	10,007,371
Admin., Support, Waste Mngt., Remediation Services	449,222	484,601	11,375,703	16,926,189
Wholesale Trade	410,877	409,023	18,116,101	22,824,939
Other Services (except Public Admin.)	325,885	355,095	7,337,514	9,979,169
Educational Services	283,373	340,497	7,158,767	10,861,885

Data: U.S. Census Bureau, County Business Patterns

Taxes and Business Climate

State and Local Taxes		
Combined Revenues ($1,000s)	**2003–4**	**2004–5**
Revenue from Property Taxes	32,333,564	34,149,967
Revenue from Sales and Gross Receipts Taxes	27,397,195	27,975,721
Revenue from Individual Income Taxes	30,744,990	34,843,704
Revenue from Corporate Income Taxes	5,362,907	6,994,100
Revenue from Other Taxes	5,587,606	7,144,127
Total Tax Revenue	101,426,262	111,107,619
Per Capita Taxes		
Property Tax Per Capita	1,677	1,773
Sales and Gross Receipts Tax Per Capita	1,421	1,452
Individual Income Tax Per Capita	1,595	1,809
Corporate Income Tax Per Capita	278	363
Other Taxes Per Capita	290	371
Total Taxes Per Capita	5,260	5,768

Data: U.S. Census Bureau; Anderson Economic Group, LLC

Business Climate Measures	
Anderson Economic Group: 2007 Business Tax Ranking (1 is Best)	22
Forbes Magazine: 2007 Best States for Business Ranking (1 is Best)	33
Tax Foundation: 2008 Business Tax Climate Ranking (1 is Best)	48
ALEC-Laffer 2007 Economic Competitiveness Ranking (1 is Best)	49
2003–4 Employer Firm Births	52,129
2003–4 Employer Firm Terminations	46,631

Data: Anderson Economic Group; Tax Foundation; Forbes Magazine; U.S. Census, Statistics of U.S. Businesses; American Legislative Exchange Council

Voting Behavior and Elected Officials

Voter Registration and Turnout (%)

	1992	1996	2000	2004
Registered Voters Who Voted	75.3	62.2	60.6	62.4
Citizens Age 18+ Who Voted	50.9	46.6	47.7	50.4

Data: Dave Leip's Atlas of U.S. Presidential Elections

Presidential Election Results (Nationwide Winner Listed First)

2004	Popular Vote (%)	Electoral Votes
George W. Bush (Republican, Incumbent)	40.1	0
John Kerry (Democrat)	58.4	31
Other	1.6	0
2000		
George W. Bush (Republican)	35.2	0
Albert Gore (Democrat)	60.2	33
Ralph Nader (Green)	3.6	0
Other	1.0	0
1996		
William Clinton (Democrat, Incumbent)	59.5	33
Robert Dole (Republican)	30.6	0
H. Ross Perot (Reformist)	8.0	0
Other	2.0	0
1992		
William Clinton (Democrat)	49.7	33
George H. W. Bush (Republican, Incumbent)	33.9	0
H. Ross Perot (Independent)	15.8	0
Other	0.6	0

Data: Dave Leip's Atlas of U.S. Presidential Elections

Governor and U.S. Congressional Seats				
Governor	**Party**	**Year Term Began**	**Term**	**Max. Consecutive Terms**
Eliot Spitzer	D	2007	First	No limit
U.S. Senators	**Party**	**Year Elected**	**Term Expires**	
Hillary Rodham Clinton	D	2000	2013	
Charles "Chuck" E. Schumer	D	1998	2011	
U.S. Representatives		**Republican**	**Democrat**	**Other**
		6	23	0

Data: National Governors Association; U.S. Senate, Office of the Clerk; U.S. House of Representatives

Business and Economic Agencies

Agency	Website Address
Business Council of New York State, Inc.	www.bcnys.org
Empire State Development	www.nylovesbiz.com/default.asp
New York State Small Business Dev. Center	www.nyssbdc.org
New York Department of State	www.dos.state.ny.us

Data: Various agency websites

North Carolina

North Carolina is located in the South Atlantic region of the United State and had a population of 8.9 million people in 2006, making it the tenth most populous state. The state's population increased by 807,192 people from 2000 to 2006, and is projected to increase to 11.5 million by 2025. This 1.4% projected annual growth rate is above the national average of 0.8%. Per capita personal income in North Carolina was $32,338 in 2006, up from $30,785 in 2005. For 2006, this was $4,291 below the national average and the seventeenth lowest in the country. The state's per capita income grew at an average annual rate of 3.0% from 2000 to 2006, compared to 3.5% nationally.

The state's workforce generally has less education than other states—82.0% of the state's adult population has graduated from high school, compared to an 84.1% national average; 24.8% hold a bachelor degree or higher (national average is 27.0%); and 8.3% hold professional or graduate degrees (national average is 9.9%). In 2005, the state's largest industry in terms of employment was manufacturing, followed by health care and

★ State Capitol

Major Urban Area

Major Roadway

Demographic and Socioeconomic Profile

Demographics and Socioeconomic Figures			
Population and Households	**2000**	**2005**	**2006**
Total Population	8,049,313	8,411,041	8,856,505
Number of Households	3,132,013	3,409,840	3,454,068
Average Household Size	2.5	2.5	2.5
Age and Ethnicity			
Median Age	35.3	36.2	36.6
Population 18 Years of Age and Older	6,087,996	6,279,024	6,701,486
Population 65 Years of Age and Older	969,822	985,875	1,071,799
Caucasian Population	5,802,165	6,005,471	6,224,663
African-American Population	1,734,154	1,765,698	1,892,469
Hispanic Population	372,964	533,087	597,382
Asian Population	111,292	146,795	162,578
Foreign-Born Population (%)	5.3	6.7	6.9
Income			
Per Capita Personal Income (USD)	$27,068	$30,785	$32,338
Median Household Income (USD)	$39,184	$40,729	$42,625
Individuals Below Poverty Level	12.3%	15.1%	14.7%

Data: U.S. Census, American Community Survey; U.S. Department of Commerce, Bureau of Economic Analysis

social assistance. The fastest growing industry was administration, support, waste management, and remediation services, with 4.8% annual growth from 1998 to 2005.

In fiscal year 2004–5, North Carolina had total tax revenues of $27.3 billion. The largest share was generated from sales and gross receipts taxes, followed by individual income taxes. The per capita tax burden in North Carolina was $3,146 for 2004–5, some $559 below the national average, but a $217 increase from 2003–4. In terms of business taxes, North Carolina ranked seventh in a report by Anderson Economic Group. The state's business climate was ranked third by Forbes Magazine and fortieth by the Tax Foundation. North Carolina was ranked nineteenth by ALEC in its state competitiveness index. One is considered best for each ranking.

Population Projections

Year	2010	2015	2020	2025
Total Population	9,345,823	10,010,770	10,709,289	11,449,153
Median Age	36.9	37.3	37.2	36.8
Population 18 Years of Age and Older	7,076,985	7,572,393	8,083,886	8,609,911
Population 65 Years of Age and Older	1,161,164	1,374,754	1,618,578	1,897,902

Data: U.S. Census Bureau

Workforce and Industry Profile

Workforce

	2000	2005	2006
Civilian Labor Force	4,123,812	4,339,807	4,464,875
Labor Force Participation Rate	67.5%	65.9%	66.3%
Unemployment Rate	3.7%	5.2%	4.8%
Average Wage Per Job (USD)	$31,068	$34,460	$35,520
Education Attainment (Population 25 Years and Older)	**(%)**	**(%)**	**(%)**
High School Graduate or Higher	78.1	82.3	82.0
Bachelors Degree or Higher	22.5	25.1	24.8
Graduate or Professional Degree	7.2	8.0	8.3

Data: U.S. Census Bureau, American Community Survey; U.S. Department of Commerce, Bureau of Economic Analysis; U.S. Department of Labor, Bureau of Labor Statistics

Industry Overview

	1998	2004	2005
Total Employees	3,223,178	3,365,633	3,409,968
Total Payroll ($1,000s)	$86,780,877	$109,572,059	$115,740,410
Total Establishments	198,690	213,057	216,994
Establishments with 1–19 Employees	170,676	181,555	185,763
Establishments with 20–49 Employees	17,002	19,828	19,642
Establishments with 50–249 Employees	9,411	10,211	10,101
Establishments with 250–999 Employees	1,426	1,279	1,293
Establishments with 1,000+ Employees	175	184	195

Data: U.S. Census Bureau, County Business Patterns

Major Industries (Ranked by 2005 Employment; Payroll in $1,000s)				
Industry	1998 Employment	2005 Employment	1998 Payroll	2005 Payroll
Manufacturing	771,282	554,442	22,452,407	20,681,882
Health Care and Social Assistance	375,399	470,820	10,495,546	16,282,077
Retail Trade	430,667	449,870	7,424,839	9,707,125
Accommodation and Food Services	260,453	315,212	2,668,813	3,894,008
Admin., Support, Waste Mngt., Remediation Services	188,349	262,070	3,608,799	6,433,258
Construction	205,750	221,783	5,926,419	7,970,603
Finance and Insurance	133,120	178,306	5,316,012	10,265,446
Professional, Scientific, Technical Services	126,888	174,892	5,000,972	9,503,601
Wholesale Trade	161,459	163,867	6,121,068	7,794,777
Other Services (except Public Admin.)	134,043	147,579	2,313,119	3,038,554

Data: U.S. Census Bureau, County Business Patterns

Taxes and Business Climate

State and Local Taxes		
Combined Revenues ($1,000s)	**2003–4**	**2004–5**
Revenue from Property Taxes	6,093,170	6,449,622
Revenue from Sales and Gross Receipts Taxes	8,951,045	9,423,309
Revenue from Individual Income Taxes	7,510,978	8,427,553
Revenue from Corporate Income Taxes	837,085	1,271,985
Revenue from Other Taxes	1,620,186	1,734,639
Total Tax Revenue	25,012,464	27,307,108
Per Capita Taxes		
Property Tax Per Capita	713	743
Sales and Gross Receipts Tax Per Capita	1,048	1,086
Individual Income Tax Per Capita	880	971
Corporate Income Tax Per Capita	98	147
Other Taxes Per Capita	190	200
Total Taxes Per Capita	2,929	3,146

Data: U.S. Census Bureau; Anderson Economic Group, LLC

Business Climate Measures	
Anderson Economic Group: 2007 Business Tax Ranking (1 is Best)	7
Forbes Magazine: 2007 Best States for Business Ranking (1 is Best)	3
Tax Foundation: 2008 Business Tax Climate Ranking (1 is Best)	40
ALEC-Laffer 2007 Economic Competitiveness Ranking (1 is Best)	19
2003–4 Employer Firm Births	21,261
2003–4 Employer Firm Terminations	18,288

Data: Anderson Economic Group; Tax Foundation; Forbes Magazine; U.S. Census, Statistics of U.S. Businesses; American Legislative Exchange Council

Voting Behavior and Elected Officials

Voter Registration and Turnout (%)

	1992	1996	2000	2004
Registered Voters Who Voted	68.4	58.3	56.8	64.0
Citizens Age 18+ Who Voted	50.1	45.6	47.8	55.4

Data: Dave Leip's Atlas of U.S. Presidential Elections

Presidential Election Results (Nationwide Winner Listed First)

2004	Popular Vote (%)	Electoral Votes
George W. Bush (Republican, Incumbent)	56.0	15
John Kerry (Democrat)	43.6	0
Other	0.4	0
2000		
George W. Bush (Republican)	56.0	14
Albert Gore (Democrat)	43.2	0
Ralph Nader (Green)	0.0	0
Other	0.8	0
1996		
William Clinton (Democrat, Incumbent)	44.0	0
Robert Dole (Republican)	48.7	14
H. Ross Perot (Reformist)	6.7	0
Other	0.6	0
1992		
William Clinton (Democrat)	42.7	0
George H. W. Bush (Republican, Incumbent)	43.4	14
H. Ross Perot (Independent)	13.7	0
Other	0.2	0

Data: Dave Leip's Atlas of U.S. Presidential Elections

Governor and U.S. Congressional Seats				
Governor	Party	Year Term Began	Term	Max. Consecutive Terms
Michael Easley	D	2005	Second	2
U.S. Senators	**Party**	**Year Elected**	**Term Expires**	
Elizabeth Dole	R	2002	2009	
Richard Burr	R	2004	2011	
U.S. Representatives		**Republican**	**Democrat**	**Other**
		6	7	0

Data: National Governors Association; U.S. Senate, Office of the Clerk; U.S. House of Representatives

Business and Economic Agencies

Agency	Website Address
North Carolina Citizens For Business & Industry	www.nccbi.org
North Carolina Department of Commerce	www.commerce.state.nc.us
North Carolina Small Business & Tech Dev. Center	www.sbtdc.org
Employment Security Comission	www.ncesc.com

Data: Various agency websites

North Dakota

North Dakota, located in the West North Central region of the United States, had a population of 635,867 people in 2006, making it the third least populous state. The state's population decreased by 6,333 people from 2000 to 2006, and is projected to decrease to 620,777 by 2025. This −0.1% projected annual growth rate compares to the projected national average of 0.8%. Per capita personal income in North Dakota was $33,034 in 2006, up from $32,053 in 2005. For 2006, this was twenty-second lowest in the country and $3,595 below the national average. From 2000 to 2006 per capita income in North Dakota grew at an average annual rate of 4.7%, compared to 3.5% nationally.

In 2005, the state's largest industry in terms of employment was health care and social assistance, followed by retail trade. The fastest growing industry was professional, scientific, and technical services, with 6.2% annual employment growth from 1998 to 2005. The state's workforce is generally less educated than other states—88.1% of the state's adult population has graduated from high school, compared to an 84.1% national average. Nationally, an average of 27.0% hold a bachelor degree

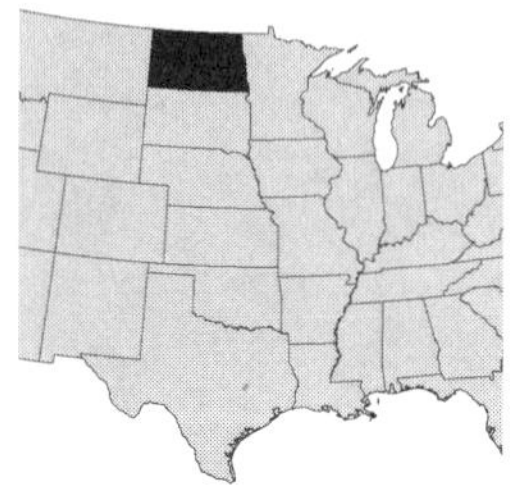

★ State Capitol

Major Urban Area

Major Roadway

Demographic and Socioeconomic Profile

Demographics and Socioeconomic Figures			
Population and Households	**2000**	**2005**	**2006**
Total Population	642,200	609,645	635,867
Number of Households	257,152	270,437	272,352
Average Household Size	2.4	2.3	2.2
Age and Ethnicity			
Median Age	36.2	39.1	37.1
Population 18 Years of Age and Older	481,301	474,382	492,255
Population 65 Years of Age and Older	94,597	86,655	92,829
Caucasian Population	593,785	557,952	578,919
African-American Population	3,673	4,981	5,999
Hispanic Population	7,568	8,553	9,332
Asian Population	3,342	5,459	4,348
Foreign-Born Population (%)	1.9	2.0	2.1
Income			
Per Capita Personal Income (USD)	$25,106	$32,053	$33,034
Median Household Income (USD)	$34,604	$41,030	$41,919
Individuals Below Poverty Level	11.9%	11.2%	11.4%

Data: U.S. Census, American Community Survey; U.S. Department of Commerce, Bureau of Economic Analysis

or higher compared to 25.6% in North Dakota. Nationally, 9.9% hold professional or graduate degrees compared to 6.5% in North Dakota.

In fiscal year 2004–5, North Dakota had total tax revenues of $2.1 billion. The largest share was generated from sales and gross receipts taxes, followed by property taxes. The per capita tax burden in North Dakota was $3,336 for 2004–5, some $369 below the national average. In terms of business taxes, the state ranked forty-second in a study from Anderson Economic Group. Forbes Magazine and the Tax Foundation ranked the state's business climate ninth and thirtieth, respectively, while ALEC ranked North Dakota twenty-fourth in its state competitiveness index. One is considered best for each ranking.

Population Projections

Year	2010	2015	2020	2025
Total Population	636,623	635,133	630,112	620,777
Median Age	38.4	39.3	40.6	41.9
Population 18 Years of Age and Older	494,659	496,436	492,483	486,949
Population 65 Years of Age and Older	97,108	107,900	125,023	142,195

Data: U.S. Census Bureau

Workforce and Industry Profile

Workforce

	2000	2005	2006
Civilian Labor Force	345,881	354,032	357,960
Labor Force Participation Rate	71.2%	72.2%	72.6%
Unemployment Rate	2.9%	3.4%	3.2%
Average Wage Per Job (USD)	$24,683	$30,850	$32,440
Education Attainment (Population 25 Years and Older)	**(%)**	**(%)**	**(%)**
High School Graduate or Higher	83.9	88.2	88.1
Bachelors Degree or Higher	22.0	25.5	25.6
Graduate or Professional Degree	5.5	6.7	6.5

Data: U.S. Census Bureau, American Community Survey; U.S. Department of Commerce, Bureau of Economic Analysis; U.S. Department of Labor, Bureau of Labor Statistics

Industry Overview

	1998	2004	2005
Total Employees	249,476	265,663	270,479
Total Payroll ($1,000s)	$5,533,810	$7,314,026	$7,779,322
Total Establishments	20,288	20,822	21,061
Establishments with 1–19 Employees	17,815	18,229	18,384
Establishments with 20–49 Employees	1,618	1,632	1,727
Establishments with 50–249 Employees	774	860	849
Establishments with 250–999 Employees	72	92	93
Establishments with 1,000+ Employees	9	9	8

Data: U.S. Census Bureau, County Business Patterns

Major Industries (Ranked by 2005 Employment; Payroll in $1,000s)				
Industry	1998 Employment	2005 Employment	1998 Payroll	2005 Payroll
Health Care and Social Assistance	45,894	50,372	1,089,193	1,609,606
Retail Trade	41,402	43,548	655,415	854,201
Accommodation and Food Services	25,850	28,662	208,591	290,993
Manufacturing	23,209	24,604	670,183	827,442
Wholesale Trade	17,000	17,233	476,356	668,191
Construction	13,980	15,128	451,087	641,985
Finance and Insurance	12,526	14,990	371,331	563,818
Other Services (except Public Admin.)	13,819	13,601	184,901	229,642
Professional, Scientific, Technical Services	7,596	11,561	233,272	417,841
Admin., Support, Waste Mngt., Remediation Services	10,953	10,837	177,802	236,809

Data: U.S. Census Bureau, County Business Patterns

Taxes and Business Climate

State and Local Taxes		
Combined Revenues ($1,000s)	**2003–4**	**2004–5**
Revenue from Property Taxes	584,622	619,912
Revenue from Sales and Gross Receipts Taxes	742,116	791,296
Revenue from Individual Income Taxes	213,982	242,008
Revenue from Corporate Income Taxes	49,807	75,836
Revenue from Other Taxes	310,520	392,334
Total Tax Revenue	1,901,047	2,121,388
Per Capita Taxes		
Property Tax Per Capita	919	975
Sales and Gross Receipts Tax Per Capita	1,165	1,244
Individual Income Tax Per Capita	336	381
Corporate Income Tax Per Capita	78	119
Other Taxes Per Capita	488	617
Total Taxes Per Capita	2,985	3,336

Data: U.S. Census Bureau; Anderson Economic Group, LLC

Business Climate Measures	
Anderson Economic Group: 2007 Business Tax Ranking (1 is Best)	42
Forbes Magazine: 2007 Best States for Business Ranking (1 is Best)	9
Tax Foundation: 2008 Business Tax Climate Ranking (1 is Best)	30
ALEC-Laffer 2007 Economic Competitiveness Ranking (1 is Best)	24
2003–4 Employer Firm Births	1,660
2003–4 Employer Firm Terminations	1,390

Data: Anderson Economic Group; Tax Foundation; Forbes Magazine; U.S. Census, Statistics of U.S. Businesses; American Legislative Exchange Council

Voting Behavior and Elected Officials

Voter Registration and Turnout

	1992	1996	2000	2004
Registered Voters Who Voted	NA	NA	NA	NA
Citizens Age 18+ Who Voted	67.3%	56.0%	59.9%	64.2%

Data: Dave Leip's Atlas of U.S. Presidential Elections; Not Available

Presidential Election Results (Nationwide Winner Listed First)

2004	Popular Vote (%)	Electoral Votes
George W. Bush (Republican, Incumbent)	62.9	3
John Kerry (Democrat)	35.5	0
Other	1.6	0
2000		
George W. Bush (Republican)	60.7	3
Albert Gore (Democrat)	33.1	0
Ralph Nader (Green)	3.3	0
Other	3.0	0
1996		
William Clinton (Democrat, Incumbent)	40.1	0
Robert Dole (Republican)	46.9	3
H. Ross Perot (Reformist)	12.2	0
Other	0.7	0
1992		
William Clinton (Democrat)	32.2	0
George H. W. Bush (Republican, Incumbent)	44.2	3
H. Ross Perot (Independent)	23.1	0
Other	0.5	0

Data: Dave Leip's Atlas of U.S. Presidential Elections

Governor and U.S. Congressional Seats				
Governor	Party	Year Term Began	Term	Max. Consecutive Terms
John Hoeven	R	2005	Second	No limit
U.S. Senators	Party	Year Elected	Term Expires	
Kent Conrad	D	1986	2013	
Byron L. Dorgan	D	1992	2011	
U.S. Representatives		Republican	Democrat	Other
		0	1	0

Data: National Governors Association; U.S. Senate, Office of the Clerk; U.S. House of Representatives

Business and Economic Agencies

Agency	Website Address
Greater North Dakota Chamber of Commerce	www.gnda.com
North Dakota Department of Commerce	www.growingnd.com
North Dakota Small Business Dev. Center	www.ndsbdc.org
North Dakota Secretary of State	www.nd.gov/sos/businessserv

Data: Various agency websites

Ohio

Ohio is located in the East North Central region of the United State and had a population of 11.5 million people in 2006, making it the seventh most populous state. The state's population increased by 124,866 people from 2000 to 2006, and is projected to increase to 11.6 million by 2025. This 0.1% projected annual growth rate is above the national average of 0.8%. Per capita personal income in Ohio was $33,217 in 2006, up from $31,849 in 2005. For 2006, this was $3,412 below the national average and the twenty-third lowest in the country. The state's per capita income grew at an average annual rate of 2.8% from 2000 to 2006, compared to 3.5% nationally.

The state's workforce generally has less education than other states—86.2% of the state's adult population has graduated from high school, compared to an 84.1% national average; 23.0% hold a bachelor degree or higher (national average is 27.0%); and 8.3% hold professional or graduate degrees (national average is 9.9%). In 2005, the state's largest industry in terms of employment was manufacturing, followed by health care and social assistance. The fastest

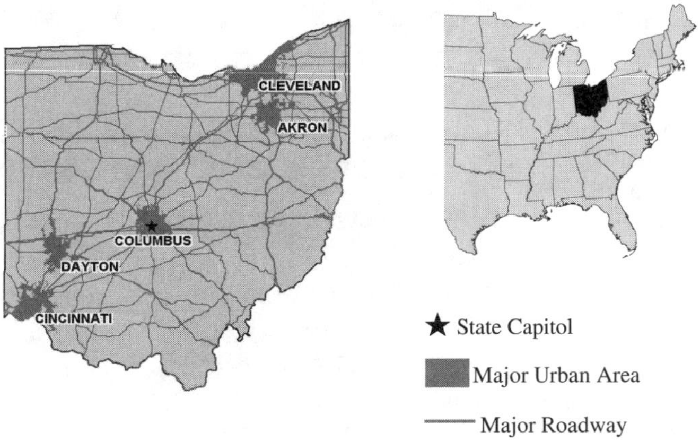

Demographic and Socioeconomic Profile

Demographics and Socioeconomic Figures			
Population and Households	**2000**	**2005**	**2006**
Total Population	11,353,140	11,155,606	11,478,006
Number of Households	4,445,773	4,507,821	4,499,506
Average Household Size	2.5	2.5	2.5
Age and Ethnicity			
Median Age	36.2	37.6	37.6
Population 18 Years of Age and Older	8,467,999	8,401,998	8,705,230
Population 65 Years of Age and Older	1,508,095	1,430,984	1,528,079
Caucasian Population	9,640,523	9,408,020	9,645,844
African-American Population	1,288,359	1,283,908	1,357,343
Hispanic Population	213,889	253,889	265,762
Asian Population	132,131	162,117	175,000
Foreign-Born Population (%)	3.0	3.5	3.6
Income			
Per Capita Personal Income (USD)	$28,207	$31,849	$33,217
Median Household Income (USD)	$40,956	$43,493	$44,532
Individuals Below Poverty Level	10.6%	13.0%	13.3%

Data: U.S. Census, American Community Survey; U.S. Department of Commerce, Bureau of Economic Analysis

growing industry was professional, scientific, and technical services, with 2.4% annual growth from 1998 to 2005.

In fiscal year 2004–5, Ohio had total tax revenues of $41.7 billion. The largest share was generated from individual income taxes, followed by sales and gross receipts taxes. The per capita tax burden in Ohio was $3,640 for 2004–5, some $65 below the national average, but a $221 increase from 2003–4. In terms of business taxes, Ohio ranked ninth in a report by Anderson Economic Group. The state's business climate was ranked thirty-eighth by Forbes Magazine and forty-sixth by the Tax Foundation. Ohio was ranked forty-seventh by ALEC in its state competitiveness index. One is considered best for each ranking.

Population Projections

Year	2010	2015	2020	2025
Total Population	11,576,181	11,635,446	11,644,058	11,605,738
Median Age	38.1	38.3	39.0	39.7
Population 18 Years of Age and Older	8,831,750	8,912,543	8,940,542	8,932,576
Population 65 Years of Age and Older	1,586,981	1,766,239	1,978,464	2,206,698

Data: U.S. Census Bureau

Workforce and Industry Profile

Workforce

	2000	2005	2006
Civilian Labor Force	5,807,036	5,891,633	5,933,957
Labor Force Participation Rate	67.3%	66.7%	66.9%
Unemployment Rate	4.0%	5.9%	5.5%
Average Wage Per Job (USD)	$32,507	$36,270	$37,360
Education Attainment (Population 25 Years and Older)	**(%)**	**(%)**	**(%)**
High School Graduate or Higher	83.0	86.3	86.2
Bachelors Degree or Higher	21.1	23.3	23.0
Graduate or Professional Degree	7.4	7.5	8.3

Data: U.S. Census Bureau, American Community Survey; U.S. Department of Commerce, Bureau of Economic Analysis; U.S. Department of Labor, Bureau of Labor Statistics

Industry Overview

	1998	2004	2005
Total Employees	4,806,046	4,762,205	4,762,618
Total Payroll ($1,000s)	$140,265,358	$162,559,634	$168,350,499
Total Establishments	270,343	271,733	270,968
Establishments with 1–19 Employees	227,768	228,346	227,995
Establishments with 20–49 Employees	25,666	26,358	25,869
Establishments with 50–249 Employees	14,702	14,957	14,952
Establishments with 250–999 Employees	1,927	1,793	1,872
Establishments with 1,000+ Employees	280	279	280

Data: U.S. Census Bureau, County Business Patterns

Major Industries (Ranked by 2005 Employment; Payroll in $1,000s)				
Industry	1998 Employment	2005 Employment	1998 Payroll	2005 Payroll
Manufacturing	994,788	792,783	37,590,541	35,677,361
Health Care and Social Assistance	628,383	715,021	17,364,658	24,680,904
Retail Trade	632,285	620,869	10,789,385	12,465,820
Accommodation and Food Services	404,645	430,134	3,839,217	4,799,826
Admin., Support, Waste Mngt., Remediation Services	298,272	335,702	5,734,863	8,293,808
Finance and Insurance	246,164	263,129	9,522,859	13,685,220
Professional, Scientific, Technical Services	207,796	244,577	8,391,803	12,704,427
Wholesale Trade	254,997	237,889	9,446,007	11,276,311
Other Services (except Public Admin.)	228,028	227,947	3,907,272	4,750,055
Construction	222,637	214,948	7,898,182	9,261,274

Data: U.S. Census Bureau, County Business Patterns

Taxes and Business Climate

State and Local Taxes		
Combined Revenues ($1,000s)	**2003–4**	**2004–5**
Revenue from Property Taxes	11,232,828	11,973,971
Revenue from Sales and Gross Receipts Taxes	12,318,284	12,743,328
Revenue from Individual Income Taxes	12,183,380	13,079,167
Revenue from Corporate Income Taxes	1,060,594	1,345,910
Revenue from Other Taxes	2,356,137	2,572,378
Total Tax Revenue	39,151,223	41,714,754
Per Capita Taxes		
Property Tax Per Capita	981	1,045
Sales and Gross Receipts Tax Per Capita	1,076	1,112
Individual Income Tax Per Capita	1,064	1,141
Corporate Income Tax Per Capita	93	117
Other Taxes Per Capita	206	224
Total Taxes Per Capita	3,419	3,640

Data: U.S. Census Bureau; Anderson Economic Group, LLC

Business Climate Measures	
Anderson Economic Group: 2007 Business Tax Ranking (1 is Best)	9
Forbes Magazine: 2007 Best States for Business Ranking (1 is Best)	38
Tax Foundation: 2008 Business Tax Climate Ranking (1 is Best)	46
ALEC-Laffer 2007 Economic Competitiveness Ranking (1 is Best)	47
2003–4 Employer Firm Births	22,254
2003–4 Employer Firm Terminations	21,847

Data: Anderson Economic Group; Tax Foundation; Forbes Magazine; U.S. Census, Statistics of U.S. Businesses; American Legislative Exchange Council

Voting Behavior and Elected Officials

Voter Registration and Turnout (%)

	1992	1996	2000	2004
Registered Voters Who Voted	75.6	66.3	62.4	70.6
Citizens Age 18+ Who Voted	60.6	54.3	55.6	65.3

Data: Dave Leip's Atlas of U.S. Presidential Elections

Presidential Election Results (Nationwide Winner Listed First)

2004	Popular Vote (%)	Electoral Votes
George W. Bush (Republican, Incumbent)	50.8	20
John Kerry (Democrat)	48.7	0
Other	0.5	0
2000		
George W. Bush (Republican)	50.0	21
Albert Gore (Democrat)	46.5	0
Ralph Nader (Green)	2.5	0
Other	1.1	0
1996		
William Clinton (Democrat, Incumbent)	47.4	21
Robert Dole (Republican)	41.0	0
H. Ross Perot (Reformist)	10.7	0
Other	1.0	0
1992		
William Clinton (Democrat)	40.2	21
George H. W. Bush (Republican, Incumbent)	38.4	0
H. Ross Perot (Independent)	21.0	0
Other	0.5	0

Data: Dave Leip's Atlas of U.S. Presidential Elections

Governor and U.S. Congressional Seats				
Governor	**Party**	**Year Term Began**	**Term**	**Max. Consecutive Terms**
Ted Strickland	D	2007	First	2
U.S. Senators	**Party**	**Year Elected**	**Term Expires**	
Sherrod Brown	D	2006	2013	
George V. Voinovich	R	1998	2011	
U.S. Representatives		**Republican**	**Democrat**	**Other**
		11	7	0

Data: National Governors Association; U.S. Senate, Office of the Clerk; U.S. House of Representatives

Business and Economic Agencies

Agency	Website Address
Ohio Chamber of Commerce	www.ohiochamber.com
Ohio Department of Development	www.odod.state.oh.us
Ohio Small Business Dev. Center	www.odod.state.oh.us/edd/osb/sbdc
Ohio Secretary of State	www.sos.state.oh.us

Data: Various agency websites

Oklahoma

Oklahoma, located in the West South Central region of the United States, had a population of 3.6 million people in 2006, making it the twenty-third least populous state. The state's population increased by 128,558 people from 2000 to 2006, and is projected to increase to 3.8 million by 2025. This 0.3% projected annual growth rate compares to the projected national average of 0.8%. Per capita personal income in Oklahoma was $32,398 in 2006, up from $30,054 in 2005. For 2006, this was eighteenth lowest in the country and $4,231 below the national average. From 2000 to 2006 per capita income in Oklahoma grew at an average annual rate of 4.8%, compared to 3.5% nationally.

In 2005, the state's largest industry in terms of employment was health care and social assistance, followed by retail trade. The fastest growing industry was professional, scientific, and technical services, with 4.1% annual employment growth from 1998 to 2005. The state's workforce is generally less educated than other states—84.3% of the state's adult population has graduated from high school, compared to an 84.1% national average. Nationally, an average of 27.0% hold a bachelor degree

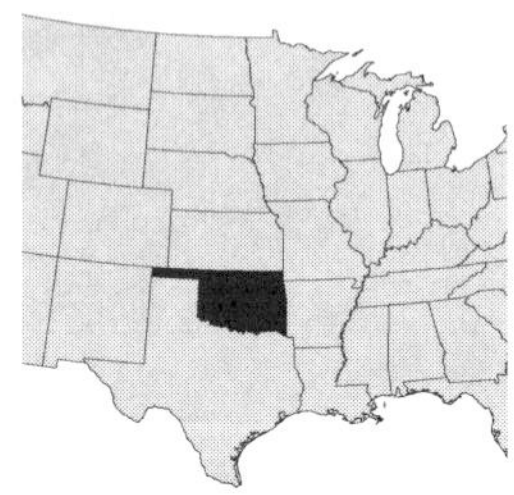

★ State Capitol

Major Urban Area

Major Roadway

Demographic and Socioeconomic Profile

Demographics and Socioeconomic Figures			
Population and Households	**2000**	**2005**	**2006**
Total Population	3,450,654	3,433,496	3,579,212
Number of Households	1,342,293	1,380,595	1,385,300
Average Household Size	2.5	2.5	2.5
Age and Ethnicity			
Median Age	35.5	36.5	36.2
Population 18 Years of Age and Older	2,560,390	2,585,083	2,684,026
Population 65 Years of Age and Older	455,700	441,763	475,637
Caucasian Population	2,624,679	2,589,660	2,698,032
African-American Population	258,532	243,094	263,271
Hispanic Population	177,768	227,767	244,822
Asian Population	45,546	54,270	59,164
Foreign-Born Population (%)	3.8	4.5	4.9
Income			
Per Capita Personal Income (USD)	$24,407	$30,054	$32,398
Median Household Income (USD)	$33,400	$37,063	$38,770
Individuals Below Poverty Level	14.7%	16.5%	17.0%

Data: U.S. Census, American Community Survey; U.S. Department of Commerce, Bureau of Economic Analysis

or higher compared to 22.1% in Oklahoma. Nationally, 9.9% hold professional or graduate degrees compared to 7.2% in Oklahoma.

In fiscal year 2004–5, Oklahoma had total tax revenues of $10.1 billion. The largest share was generated from sales and gross receipts taxes, followed by individual income taxes. The per capita tax burden in Oklahoma was $2,849 for 2004–5, some $856 below the national average. In terms of business taxes, the state ranked seventeenth in a study from Anderson Economic Group. Forbes Magazine and the Tax Foundation ranked the state's business climate thirtieth and nineteenth, respectively, while ALEC ranked Oklahoma thirteenth in its state competitiveness index. One is considered best for each ranking.

Population Projections

Year	2010	2015	2020	2025
Total Population	3,591,516	3,661,694	3,735,690	3,820,994
Median Age	36.8	37.3	37.9	38.0
Population 18 Years of Age and Older	2,696,443	2,746,485	2,801,647	2,870,485
Population 65 Years of Age and Older	494,966	553,761	625,384	702,307

Data: U.S. Census Bureau

Workforce and Industry Profile

Workforce

	2000	2005	2006
Civilian Labor Force	1,661,045	1,704,988	1,719,628
Labor Force Participation Rate	64.4%	63.8%	63.7%
Unemployment Rate	3.1%	4.4%	4.0%
Average Wage Per Job (USD)	$26,988	$31,460	$32,570
Education Attainment (Population 25 Years and Older)	**(%)**	**(%)**	**(%)**
High School Graduate or Higher	80.6	84.3	84.3
Bachelors Degree or Higher	20.3	22.4	22.1
Graduate or Professional Degree	6.8	7.2	7.2

Data: U.S. Census Bureau, American Community Survey; U.S. Department of Commerce, Bureau of Economic Analysis; U.S. Department of Labor, Bureau of Labor Statistics

Industry Overview

	1998	2004	2005
Total Employees	1,167,709	1,195,043	1,220,285
Total Payroll ($1,000s)	$28,667,008	$35,597,604	$37,620,071
Total Establishments	84,881	87,440	88,548
Establishments with 1–19 Employees	73,827	76,061	76,986
Establishments with 20–49 Employees	7,124	7,363	7,462
Establishments with 50–249 Employees	3,453	3,527	3,587
Establishments with 250–999 Employees	420	423	445
Establishments with 1,000+ Employees	57	66	68

Data: U.S. Census Bureau, County Business Patterns

Major Industries (Ranked by 2005 Employment; Payroll in $1,000s)				
Industry	1998 Employment	2005 Employment	1998 Payroll	2005 Payroll
Health Care and Social Assistance	171,498	187,899	4,149,804	5,821,233
Retail Trade	165,852	168,914	2,605,428	3,350,298
Manufacturing	168,140	140,428	5,241,720	5,556,517
Accommodation and Food Services	104,489	121,362	956,839	1,279,470
Admin., Support, Waste Mngt., Remediation Services	79,011	98,357	1,404,856	2,359,530
Professional, Scientific, Technical Services	49,645	65,621	1,721,291	2,718,604
Construction	54,900	61,415	1,478,200	2,036,409
Other Services (except Public Admin.)	61,363	61,305	962,404	1,136,855
Finance and Insurance	57,364	58,568	1,825,437	2,359,868
Wholesale Trade	61,096	55,771	1,919,885	2,311,890

Data: U.S. Census Bureau, County Business Patterns

Taxes and Business Climate

State and Local Taxes		
Combined Revenues ($1,000s)	**2003–4**	**2004–5**
Revenue from Property Taxes	1,637,457	1,718,634
Revenue from Sales and Gross Receipts Taxes	3,638,525	3,891,471
Revenue from Individual Income Taxes	2,319,123	2,468,609
Revenue from Corporate Income Taxes	133,309	168,890
Revenue from Other Taxes	1,706,529	1,825,498
Total Tax Revenue	9,434,943	10,073,102
Per Capita Taxes		
Property Tax Per Capita	465	486
Sales and Gross Receipts Tax Per Capita	1,032	1,101
Individual Income Tax Per Capita	658	698
Corporate Income Tax Per Capita	38	48
Other Taxes Per Capita	484	516
Total Taxes Per Capita	2,677	2,849

Data: U.S. Census Bureau; Anderson Economic Group, LLC

Business Climate Measures	
Anderson Economic Group: 2007 Business Tax Ranking (1 is Best)	17
Forbes Magazine: 2007 Best States for Business Ranking (1 is Best)	30
Tax Foundation: 2008 Business Tax Climate Ranking (1 is Best)	19
ALEC-Laffer 2007 Economic Competitiveness Ranking (1 is Best)	13
2003–4 Employer Firm Births	8,334
2003–4 Employer Firm Terminations	7,421

Data: Anderson Economic Group; Tax Foundation; Forbes Magazine; U.S. Census, Statistics of U.S. Businesses; American Legislative Exchange Council

Voting Behavior and Elected Officials

Voter Registration and Turnout (%)

	1992	1996	2000	2004
Registered Voters Who Voted	60.4	61.0	55.3	68.3
Citizens Age 18+ Who Voted	59.7	49.7	48.2	55.6

Data: Dave Leip's Atlas of U.S. Presidential Elections

Presidential Election Results (Nationwide Winner Listed First)

2004	Popular Vote (%)	Electoral Votes
George W. Bush (Republican, Incumbent)	65.6	7
John Kerry (Democrat)	34.4	0
Other	0.0	0
2000		
George W. Bush (Republican)	60.3	8
Albert Gore (Democrat)	38.4	0
Ralph Nader (Green)	0.0	0
Other	1.3	0
1996		
William Clinton (Democrat, Incumbent)	40.5	0
Robert Dole (Republican)	48.3	8
H. Ross Perot (Reformist)	10.8	0
Other	0.5	0
1992		
William Clinton (Democrat)	34.0	0
George H. W. Bush (Republican, Incumbent)	42.7	8
H. Ross Perot (Independent)	23.0	0
Other	0.3	0

Data: Dave Leip's Atlas of U.S. Presidential Elections

Governor and U.S. Congressional Seats				
Governor	**Party**	**Year Term Began**	**Term**	**Max. Consecutive Terms**
Brad Henry	D	2007	Second	2
U.S. Senators	**Party**	**Year Elected**	**Term Expires**	
James M. Inhofe	R	1994	2009	
Tom Coburn	R	2004	2011	
U.S. Representatives		**Republican**	**Democrat**	**Other**
		4	1	0

Data: National Governors Association; U.S. Senate, Office of the Clerk; U.S. House of Representatives

Business and Economic Agencies

Agency	Website Address
The State Chamber	www.okstatechamber.com
Oklahoma Advantage, Oklahoma Department of Commerce	www.okcommerce.gov
Oklahoma Small Business Dev. Center	www.osbdc.org
Oklahoma Secretary of State	www.sos.state.ok.us/business/business_filing.htm

Data: Various agency websites

Oregon

With a population of 3.7 million people, Oregon was the twenty-fourth least populous state in the United States in 2006. From 2000 to 2006 the state's population increased by 279,359 people, and is projected to increase to 4.5 million by 2025. This1.1% projected annual growth rate compares to the projected national average of 0.8%. The state's 2006 per capita personal income of $33,252 was higher compared to $31,507 in 2005 and twenty-fourth lowest in the United States, some $3,377 below the national average. Per capita income in Oregon grew at an average annual rate of 2.9% from 2000 to 2006, compared to 3.5% nationally.

Oregon's largest industry in terms of 2005 employment was retail trade. The fastest growing industry was profes sional, scientific, and technical services, with 2.7% annual employment growth from 1998 to 2005. The second fastest growing industry was health care and social assistance. The state's workforce is generally more educated than other states—87.6% of the state's adult population has graduated from high school, compared to an 84.1% national average;

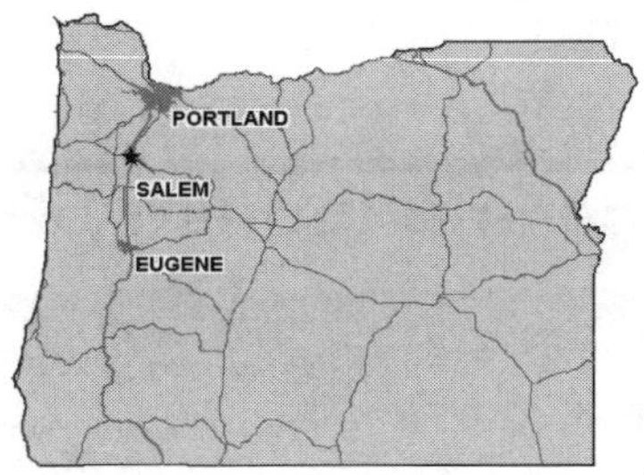

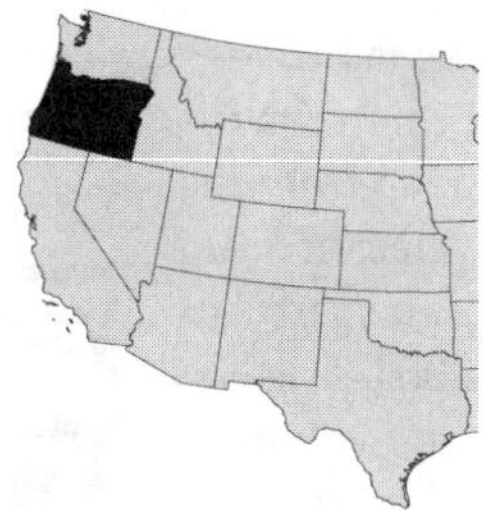

★ State Capitol

Major Urban Area

Major Roadway

Demographic and Socioeconomic Profile

Demographics and Socioeconomic Figures			
Population and Households	**2000**	**2005**	**2006**
Total Population	3,421,399	3,560,109	3,700,758
Number of Households	1,333,723	1,425,340	1,449,662
Average Household Size	2.5	2.5	2.5
Age and Ethnicity			
Median Age	36.3	37.0	37.6
Population 18 Years of Age and Older	2,577,129	2,713,648	2,843,141
Population 65 Years of Age and Older	437,887	447,408	476,865
Caucasian Population	2,957,510	3,089,729	3,186,177
African-American Population	53,032	58,309	63,631
Hispanic Population	273,938	353,433	379,034
Asian Population	99,136	125,049	135,746
Foreign-Born Population (%)	8.5	9.7	9.7
Income			
Per Capita Personal Income (USD)	$28,097	$31,507	$33,252
Median Household Income (USD)	$40,916	$42,944	$46,230
Individuals Below Poverty Level	11.6%	14.1%	13.3%

Data: U.S. Census, American Community Survey; U.S. Department of Commerce, Bureau of Economic Analysis

27.6% hold a bachelor degree or higher (national average is 27.0%); and 10.0% hold professional or graduate degrees compared to the national average of 9.9%.

Oregon's total tax revenue was $11.1 billion for fiscal year 2004–5, up from the 2003–4 total revenue of $10.5 billion. The largest share of tax revenue in 2004–5 was generated from individual income taxes, followed by property taxes. On a per capita basis, residents of Oregon paid taxes of $3,060, compared to the national average of $3,705 for 2004–5. In terms of business taxes, the state ranked thirty-third in a study from Anderson Economic Group. Forbes Magazine and the Tax Foundation ranked the state's business climate twenty-eighth and tenth, respectively, while ALEC ranked Oregon at thirty-sixth in its state competitiveness index. One is considered best for each ranking.

Population Projections

Year	2010	2015	2020	2025
Total Population	3,790,996	4,012,924	4,260,393	4,536,418
Median Age	37.6	37.9	38.5	38.9
Population 18 Years of Age and Older	2,927,830	3,097,346	3,279,891	3,483,880
Population 65 Years of Age and Older	494,328	590,784	704,866	805,717

Data: U.S. Census Bureau

Workforce and Industry Profile

Workforce

	2000	2005	2006
Civilian Labor Force	1,810,150	1,870,407	1,898,847
Labor Force Participation Rate	68.5%	65.6%	65.3%
Unemployment Rate	5.1%	6.2%	5.4%
Average Wage Per Job (USD)	$32,774	$37,280	$38,570
Education Attainment (Population 25 Years and Older)	**(%)**	**(%)**	**(%)**
High School Graduate or Higher	85.1	87.5	87.6
Bachelors Degree or Higher	25.1	27.7	27.6
Graduate or Professional Degree	8.7	10.0	10.0

Data: U.S. Census Bureau, American Community Survey; U.S. Department of Commerce, Bureau of Economic Analysis; U.S. Department of Labor, Bureau of Labor Statistics

Industry Overview

	1998	2004	2005
Total Employees	1,310,750	1,355,542	1,409,576
Total Payroll ($1,000s)	$37,722,920	$46,346,936	$50,019,294
Total Establishments	99,183	105,449	108,571
Establishments with 1–19 Employees	86,688	92,522	95,175
Establishments with 20–49 Employees	8,151	8,383	8,660
Establishments with 50–249 Employees	3,831	4,036	4,182
Establishments with 250–999 Employees	456	439	484
Establishments with 1,000+ Employees	57	69	70

Data: U.S. Census Bureau, County Business Patterns

Major Industries (Ranked by 2005 Employment; Payroll in $1,000s)				
Industry	1998 Employment	2005 Employment	1998 Payroll	2005 Payroll
Retail Trade	182,706	199,261	3,622,503	4,708,601
Manufacturing	211,636	184,708	7,624,969	7,987,583
Health Care and Social Assistance	150,105	180,291	4,199,706	6,773,806
Accommodation and Food Services	125,462	140,934	1,363,861	1,944,540
Admin., Support, Waste Mngt., Remediation Services	81,555	92,640	1,621,416	2,249,439
Construction	78,753	85,319	2,718,801	3,532,998
Wholesale Trade	77,517	75,899	2,950,647	3,629,651
Professional, Scientific, Technical Services	62,828	75,596	2,380,263	3,692,635
Finance and Insurance	59,843	68,114	2,501,220	3,586,248
Other Services (except Public Admin.)	57,303	62,299	1,028,385	1,435,665

Data: U.S. Census Bureau, County Business Patterns

Taxes and Business Climate

State and Local Taxes		
Combined Revenues ($1,000s)	**2003–4**	**2004–5**
Revenue from Property Taxes	3,459,371	3,562,960
Revenue from Sales and Gross Receipts Taxes	1,014,307	971,506
Revenue from Individual Income Taxes	4,370,854	4,829,181
Revenue from Corporate Income Taxes	320,065	365,347
Revenue from Other Taxes	1,309,613	1,377,997
Total Tax Revenue	10,474,210	11,106,991
Per Capita Taxes		
Property Tax Per Capita	963	982
Sales and Gross Receipts Tax Per Capita	282	268
Individual Income Tax Per Capita	1,217	1,330
Corporate Income Tax Per Capita	89	101
Other Taxes Per Capita	365	380
Total Taxes Per Capita	2,917	3,060

Data: U.S. Census Bureau; Anderson Economic Group, LLC

Business Climate Measures

Anderson Economic Group: 2007 Business Tax Ranking (1 is Best)	33
Forbes Magazine: 2007 Best States for Business Ranking (1 is Best)	28
Tax Foundation: 2008 Business Tax Climate Ranking (1 is Best)	10
ALEC-Laffer 2007 Economic Competitiveness Ranking (1 is Best)	36
2003–4 Employer Firm Births	10,774
2003–4 Employer Firm Terminations	9,190

Data: Anderson Economic Group; Tax Foundation; Forbes Magazine; U.S. Census, Statistics of U.S. Businesses; American Legislative Exchange Council

Voting Behavior and Elected Officials

Voter Registration and Turnout (%)

	1992	1996	2000	2004
Registered Voters Who Voted	82.4	70.2	78.5	85.8
Citizens Age 18+ Who Voted	65.7	57.1	59.5	67.8

Data: Dave Leip's Atlas of U.S. Presidential Elections

Presidential Election Results (Nationwide Winner Listed First)

2004	Popular Vote (%)	Electoral Votes
George W. Bush (Republican, Incumbent)	47.2	0
John Kerry (Democrat)	51.4	7
Other	1.5	0
2000		
George W. Bush (Republican)	46.5	0
Albert Gore (Democrat)	47.0	7
Ralph Nader (Green)	5.0	0
Other	1.5	0
1996		
William Clinton (Democrat, Incumbent)	47.2	7
Robert Dole (Republican)	39.1	0
H. Ross Perot (Reformist)	8.8	0
Other	5.0	0
1992		
William Clinton (Democrat)	42.5	7
George H. W. Bush (Republican, Incumbent)	32.5	0
H. Ross Perot (Independent)	24.2	0
Other	0.8	0

Data: Dave Leip's Atlas of U.S. Presidential Elections

Governor and U.S. Congressional Seats

Governor	Party	Year Term Began	Term	Max. Consecutive Terms
Ted Kulongoski	D	2007	Second	2
U.S. Senators	**Party**	**Year Elected**	**Term Expires**	
Gordon H. Smith	R	1996	2009	
Ron Wyden	D	1996	2011	
U.S. Representatives		**Republican**	**Democrat**	**Other**
		1	4	0

Data: National Governors Association; U.S. Senate, Office of the Clerk; U.S. House of Representatives

Business and Economic Agencies

Agency	Website Address
Associated Oregon Industries, Inc.	www.aoi.org
Oregon Economic and Community Development Department	econ.oregon.gov
Oregon Small Busines Development Center	www.bizcenter.org
Oregon Secretary of State, Corporation Division	www.filinginoregon.com

Data: Various agency websites

Pennsylvania

Pennsylvania is located in the Mid-Atlantic region of the United States and had a population of 12.4 million people in 2006, making it the sixth most populous state. The state's population increased by 159,657 people from 2000 to 2006, and is projected to increase to 12.8 million by 2025. This 0.2% projected annual growth rate is below the national average of 0.8%. Per capita personal income in Pennsylvania was $36,689 in 2006, up from $34,810 in 2005. For 2006, this was $60 above the national average and the nineteenth highest in the country. The state's per capita income grew at an average annual rate of 3.6% from 2000 to 2006, compared to 3.5% nationally.

The state's workforce generally has less education than other states—86.2% of the state's adult population has graduated from high school, compared to an 84.1% national average; 25.4% hold a bachelor degree or higher (national average is 27.0%); and 9.6% hold professional or graduate degrees (national average is 9.9%). In 2005, the state's largest industry in terms of employment was health care and social assistance, followed by retail trade. The fastest growing industry was professional,

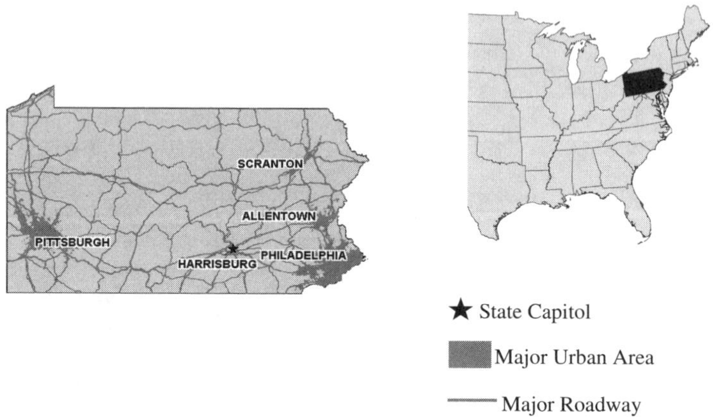

Demographic and Socioeconomic Profile

Demographics and Socioeconomic Figures			
Population and Households	**2000**	**2005**	**2006**
Total Population	12,281,054	11,979,147	12,440,621
Number of Households	4,777,003	4,860,140	4,845,603
Average Household Size	2.5	2.5	2.5
Age and Ethnicity			
Median Age	38.0	39.7	39.6
Population 18 Years of Age and Older	9,362,066	9,179,373	9,633,087
Population 65 Years of Age and Older	1,920,257	1,754,466	1,883,234
Caucasian Population	10,486,177	10,132,144	10,429,732
African-American Population	1,211,669	1,208,536	1,289,799
Hispanic Population	392,121	484,679	527,142
Asian Population	216,631	266,473	289,289
Foreign-Born Population (%)	4.1	5.0	5.1
Income			
Per Capita Personal Income (USD)	$29,695	$34,810	$36,689
Median Household Income (USD)	$40,106	$44,537	$46,259
Individuals Below Poverty Level	11.0%	11.9%	12.1%

Data: U.S. Census, American Community Survey; U.S. Department of Commerce, Bureau of Economic Analysis

scientific, and technical services, with 1.9% annual growth from 1998 to 2005.

In fiscal year 2004–5, Pennsylvania had total tax revenues of $46.0 billion. The largest share was generated from sales and gross receipts taxes, followed by property taxes. The per capita tax burden in Pennsylvania was $3,721 for 2004–5, just $16 above the national average, and a $274 increase from 2003–4. In terms of business taxes, Pennsylvania ranked twenty-fourth in a report by Anderson Economic Group. The state's business climate was ranked thirty-ninth by Forbes Magazine and twenty-seventh by the Tax Foundation. Pennsylvania was ranked thirty-seventh by ALEC in its state competitiveness index. One is considered best for each ranking.

Population Projections

Year	2010	2015	2020	2025
Total Population	12,584,487	12,710,938	12,787,354	12,801,945
Median Age	40.0	40.3	40.6	41.4
Population 18 Years of Age and Older	9,836,892	9,970,245	10,016,274	10,023,766
Population 65 Years of Age and Older	1,956,235	2,148,982	2,403,118	2,688,781

Data: U.S. Census Bureau

Workforce and Industry Profile

Workforce

	2000	2005	2006
Civilian Labor Force	6,085,833	6,279,472	6,306,050
Labor Force Participation Rate	64.1%	64.6%	64.5%
Unemployment Rate	4.2%	5.0%	4.7%
Average Wage Per Job (USD)	$34,015	$36,320	$37,580
Education Attainment (Population 25 Years and Older)	**(%)**	**(%)**	**(%)**
High School Graduate or Higher	81.9	86.7	86.2
Bachelors Degree or Higher	22.4	25.7	25.4
Graduate or Professional Degree	8.4	9.8	9.6

Data: U.S. Census Bureau, American Community Survey; U.S. Department of Commerce, Bureau of Economic Analysis; U.S. Department of Labor, Bureau of Labor Statistics

Industry Overview

	1998	2004	2005
Total Employees	4,906,190	5,107,044	5,082,630
Total Payroll ($1,000s)	$145,569,019	$181,784,478	$189,692,284
Total Establishments	292,659	301,557	303,333
Establishments with 1–19 Employees	250,822	256,868	258,823
Establishments with 20–49 Employees	25,263	27,113	26,891
Establishments with 50–249 Employees	14,282	15,214	15,284
Establishments with 250–999 Employees	1,971	2,050	2,025
Establishments with 1,000+ Employees	321	312	310

Data: U.S. Census Bureau, County Business Patterns

Major Industries (Ranked by 2005 Employment; Payroll in $1,000s)				
Industry	1998 Employment	2005 Employment	1998 Payroll	2005 Payroll
Health Care and Social Assistance	740,333	837,643	20,979,688	29,533,070
Retail Trade	645,472	668,973	11,092,400	14,205,271
Manufacturing	818,215	663,605	28,636,023	28,643,809
Accommodation and Food Services	364,480	404,683	3,736,716	5,053,740
Professional, Scientific, Technical Services	266,917	304,291	12,571,204	18,452,450
Admin., Support, Waste Mngt., Remediation Services	278,403	295,723	5,632,982	7,639,549
Finance and Insurance	272,427	295,538	11,510,271	17,612,704
Other Services (except Public Admin.)	239,673	250,423	4,148,515	5,349,986
Construction	225,797	242,100	8,279,710	11,463,841
Wholesale Trade	234,940	238,710	9,203,086	11,945,383

Data: U.S. Census Bureau, County Business Patterns

Taxes and Business Climate

State and Local Taxes		
Combined Revenues ($1,000s)	**2003–4**	**2004–5**
Revenue from Property Taxes	12,518,226	13,390,534
Revenue from Sales and Gross Receipts Taxes	12,917,786	13,637,892
Revenue from Individual Income Taxes	10,311,095	11,461,650
Revenue from Corporate Income Taxes	1,677,998	1,703,295
Revenue from Other Taxes	5,292,752	5,825,887
Total Tax Revenue	42,717,857	46,019,258
Per Capita Taxes		
Property Tax Per Capita	1,010	1,083
Sales and Gross Receipts Tax Per Capita	1,042	1,103
Individual Income Tax Per Capita	832	927
Corporate Income Tax Per Capita	135	138
Other Taxes Per Capita	427	471
Total Taxes Per Capita	3,447	3,721

Data: U.S. Census Bureau; Anderson Economic Group, LLC

Business Climate Measures

Anderson Economic Group: 2007 Business Tax Ranking (1 is Best)	24
Forbes Magazine: 2007 Best States for Business Ranking (1 is Best)	39
Tax Foundation: 2008 Business Tax Climate Ranking (1 is Best)	27
ALEC-Laffer 2007 Economic Competitiveness Ranking (1 is Best)	37
2003–4 Employer Firm Births	25,364
2003–4 Employer Firm Terminations	23,431

Data: Anderson Economic Group; Tax Foundation; Forbes Magazine; U.S. Census, Statistics of U.S. Businesses; American Legislative Exchange Council

Voting Behavior and Elected Officials

Voter Registration and Turnout (%)

	1992	1996	2000	2004
Registered Voters Who Voted	82.8	66.2	63.1	69.0
Citizens Age 18+ Who Voted	54.3	49.0	52.5	60.5

Data: Dave Leip's Atlas of U.S. Presidential Elections

Presidential Election Results (Nationwide Winner Listed First)

2004	Popular Vote (%)	Electoral Votes
George W. Bush (Republican, Incumbent)	48.4	0
John Kerry (Democrat)	50.9	21
Other	0.7	0
2000		
George W. Bush (Republican)	46.4	0
Albert Gore (Democrat)	50.6	23
Ralph Nader (Green)	2.1	0
Other	0.9	0
1996		
William Clinton (Democrat, Incumbent)	49.2	23
Robert Dole (Republican)	40.0	0
H. Ross Perot (Reformist)	9.6	0
Other	1.3	0
1992		
William Clinton (Democrat)	45.2	23
George H. W. Bush (Republican, Incumbent)	36.1	0
H. Ross Perot (Independent)	18.2	0
Other	0.5	0

Data: Dave Leip's Atlas of U.S. Presidential Elections

Governor and U.S. Congressional Seats				
Governor	**Party**	**Year Term Began**	**Term**	**Max. Consecutive Terms**
Edward Rendell	D	2007	Second	2
U.S. Senators	**Party**	**Year Elected**	**Term Expires**	
Bob Casey, Jr.	D	2006	2013	
Arlen Specter	R	1980	2011	
U.S. Representatives		**Republican**	**Democrat**	**Other**
		8	11	0

Data: National Governors Association; U.S. Senate, Office of the Clerk; U.S. House of Representatives

Business and Economic Agencies

Agency	Website Address
Pennsylvania Chamber of Business & Industry	www.pachamber.org
Pennsylvania Department of Community and Economic Development	www.newpa.com
Pennsylvania Small Business Dev. Center	www.pasbdc.org
Pennsylvania Department of State	www.dos.state.pa.us/corps

Data: Various agency websites

Rhode Island

Rhode Island, located in the New England region of the United States, had a population of 1.1 million people in 2006, making it the eighth least populous state. The state's population increased by 19,291 people from 2000 to 2006, and is projected to increase to 1.2 million by 2025. This 0.4% projected annual growth rate compares to the projected national average of 0.8%. Per capita personal income in Rhode Island was $37,261 in 2006, up from $35,757 in 2005. For 2006, this was seventeenth highest in the country and $632 above the national average. From 2000 to 2006 per capita income in Rhode Island grew at an average annual rate of 4.1%, compared to 3.5% nationally.

In 2005, the state's largest industry in terms of employment was health care and social assistance, followed by manufacturing. The fastest growing industry was professional, scientific, and technical services, with 5.2% annual employment growth from 1998 to 2005. The state's workforce is generally more educated than other states—82.4% of the state's adult population has graduated from high school, compared to an 84.1% national

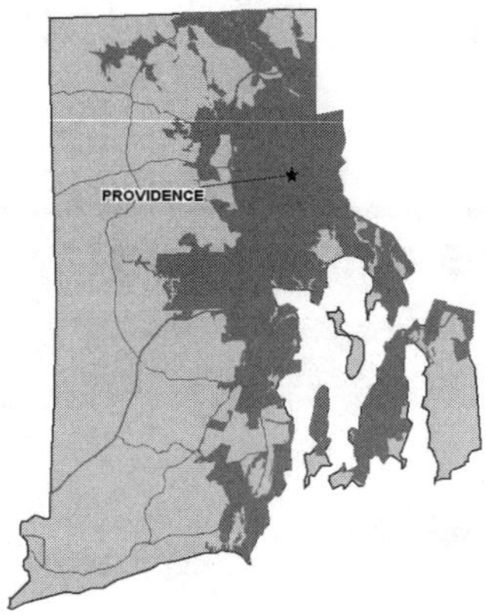

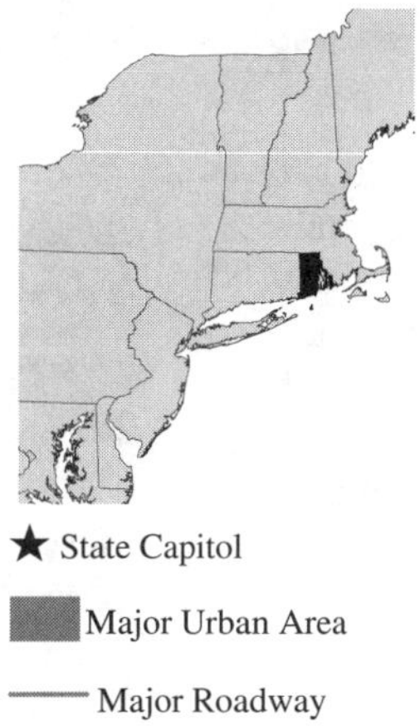

Demographic and Socioeconomic Profile

Demographics and Socioeconomic Figures			
Population and Households	**2000**	**2005**	**2006**
Total Population	1,048,319	1,032,662	1,067,610
Number of Households	408,424	406,089	405,627
Average Household Size	2.5	2.5	2.5
Age and Ethnicity			
Median Age	36.7	38.4	38.4
Population 18 Years of Age and Older	800,810	788,331	830,163
Population 65 Years of Age and Older	152,719	139,961	147,444
Caucasian Population	890,766	856,314	882,370
African-American Population	45,236	51,843	54,396
Hispanic Population	90,452	112,722	117,708
Asian Population	23,825	26,803	29,406
Foreign-Born Population (%)	11.4	12.6	12.6
Income			
Per Capita Personal Income (USD)	$29,214	$35,757	$37,261
Median Household Income (USD)	$42,090	$51,458	$51,814
Individuals Below Poverty Level	11.9%	12.3%	11.1%

Data: U.S. Census, American Community Survey; U.S. Department of Commerce, Bureau of Economic Analysis

average. Nationally, an average of 27.0% hold a bachelor degree or higher compared to 29.6% in Rhode Island. Nationally, 9.9% hold professional or graduate degrees compared to 11.3% in Rhode Island.

In fiscal year 2004–5, Rhode Island had total tax revenues of $4.5 billion. The largest share was generated from property taxes, followed by sales and gross receipts taxes. The per capita tax burden in Rhode Island was $4,218 for 2004–5, some $513 above below the national average. In terms of business taxes, the state ranked thirty-ninth in a report from Anderson Economic Group. Forbes Magazine and the Tax Foundation ranked the state's business climate forty-fifth and fiftieth, respectively, while ALEC ranked Rhode Island forty-eighth in its state competitiveness index. One is considered best for each ranking.

Population Projections

Year	2010	2015	2020	2025
Total Population	1,116,652	1,139,543	1,154,230	1,157,855
Median Age	38.2	38.2	39.2	39.7
Population 18 Years of Age and Older	867,379	891,204	900,219	901,037
Population 65 Years of Age and Older	157,358	175,242	197,972	224,508

Data: U.S. Census Bureau

Workforce and Industry Profile

Workforce

	2000	2005	2006
Civilian Labor Force	543,404	568,610	577,338
Labor Force Participation Rate	66.8%	67.5%	68.5%
Unemployment Rate	4.2%	5.1%	5.1%
Average Wage Per Job (USD)	$32,615	$38,980	$40,580
Education Attainment (Population 25 Years and Older)	**(%)**	**(%)**	**(%)**
High School Graduate or Higher	78.0	83.5	82.4
Bachelors Degree or Higher	25.6	29.3	29.6
Graduate or Professional Degree	9.7	11.5	11.3

Data: U.S. Census Bureau, American Community Survey; U.S. Department of Commerce, Bureau of Economic Analysis; U.S. Department of Labor, Bureau of Labor Statistics

Industry Overview

	1998	2004	2005
Total Employees	402,485	434,706	442,291
Total Payroll ($1,000s)	$11,115,638	$15,025,183	$15,756,079
Total Establishments	28,245	30,011	30,331
Establishments with 1–19 Employees	24,651	25,940	26,255
Establishments with 20–49 Employees	2,242	2,556	2,546
Establishments with 50–249 Employees	1,165	1,344	1,366
Establishments with 250–999 Employees	162	146	137
Establishments with 1,000+ Employees	25	25	27

Data: U.S. Census Bureau, County Business Patterns

Major Industries (Ranked by 2005 Employment; Payroll in $1,000s)				
Industry	1998 Employment	2005 Employment	1998 Payroll	2005 Payroll
Health Care and Social Assistance	68,633	82,286	1,914,868	2,825,111
Manufacturing	74,181	58,738	2,341,311	2,366,601
Retail Trade	46,781	54,724	834,011	1,284,483
Accommodation and Food Services	33,837	42,638	384,469	611,147
Finance and Insurance	24,277	33,032	917,996	1,989,292
Admin., Support, Waste Mngt., Remediation Services	28,065	22,929	563,833	563,367
Professional, Scientific, Technical Services	15,973	22,718	632,606	1,141,686
Educational Services	18,410	22,070	429,108	668,237
Construction	16,290	20,041	614,594	993,532
Other Services (except Public Admin.)	16,913	19,741	314,071	463,394

Data: U.S. Census Bureau, County Business Patterns

Taxes and Business Climate

State and Local Taxes		
Combined Revenues ($1,000s)	**2003–4**	**2004–5**
Revenue from Property Taxes	1,759,134	1,819,413
Revenue from Sales and Gross Receipts Taxes	1,310,984	1,386,537
Revenue from Individual Income Taxes	899,939	998,042
Revenue from Corporate Income Taxes	69,479	113,326
Revenue from Other Taxes	162,730	182,306
Total Tax Revenue	4,202,266	4,499,624
Per Capita Taxes		
Property Tax Per Capita	1,629	1,706
Sales and Gross Receipts Tax Per Capita	1,214	1,300
Individual Income Tax Per Capita	833	936
Corporate Income Tax Per Capita	64	106
Other Taxes Per Capita	151	171
Total Taxes Per Capita	3,891	4,218

Data: U.S. Census Bureau; Anderson Economic Group, LLC

Business Climate Measures

Anderson Economic Group: 2007 Business Tax Ranking (1 is Best)	39
Forbes Magazine: 2007 Best States for Business Ranking (1 is Best)	45
Tax Foundation: 2008 Business Tax Climate Ranking (1 is Best)	50
ALEC-Laffer 2007 Economic Competitiveness Ranking (1 is Best)	48
2003–4 Employer Firm Births	2,864
2003–4 Employer Firm Terminations	2,234

Data: Anderson Economic Group; Tax Foundation; Forbes Magazine; U.S. Census, Statistics of U.S. Businesses; American Legislative Exchange Council

Voting Behavior and Elected Officials

Voter Registration and Turnout (%)

	1992	1996	2000	2004
Registered Voters Who Voted	81.8	64.8	60.9	61.7
Citizens Age 18+ Who Voted	58.4	52.0	51.1	52.5

Data: Dave Leip's Atlas of U.S. Presidential Elections

Presidential Election Results (Nationwide Winner Listed First)

2004	Popular Vote (%)	Electoral Votes
George W. Bush (Republican, Incumbent)	38.7	0
John Kerry (Democrat)	59.4	4
Other	1.9	0
2000		
George W. Bush (Republican)	31.9	0
Albert Gore (Democrat)	61.0	4
Ralph Nader (Green)	6.1	0
Other	1.0	0
1996		
William Clinton (Democrat, Incumbent)	59.7	4
Robert Dole (Republican)	26.8	0
H. Ross Perot (Reformist)	11.2	0
Other	2.3	0
1992		
William Clinton (Democrat)	47.0	4
George H. W. Bush (Republican, Incumbent)	29.0	0
H. Ross Perot (Independent)	23.2	0
Other	0.8	0

Data: Dave Leip's Atlas of U.S. Presidential Elections

Governor and U.S. Congressional Seats				
Governor	**Party**	**Year Term Began**	**Term**	**Max. Consecutive Terms**
Don Carcieri	R	2007	Second	2
U.S. Senators	**Party**	**Year Elected**	**Term Expires**	
Jack Reed	D	1996	2009	
Sheldon Whitehouse	D	2006	2013	
U.S. Representatives		**Republican**	**Democrat**	**Other**
		0	2	0

Data: National Governors Association; U.S. Senate, Office of the Clerk; U.S. House of Representatives

Business and Economic Agencies

Agency	Website Address
Narragansett Rhode Island Chamber of Commerce	www.narragansettri.com/chamber/
Rhode Island Economic Development Corporation	www.riedc.com
Rhode Island Small Business Dev. Center	www.risbdc.org
Rhode Island Secretary of State	www.sec.state.ri.us/corps

Data: Various agency websites

South Carolina

With a population of 4.3 million people, South Carolina was the twenty-seventh least populous state in the United States in 2006. From 2000 to 2006 the state's population increased by 309,237 people, and is projected to increase to 5.0 million by 2025. This 0.8% projected annual growth rate is equal to the projected national average. The state's 2006 per capita personal income of $29,668 was higher compared to $28,427 in 2005 and fourth lowest in the United States, some $6,941 below the national average. Per capita income in South Carolina grew at an average annual rate of 3.3% from 2000 to 2006, compared to 3.5% nationally.

South Carolina's largest industry in terms of 2005 employment was maunfacturing. The fastest growing industry was professional, scientific, and technical services, with 4.0% annual employment growth from 1998 to 2005. The second fastest growing industry was health care and social assistance. The state's workforce is generally less educated than other states—81.3% of the state's adult population has graduated from high school, compared to an 84.1% national average;

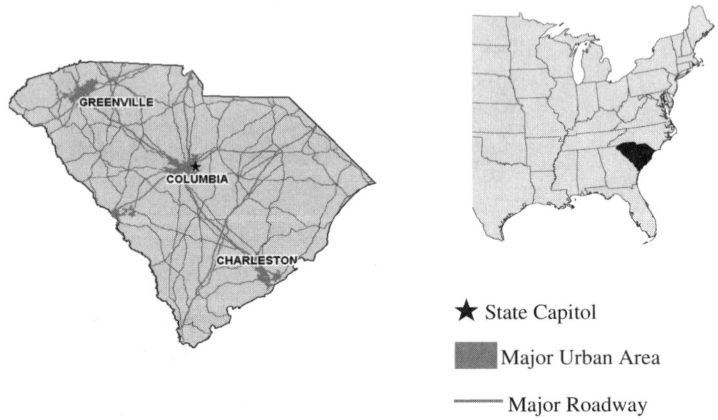

Demographic and Socioeconomic Profile

Demographics and Socioeconomic Figures			
Population and Households	**2000**	**2005**	**2006**
Total Population	4,012,012	4,113,961	4,321,249
Number of Households	1,533,854	1,635,907	1,656,978
Average Household Size	2.5	2.5	2.5
Age and Ethnicity			
Median Age	35.4	37.1	37.1
Population 18 Years of Age and Older	3,002,919	3,091,757	3,282,383
Population 65 Years of Age and Older	485,845	505,588	553,855
Caucasian Population	2,695,678	2,774,429	2,908,324
African-American Population	1,182,727	1,174,488	1,237,900
Hispanic Population	92,828	135,041	148,632
Asian Population	36,505	44,560	46,939
Foreign-Born Population (%)	2.9	4.2	4.1
Income			
Per Capita Personal Income (USD)	$24,424	$28,427	$29,688
Median Household Income (USD)	$37,082	$39,316	$41,100
Individuals Below Poverty Level	14.1%	15.6%	15.7%

Data: U.S. Census, American Community Survey; U.S. Department of Commerce, Bureau of Economic Analysis

22.7% hold a bachelor degree or higher (national average is 27.0%). Nationally, 9.9% hold professional or graduate degrees compared to 7.9% in South Carolina.

South Carolina's total tax revenue was $11.8 billion for fiscal year 2004–5, up from the 2003–4 total revenue of $11.2 billion. The largest share of tax revenue in 2004–5 was generated from sales and gross receipts taxes, followed by property taxes. On a per capita basis, residents of South Carolina paid taxes of $2,773, compared to the national average of $3,705 for 2004–5. In terms of business taxes, the state ranked thirty-second in a study from Anderson Economic Group. Forbes Magazine and the Tax Foundation ranked the state's business climate twenty-third and twenty-sixth, respectively, while ALEC ranked South Carolina twenty-fifth in its state competitiveness index. One is considered best for each ranking.

Population Projections

Year	2010	2015	2020	2025
Total Population	4,446,704	4,642,137	4,822,577	4,989,550
Median Age	38.4	39.4	40.3	41.0
Population 18 Years of Age and Older	3,410,355	3,580,984	3,737,193	3,878,805
Population 65 Years of Age and Older	605,660	729,179	866,250	1,009,242

Data: U.S. Census Bureau

Workforce and Industry Profile

Workforce

	2000	2005	2006
Civilian Labor Force	1,972,850	2,079,339	2,126,439
Labor Force Participation Rate	65.2%	64.1%	64.3%
Unemployment Rate	3.6%	6.7%	6.5%
Average Wage Per Job (USD)	$28,179	$32,250	$33,400
Education Attainment (Population 25 Years and Older)	**(%)**	**(%)**	**(%)**
High School Graduate or Higher	76.3	81.7	81.3
Bachelors Degree or Higher	20.4	23.0	22.7
Graduate or Professional Degree	6.9	7.9	7.9

Data: U.S. Census Bureau, American Community Survey; U.S. Department of Commerce, Bureau of Economic Analysis; U.S. Department of Labor, Bureau of Labor Statistics

Industry Overview

	1998	2004	2005
Total Employees	1,526,106	1,560,573	1,584,914
Total Payroll ($1,000s)	$38,559,169	$46,656,784	$49,450,267
Total Establishments	94,985	101,165	103,416
Establishments with 1–19 Employees	82,048	86,748	88,962
Establishments with 20–49 Employees	7,980	9,134	9,158
Establishments with 50–249 Employees	4,195	4,605	4,595
Establishments with 250–999 Employees	670	594	614
Establishments with 1,000+ Employees	92	84	87

Data: U.S. Census Bureau, County Business Patterns

Major Industries (Ranked by 2005 Employment; Payroll in $1,000s)				
Industry	1998 Employment	2005 Employment	1998 Payroll	2005 Payroll
Manufacturing	343,295	271,326	10,898,250	10,958,564
Retail Trade	213,800	220,737	3,393,667	4,511,411
Health Care and Social Assistance	161,581	196,457	4,600,631	6,935,358
Accommodation and Food Services	145,493	173,653	1,490,773	2,150,063
Admin., Support, Waste Mngt., Remediation Services	122,913	129,611	2,183,375	2,913,796
Construction	111,427	108,276	2,973,943	3,594,290
Other Services (except Public Admin.)	67,783	77,373	1,076,923	1,526,250
Professional, Scientific, Technical Services	58,476	76,896	2,264,270	3,778,332
Finance and Insurance	58,771	65,591	1,972,715	2,784,533
Wholesale Trade	60,762	63,718	2,056,717	2,822,820

Data: U.S. Census Bureau, County Business Patterns

Taxes and Business Climate

State and Local Taxes		
Combined Revenues ($1,000s)	**2003–4**	**2004–5**
Revenue from Property Taxes	3,704,419	3,738,818
Revenue from Sales and Gross Receipts Taxes	4,011,717	4,230,882
Revenue from Individual Income Taxes	2,438,712	2,691,473
Revenue from Corporate Income Taxes	196,510	246,935
Revenue from Other Taxes	825,248	892,532
Total Tax Revenue	11,176,606	11,800,640
Per Capita Taxes		
Property Tax Per Capita	882	879
Sales and Gross Receipts Tax Per Capita	956	994
Individual Income Tax Per Capita	581	633
Corporate Income Tax Per Capita	47	58
Other Taxes Per Capita	197	210
Total Taxes Per Capita	2,662	2,773

Data: U.S. Census Bureau; Anderson Economic Group, LLC

Business Climate Measures	
Anderson Economic Group: 2007 Business Tax Ranking (1 is Best)	32
Forbes Magazine: 2007 Best States for Business Ranking (1 is Best)	23
Tax Foundation: 2008 Business Tax Climate Ranking (1 is Best)	26
ALEC-Laffer 2007 Economic Competitiveness Ranking (1 is Best)	25
2003–4 Employer Firm Births	10,111
2003–4 Employer Firm Terminations	8,656

Data: Anderson Economic Group; Tax Foundation; Forbes Magazine; U.S. Census, Statistics of U.S. Businesses; American Legislative Exchange Council

Voting Behavior and Elected Officials

Voter Registration and Turnout (%)

	1992	1996	2000	2004
Registered Voters Who Voted	78.2	63.3	61.1	69.9
Citizens Age 18+ Who Voted	45.0	41.5	46.1	51.8

Data: Dave Leip's Atlas of U.S. Presidential Elections

Presidential Election Results (Nationwide Winner Listed First)

2004	Popular Vote (%)	Electoral Votes
George W. Bush (Republican, Incumbent)	58.0	8
John Kerry (Democrat)	40.9	0
Other	1.1	0
2000		
George W. Bush (Republican)	56.8	8
Albert Gore (Democrat)	40.9	0
Ralph Nader (Green)	1.5	0
Other	0.8	0
1996		
William Clinton (Democrat, Incumbent)	44.0	0
Robert Dole (Republican)	49.9	8
H. Ross Perot (Reformist)	5.6	0
Other	0.7	0
1992		
William Clinton (Democrat)	39.9	0
George H. W. Bush (Republican, Incumbent)	48.0	8
H. Ross Perot (Independent)	11.6	0
Other	0.6	0

Data: Dave Leip's Atlas of U.S. Presidential Elections

Governor and U.S. Congressional Seats				
Governor	**Party**	**Year Term Began**	**Term**	**Max. Consecutive Terms**
Mark Sanford	R	2007	Second	2
U.S. Senators	**Party**	**Year Elected**	**Term Expires**	
Lindsey Graham	R	2002	2009	
Jim DeMint	R	2004	2011	
U.S. Representatives		**Republican**	**Democrat**	**Other**
		4	2	0

Data: National Governors Association; U.S. Senate, Office of the Clerk; U.S. House of Representatives

Business and Economic Agencies

Agency	Website Address
South Carolina Chamber of Commerce	www.scchamber.net
South Carolina Economic Development Directory	www.sciway.net/econ
South Carolina Small Business Dev. Center	scsbdc.moore.sc.edu
South Carolina Secretary of State	www.scsos.com

Data: Various agency websites

South Dakota

South Dakota is located in the West North Central region of the United States and had a population of 781,919 people in 2006, making it the fifth least populous state. The state's population increased by 27,075 people from 2000 to 2006, and is projected to increase to 801,845 by 2025. This 0.1% projected annual growth rate is below the national average of 0.8%. Per capita personal income in South Dakota was $32,405 in 2006, up from $31,811 in 2005. For 2006, this was $4,224 below the national average and the nineteenth lowest in the country. The state's per capita income grew at an average annual rate of 3.9% from 2000 to 2006, compared to 3.5% nationally.

The state's workforce generally has less education than other states—88.3% of the state's adult population has graduated from high school, compared to an 84.1% national average; 24.9% hold a bachelor degree or higher (national average is 27.0%); and 7.3% hold professional or graduate degrees (national average is 9.9%). In 2005, the state's largest industry in terms of employment was health care and social assistance, followed by

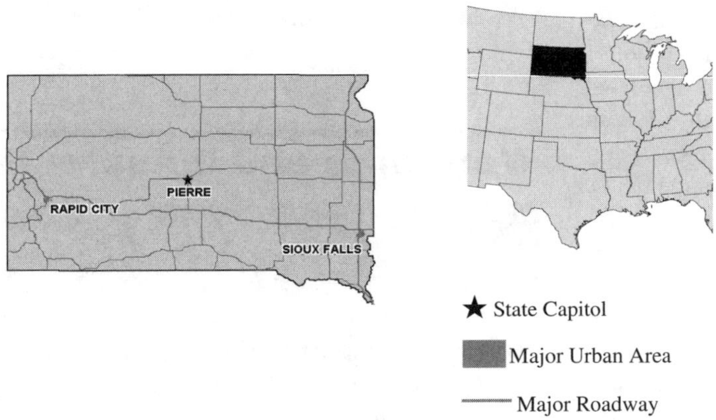

Demographic and Socioeconomic Profile

Demographics and Socioeconomic Figures			
Population and Households	**2000**	**2005**	**2006**
Total Population	754,844	746,033	781,919
Number of Households	290,245	310,331	312,477
Average Household Size	2.5	2.4	2.4
Age and Ethnicity			
Median Age	35.6	37.0	37.3
Population 18 Years of Age and Older	552,118	559,788	587,942
Population 65 Years of Age and Older	108,116	101,090	111,639
Caucasian Population	669,477	656,165	681,785
African-American Population	4,518	6,166	5,262
Hispanic Population	10,386	14,140	15,544
Asian Population	4,729	4,756	7,064
Foreign-Born Population (%)	1.8	2.3	2.2
Income			
Per Capita Personal Income (USD)	$25,720	$31,811	$32,405
Median Household Income (USD)	$35,282	$40,310	$42,791
Individuals Below Poverty Level	13.2%	13.6%	13.6%

Data: U.S. Census, American Community Survey; U.S. Department of Commerce, Bureau of Economic Analysis

retail trade. The fastest growing industry was professional, scientific, and technical services, with 3.8% annual growth from 1998 to 2005.

In fiscal year 2004–5, South Dakota had total tax revenues of $2.1 billion. The largest share was generated from sales and gross receipts taxes, followed by property taxes. The per capita tax burden in South Dakota was $2,697 for 2004–5, some $1,008 below the national average, but a $82 increase from 2003–4. In terms of business taxes, South Dakota ranked eighth in a study from Anderson Economic Group. The state's business climate was ranked twenty-fifth by Forbes Magazine and second by the Tax Foundation. South Dakota was ranked third by ALEC in its state competitiveness index. One is considered best for each ranking.

Population Projections

Year	2010	2015	2020	2025
Total Population	786,399	796,954	801,939	801,845
Median Age	37.5	38.3	39.6	40.8
Population 18 Years of Age and Older	592,247	600,551	604,727	605,728
Population 65 Years of Age and Older	114,459	127,974	148,398	169,663

Data: U.S. Census Bureau

Workforce and Industry Profile

Workforce

	2000	2005	2006
Civilian Labor Force	408,685	427,307	430,992
Labor Force Participation Rate	72.8%	72.9%	72.7%
Unemployment Rate	2.7%	3.7%	3.2%
Average Wage Per Job (USD)	$24,802	$29,170	$30,460
Education Attainment (Population 25 Years and Older)	**(%)**	**(%)**	**(%)**
High School Graduate or Higher	84.6	88.6	88.3
Bachelors Degree or Higher	21.5	24.7	24.9
Graduate or Professional Degree	6.0	7.0	7.3

Data: U.S. Census Bureau, American Community Survey; U.S. Department of Commerce, Bureau of Economic Analysis; U.S. Department of Labor, Bureau of Labor Statistics

Industry Overview

	1998	2004	2005
Total Employees	289,422	308,010	310,802
Total Payroll ($1,000s)	$6,403,476	$8,433,346	$8,860,458
Total Establishments	23,521	24,787	25,205
Establishments with 1–19 Employees	20,842	21,863	22,276
Establishments with 20–49 Employees	1,762	1,892	1,903
Establishments with 50–249 Employees	815	929	915
Establishments with 250–999 Employees	93	94	102
Establishments with 1,000+ Employees	9	9	9

Data: U.S. Census Bureau, County Business Patterns

Major Industries (Ranked by 2005 Employment; Payroll in $1,000s)				
Industry	1998 Employment	2005 Employment	1998 Payroll	2005 Payroll
Health Care and Social Assistance	48,237	55,631	1,200,868	1,947,125
Retail Trade	47,784	49,526	771,746	982,171
Manufacturing	48,082	39,397	1,371,454	1,313,973
Accommodation and Food Services	29,168	34,689	254,740	383,876
Finance and Insurance	20,034	23,964	564,637	907,331
Construction	13,992	17,683	402,173	628,966
Wholesale Trade	16,089	14,318	431,329	520,909
Other Services (except Public Admin.)	12,924	14,059	186,226	251,226
Professional, Scientific, Technical Services	7,499	9,716	193,922	331,875
Admin., Support, Waste Mngt., Remediation Services	8,289	9,566	134,475	191,443

Data: U.S. Census Bureau, County Business Patterns

Taxes and Business Climate

State and Local Taxes		
Combined Revenues ($1,000s)	**2003–4**	**2004–5**
Revenue from Property Taxes	705,183	730,122
Revenue from Sales and Gross Receipts Taxes	1,070,896	1,123,745
Revenue from Individual Income Taxes	11	0
Revenue from Corporate Income Taxes	47,108	49,142
Revenue from Other Taxes	192,730	200,811
Total Tax Revenue	2,015,928	2,103,820
Per Capita Taxes		
Property Tax Per Capita	915	936
Sales and Gross Receipts Tax Per Capita	1,389	1,441
Individual Income Tax Per Capita	0	0
Corporate Income Tax Per Capita	61	63
Other Taxes Per Capita	250	257
Total Taxes Per Capita	2,615	2,697

Data: U.S. Census Bureau; Anderson Economic Group, LLC

Business Climate Measures	
Anderson Economic Group: 2007 Business Tax Ranking (1 is Best)	8
Forbes Magazine: 2007 Best States for Business Ranking (1 is Best)	25
Tax Foundation: 2008 Business Tax Climate Ranking (1 is Best)	2
ALEC-Laffer 2007 Economic Competitiveness Ranking (1 is Best)	3
2003–4 Employer Firm Births	2,202
2003–4 Employer Firm Terminations	1,862

Data: Anderson Economic Group; Tax Foundation; Forbes Magazine; U.S. Census, Statistics of U.S. Businesses; American Legislative Exchange Council

Voting Behavior and Elected Officials

Voter Registration and Turnout (%)

	1992	1996	2000	2004
Registered Voters Who Voted	75.0	70.4	67.1	77.3
Citizens Age 18+ Who Voted	67.0	60.5	57.3	68.2

Data: Dave Leip's Atlas of U.S. Presidential Elections

Presidential Election Results (Nationwide Winner Listed First)

2004	Popular Vote (%)	Electoral Votes
George W. Bush (Republican, Incumbent)	59.9	3
John Kerry (Democrat)	38.4	0
Other	1.7	0
2000		
George W. Bush (Republican)	60.3	3
Albert Gore (Democrat)	37.6	0
Ralph Nader (Green)	0.0	0
Other	2.1	0
1996		
William Clinton (Democrat, Incumbent)	43.0	0
Robert Dole (Republican)	46.5	3
H. Ross Perot (Reformist)	9.7	0
Other	0.8	0
1992		
William Clinton (Democrat)	37.1	0
George H. W. Bush (Republican, Incumbent)	40.7	3
H. Ross Perot (Independent)	21.8	0
Other	0.4	0

Data: Dave Leip's Atlas of U.S. Presidential Elections

Governor and U.S. Congressional Seats

Governor	Party	Year Term Began	Term	Max. Consecutive Terms
Michael Rounds	R	2007	Second	2
U.S. Senators	**Party**	**Year Elected**	**Term Expires**	
Tim Johnson	D	1996	2009	
John Thune	R	2004	2011	
U.S. Representatives		**Republican**	**Democrat**	**Other**
		0	1	0

Data: National Governors Association; U.S. Senate, Office of the Clerk; U.S. House of Representatives

Business and Economic Agencies

Agency	Website Address
South Dakota Chamber of Commerce & Industry	www.sdchamber.biz
South Dakota's Governor's Office of Economic Development	www.sdreadytowork.com
South Dakota Small Business Dev. Center	www.sdsbdc.org
South Dakota Secretary of State	www.sdsos.gov/busineservices/busineservices_overview.shtm

Data: Various agency websites

Tennessee

Tennessee, located in the East South Central region of the United States, had a population of 6.0 million people in 2006, making it the seventeenth least populous state. The state's population increased by 349,520 people from 2000 to 2006, and is projected to increase to 7.1 million by 2025. This 0.8% projected annual growth rate compares to the projected national average of 0.8%. Per capita personal income in Tennessee was $32,305 in 2006, up from $31,001 in 2005. For 2006, this was sixteenth lowest in the country and $4,324 below the national average. From 2000 to 2006 per capita income in Tennessee grew at an average annual rate of 3.6%, compared to 3.5% nationally.

In 2005, the state's largest industry in terms of employment was manufacturing, followed by health care and social assistance. The fastest growing industry was transportation and warehousing, with 5.0% annual employment growth from 1998 to 2005. The state's workforce is generally less educated than other states—80.9% of the state's adult population has graduated from high school, compared to an 84.1% national average. Nationally, an average of 27.0% hold a bachelor degree

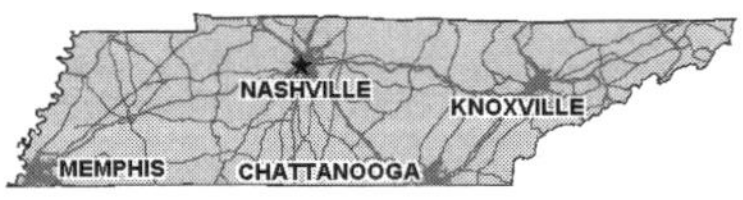

★ State Capitol

Major Urban Area

Major Roadway

Demographic and Socioeconomic Profile

Demographics and Socioeconomic Figures			
Population and Households	**2000**	**2005**	**2006**
Total Population	5,689,283	5,810,590	6,038,803
Number of Households	2,232,905	2,366,130	2,375,123
Average Household Size	2.5	2.5	2.5
Age and Ethnicity			
Median Age	35.9	37.3	37.2
Population 18 Years of Age and Older	4,292,047	4,427,784	4,591,753
Population 65 Years of Age and Older	702,839	708,653	767,093
Caucasian Population	4,562,454	4,625,715	4,781,578
African-American Population	929,864	954,287	1,011,726
Hispanic Population	119,425	172,704	187,747
Asian Population	54,132	73,824	76,208
Foreign-Born Population (%)	2.8	3.8	3.9
Income			
Per Capita Personal Income (USD)	$26,097	$31,001	$32,305
Median Household Income (USD)	$36,360	$38,874	$40,315
Individuals Below Poverty Level	13.5%	15.5%	16.2%

Data: U.S. Census, American Community Survey; U.S. Department of Commerce, Bureau of Economic Analysis

or higher compared to 21.7% in Tennessee. Nationally, 9.9% hold professional or graduate degrees compared to 7.5% in Tennessee.

In fiscal year 2004–5, Tennessee had total tax revenues of $16.0 billion. The largest share was generated from sales and gross receipts taxes, followed by property taxes. The per capita tax burden in Tennessee was $2,670 for 2004–5, some $1,035 below the national average. In terms of business taxes, the state ranked third in a study from Anderson Economic Group. Forbes Magazine and the Tax Foundation ranked the state's business climate thirteenth and sixteenth, respectively, while ALEC ranked Tennessee fifth in its state competitiveness index. One is considered best for each ranking.

Population Projections

Year	2010	2015	2020	2025
Total Population	6,230,852	6,502,017	6,780,670	7,073,125
Median Age	37.9	38.2	38.6	38.5
Population 18 Years of Age and Older	4,751,937	4,963,306	5,173,458	5,383,849
Population 65 Years of Age and Older	829,023	968,919	1,121,063	1,279,981

Data: U.S. Census Bureau

Workforce and Industry Profile

Workforce

	2000	2005	2006
Civilian Labor Force	2,871,539	2,920,400	2,990,152
Labor Force Participation Rate	65.9%	63.6%	64.1%
Unemployment Rate	4.0%	5.6%	5.2%
Average Wage Per Job (USD)	$30,554	$33,260	$34,240
Education Attainment (Population 25 Years and Older)	**(%)**	**(%)**	**(%)**
High School Graduate or Higher	75.9	81.2	80.9
Bachelors Degree or Higher	19.6	21.8	21.7
Graduate or Professional Degree	6.8	7.6	7.5

Data: U.S. Census Bureau, American Community Survey; U.S. Department of Commerce, Bureau of Economic Analysis; U.S. Department of Labor, Bureau of Labor Statistics

Industry Overview

	1998	2004	2005
Total Employees	2,299,348	2,347,335	2,378,754
Total Payroll ($1,000s)	$62,441,176	$76,922,192	$80,959,818
Total Establishments	131,110	131,691	133,098
Establishments with 1–19 Employees	111,021	110,585	111,913
Establishments with 20–49 Employees	12,072	12,920	12,992
Establishments with 50–249 Employees	6,894	7,067	7,050
Establishments with 250–999 Employees	992	986	995
Establishments with 1,000+ Employees	131	133	148

Data: U.S. Census Bureau, County Business Patterns

Major Industries (Ranked by 2005 Employment; Payroll in $1,000s)				
Industry	1998 Employment	2005 Employment	1998 Payroll	2005 Payroll
Manufacturing	482,811	396,245	15,020,254	15,564,711
Health Care and Social Assistance	281,083	332,418	8,307,173	12,325,142
Retail Trade	311,720	320,100	5,322,361	6,874,676
Accommodation and Food Services	189,001	219,970	2,078,502	2,724,314
Admin., Support, Waste Mngt., Remediation Services	157,976	180,064	3,011,742	4,376,109
Transportation and Warehousing	86,518	121,632	2,745,830	4,315,420
Finance and Insurance	101,293	116,540	4,003,336	6,237,489
Wholesale Trade	125,204	116,259	4,390,902	5,574,316
Construction	120,575	112,611	3,762,360	4,298,881
Other Services (except Public Admin.)	109,070	112,464	1,858,267	2,364,299

Data: U.S. Census Bureau, County Business Patterns

Taxes and Business Climate

State and Local Taxes		
Combined Revenues ($1,000s)	2003–4	2004–5
Revenue from Property Taxes	3,585,440	3,894,418
Revenue from Sales and Gross Receipts Taxes	8,846,308	9,381,111
Revenue from Individual Income Taxes	139,991	155,333
Revenue from Corporate Income Taxes	694,798	805,601
Revenue from Other Taxes	1,680,101	1,756,673
Total Tax Revenue	14,946,638	15,993,136
Per Capita Taxes		
Property Tax Per Capita	608	650
Sales and Gross Receipts Tax Per Capita	1,501	1,566
Individual Income Tax Per Capita	24	26
Corporate Income Tax Per Capita	118	135
Other Taxes Per Capita	285	293
Total Taxes Per Capita	2,536	2,670

Data: U.S. Census Bureau; Anderson Economic Group, LLC

Business Climate Measures	
Anderson Economic Group: 2007 Business Tax Ranking (1 is Best)	3
Forbes Magazine: 2007 Best States for Business Ranking (1 is Best)	13
Tax Foundation: 2008 Business Tax Climate Ranking (1 is Best)	16
ALEC-Laffer 2007 Economic Competitiveness Ranking (1 is Best)	5
2003–4 Employer Firm Births	12,730
2003–4 Employer Firm Terminations	11,260

Data: Anderson Economic Group; Tax Foundation; Forbes Magazine; U.S. Census, Statistics of U.S. Businesses; American Legislative Exchange Council

Voting Behavior and Elected Officials

Voter Registration and Turnout (%)

	1992	1996	2000	2004
Registered Voters Who Voted	72.7	66.5	65.3	73.1
Citizens Age 18+ Who Voted	52.4	46.9	48.4	54.8

Data: Dave Leip's Atlas of U.S. Presidential Elections

Presidential Election Results (Nationwide Winner Listed First)

2004	Popular Vote (%)	Electoral Votes
George W. Bush (Republican, Incumbent)	56.8	11
John Kerry (Democrat)	42.5	0
Other	0.7	0
2000		
George W. Bush (Republican)	51.2	11
Albert Gore (Democrat)	47.3	0
Ralph Nader (Green)	1.0	0
Other	0.6	0
1996		
William Clinton (Democrat, Incumbent)	48.0	11
Robert Dole (Republican)	45.6	0
H. Ross Perot (Reformist)	5.6	0
Other	0.8	0
1992		
William Clinton (Democrat)	47.1	11
George H. W. Bush (Republican, Incumbent)	42.4	0
H. Ross Perot (Independent)	10.1	0
Other	0.4	0

Data: Dave Leip's Atlas of U.S. Presidential Elections

Governor and U.S. Congressional Seats

Governor	Party	Year Term Began	Term	Max. Consecutive Terms
Phil Bredesen	D	2007	Second	2
U.S. Senators	**Party**	**Year Elected**	**Term Expires**	
Lamar Alexandar	R	2002	2009	
Bob Corker	R	2006	2013	
U.S. Representatives		**Republican**	**Democrat**	**Other**
		4	5	0

Data: National Governors Association; U.S. Senate, Office of the Clerk; U.S. House of Representatives

Business and Economic Agencies

Agency	Website Address
Tennessee Chamber of Commerce & Industry	www.tnchamber.org
Tennessee Department of Economic and Community Development	www.state.tn.us/ecd
Tennessee Small Business Development Centers	www.tsbdc.org
Tennessee Department of State, Division of Business Services	www.state.tn.us/sos/bus_svc

Data: Various agency websites

Texas

With a population of 23.5 million people, Texas was the second most populous state in the United States in 2006. From 2000 to 2006 the state's population increased by 2,655,963 people, and is projected to increase to 30.9 million by 2025. This 1.4% projected annual growth rate compares to the projected national average of 0.8%. The state's 2006 per capita personal income of $35,058 was higher compared to $33,160 in 2005 and thirtieth lowest in the United States, some $1,571 below the national average. Per capita income in Texas grew at an average annual rate of 3.6% from 2000 to 2006, compared to 3.5% nationally.

Texas' largest industry in terms of 2005 employment was health care and social assistance. The fastest growing industry was professional, scientific, and technical services, with 3.3% annual employment growth from 1998 to 2005. The second fastest growing industry was finance and insurance. The state's workforce is generally less educated than other states—78.6% of the state's adult population has graduated from high school, compared to an 84.1% national average; 24.7% hold a

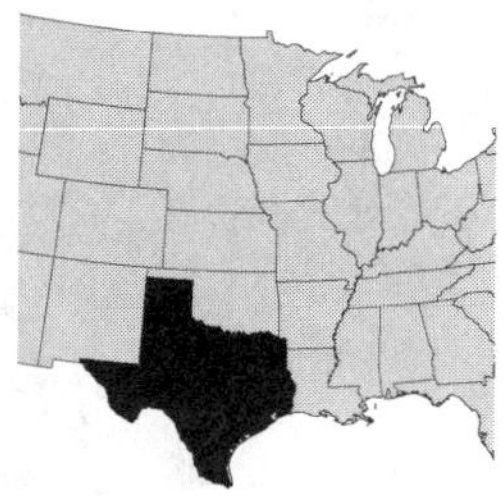

★ State Capitol

Major Urban Area

Major Roadway

Demographic and Socioeconomic Profile

Demographics and Socioeconomic Figures			
Population and Households	**2000**	**2005**	**2006**
Total Population	20,851,820	22,270,165	23,507,783
Number of Households	7,393,354	7,978,095	8,109,388
Average Household Size	2.7	2.8	2.8
Age and Ethnicity			
Median Age	32.3	33.2	33.1
Population 18 Years of Age and Older	14,977,890	15,969,874	17,004,929
Population 65 Years of Age and Older	2,067,467	2,147,849	2,329,442
Caucasian Population	14,797,985	16,021,256	16,405,937
African-American Population	2,385,554	2,442,350	2,718,515
Hispanic Population	6,670,122	7,903,079	8,385,118
Asian Population	555,928	726,027	787,208
Foreign-Born Population (%)	13.9	15.9	15.9
Income			
Per Capita Personal Income (USD)	$28,313	$33,160	$35,058
Median Household Income (USD)	$39,927	$42,139	$44,922
Individuals Below Poverty Level	15.4%	17.6%	16.9%

Data: U.S. Census, American Community Survey; U.S. Department of Commerce, Bureau of Economic Analysis

bachelor degree or higher (national average is 27.0%); and 8.1% hold professional or graduate degrees compared to the national average of 9.9%.

Texas' total tax revenue was $69.1 billion for fiscal year 2004–5, up from the 2003–4 total revenue of $64.7 billion. The largest share of tax revenue in 2004–5 was generated from sales and gross receipts taxes, followed by property taxes. On a per capita basis, residents of Texas paid taxes of $3,026, compared to the national average of $3,705 for 2004–5. In terms of business taxes, the state ranked twenty-ninth in a study from Anderson Economic Group. Forbes Magazine and the Tax Foundation ranked the state's business climate fourth and eighth, respectively, while ALEC ranked Texas tenth in its state competitiveness index. One is considered best for each ranking.

Population Projections

Year	2010	2015	2020	2025
Total Population	24,648,888	26,585,801	28,634,896	30,865,134
Median Age	33.4	33.8	34.3	34.6
Population 18 Years of Age and Older	17,863,480	19,209,583	20,666,629	22,405,639
Population 65 Years of Age and Older	2,587,383	3,112,883	3,755,814	4,500,152

Data: U.S. Census Bureau

Workforce and Industry Profile

Workforce

	2000	2005	2006
Civilian Labor Force	10,347,847	11,282,845	11,487,496
Labor Force Participation Rate	68.1%	67.1%	66.7%
Unemployment Rate	4.4%	5.4%	4.9%
Average Wage Per Job (USD)	$34,941	$35,470	$36,410
Education Attainment (Population 25 Years and Older)	**(%)**	**(%)**	**(%)**
High School Graduate or Higher	75.7	78.8	78.6
Bachelors Degree or Higher	23.2	25.1	24.7
Graduate or Professional Degree	7.6	8.2	8.1

Data: U.S. Census Bureau, American Community Survey; U.S. Department of Commerce, Bureau of Economic Analysis; U.S. Department of Labor, Bureau of Labor Statistics

Industry Overview

	1998	2004	2005
Total Employees	7,570,820	8,118,483	8,305,102
Total Payroll ($1,000s)	$229,185,833	$293,572,510	$315,809,126
Total Establishments	462,875	491,092	497,758
Establishments with 1–19 Employees	395,406	418,144	423,838
Establishments with 20–49 Employees	41,631	44,948	45,386
Establishments with 50–249 Employees	22,411	24,363	24,822
Establishments with 250–999 Employees	2,981	3,138	3,229
Establishments with 1,000+ Employees	446	499	483

Data: U.S. Census Bureau, County Business Patterns

Major Industries (Ranked by 2005 Employment; Payroll in $1,000s)				
Industry	1998 Employment	2005 Employment	1998 Payroll	2005 Payroll
Health Care and Social Assistance	911,042	1,097,308	24,604,759	38,168,221
Retail Trade	977,678	1,080,932	18,492,576	24,317,534
Manufacturing	986,892	816,221	36,331,404	38,224,668
Accommodation and Food Services	661,430	800,903	7,361,124	10,304,662
Admin., Support, Waste Mngt., Remediation Services	678,374	786,867	14,845,110	21,371,464
Professional, Scientific, Technical Services	413,798	519,075	19,768,171	31,442,127
Construction	457,076	501,694	14,281,869	19,869,823
Wholesale Trade	436,035	450,206	17,141,752	23,894,136
Finance and Insurance	360,254	441,384	15,639,191	24,080,494
Other Services (except Public Admin.)	373,791	404,458	6,532,243	8,908,953

Data: U.S. Census Bureau, County Business Patterns

Taxes and Business Climate

State and Local Taxes		
Combined Revenues ($1,000s)	2003–4	2004–5
Revenue from Property Taxes	28,176,329	30,275,679
Revenue from Sales and Gross Receipts Taxes	29,656,098	31,110,381
Revenue from Individual Income Taxes	0	0
Revenue from Corporate Income Taxes	0	1
Revenue from Other Taxes	6,906,345	7,747,801
Total Tax Revenue	64,738,772	69,133,862
Per Capita Taxes		
Property Tax Per Capita	1,254	1,325
Sales and Gross Receipts Tax Per Capita	1,320	1,362
Individual Income Tax Per Capita	0	0
Corporate Income Tax Per Capita	0	0
Other Taxes Per Capita	307	339
Total Taxes Per Capita	2,881	3,026

Data: U.S. Census Bureau; Anderson Economic Group, LLC

Business Climate Measures	
Anderson Economic Group: 2007 Business Tax Ranking (1 is Best)	29
Forbes Magazine: 2007 Best States for Business Ranking (1 is Best)	4
Tax Foundation: 2008 Business Tax Climate Ranking (1 is Best)	8
ALEC-Laffer 2007 Economic Competitiveness Ranking (1 is Best)	10
2003–4 Employer Firm Births	52,915
2003–4 Employer Firm Terminations	47,394

Data: Anderson Economic Group; Tax Foundation; Forbes Magazine; U.S. Census, Statistics of U.S. Businesses; American Legislative Exchange Council

Voting Behavior and Elected Officials

Voter Registration and Turnout (%)

	1992	1996	2000	2004
Registered Voters Who Voted	72.9	58.8	62.4	67.4
Citizens Age 18+ Who Voted	49.1	41.3	42.8	46.7

Data: Dave Leip's Atlas of U.S. Presidential Elections

Presidential Election Results (Nationwide Winner Listed First)

2004	Popular Vote (%)	Electoral Votes
George W. Bush (Republican, Incumbent)	61.1	34
John Kerry (Democrat)	38.2	0
Other	0.7	0
2000		
George W. Bush (Republican)	59.3	32
Albert Gore (Democrat)	38.0	0
Ralph Nader (Green)	2.2	0
Other	0.6	0
1996		
William Clinton (Democrat, Incumbent)	43.8	0
Robert Dole (Republican)	48.8	32
H. Ross Perot (Reformist)	6.8	0
Other	0.7	0
1992		
William Clinton (Democrat)	37.1	0
George H. W. Bush (Republican, Incumbent)	40.6	32
H. Ross Perot (Independent)	22.0	0
Other	0.4	0

Data: Dave Leip's Atlas of U.S. Presidential Elections

Governor and U.S. Congressional Seats				
Governor	**Party**	**Year Term Began**	**Term**	**Max. Consecutive Terms**
Rick Perry	R	2007	Second	No limit
U.S. Senators	**Party**	**Year Elected**	**Term Expires**	
John Cornyn	R	2002	2009	
Kay Bailey Hutchison	R	1993	2013	
U.S. Representatives		**Republican**	**Democrat**	**Other**
		19	13	0

Data: National Governors Association; U.S. Senate, Office of the Clerk; U.S. House of Representatives

Business and Economic Agencies

Agency	Website Address
Texas Association of Business	www.txbiz.org
Office of the Governor, Economic Development Office and Tourism	www.governor.state.tx.us/ecodevo
Texas Small Business Development Center	www.business.txstate.edu/sbdc
Texas Secretary of State, Corporations Section	www.sos.state.tx.us/corp

Data: Various agency websites

Utah

Utah had a population of 2.6 million people in 2006, making it the seventeenth least populous state. The state's population increased by 316,894 people from 2000 to 2006, and is projected to increase to 3.2 million by 2025. This 1.2% projected annual growth rate is above the national average of 0.8%. Per capita personal income in Utah was $29,769 in 2006, up from $28,176 in 2005. For 2006, this was $6,860 below the national average and the seventh highest in the country. The state's per capita income grew at an average annual rate of 3.7% from 2000 to 2006, compared to 3.5% nationally.

The state's workforce generally has more education than other states—90.2% of the state's adult population has graduated from high school, compared to an 84.1% national average; 28.6% hold a bachelor degree or higher (national average is 27.0%); and 9.4% hold professional or graduate degrees (national average is 9.9%). In 2005, the state's largest industry in terms of employment was retail trade, followed by manufacturing. The fastest growing industry was professional, scientific, and technical services, with 5.8% annual growth from 1998 to 2005.

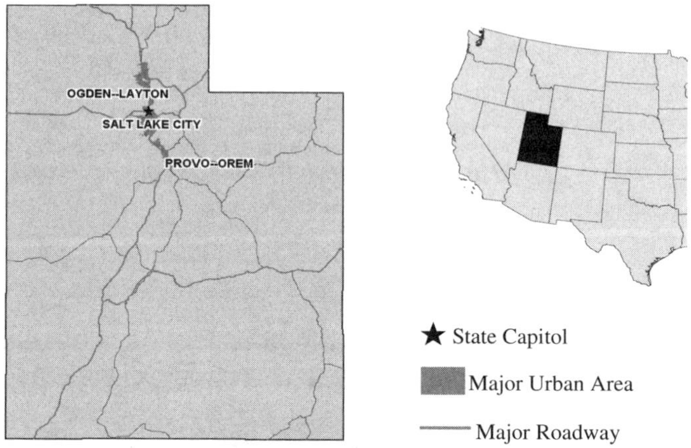

Demographic and Socioeconomic Profile

Demographics and Socioeconomic Figures			
Population and Households	**2000**	**2005**	**2006**
Total Population	2,233,169	2,427,350	2,550,063
Number of Households	701,281	791,929	814,028
Average Household Size	3.1	3.1	3.1
Age and Ethnicity			
Median Age	27.1	28.5	28.4
Population 18 Years of Age and Older	1,516,338	1,688,413	1,757,891
Population 65 Years of Age and Older	190,531	205,548	223,960
Caucasian Population	1,991,560	2,178,777	2,271,604
African-American Population	16,150	18,325	22,742
Hispanic Population	200,005	264,084	286,113
Asian Population	36,878	46,962	49,079
Foreign-Born Population (%)	7.1	7.9	8.3
Income			
Per Capita Personal Income (USD)	$23,878	$28,176	$29,769
Median Household Income (USD)	$45,726	$47,934	$51,309
Individuals Below Poverty Level	9.4%	10.2%	10.6%

Data: U.S. Census, American Community Survey; U.S. Department of Commerce, Bureau of Economic Analysis

In fiscal year 2004–5, Utah had total tax revenues of $7.3 billion. The largest share was generated from sales and gross receipts taxes, followed by individual income taxes. The per capita tax burden in Utah was $2,916 for 2004–5, some $789 below the national average, and a $181 increase from 2003–4. In terms of business taxes, Utah ranked twelfth in a report by Anderson Economic Group. The state's business climate was ranked second by Forbes Magazine and seventeenth by the Tax Foundation. Utah was ranked first by ALEC in its state competitiveness index. One is considered best for each ranking.

Population Projections

Year	2010	2015	2020	2025
Total Population	2,595,013	2,783,040	2,990,094	3,225,680
Median Age	29.5	30.1	30.3	30.4
Population 18 Years of Age and Older	1,776,028	1,910,568	2,069,975	2,244,888
Population 65 Years of Age and Older	234,798	280,969	341,095	405,543

Data: U.S. Census Bureau

Workforce and Industry Profile

Workforce

	2000	2005	2006
Civilian Labor Force	1,136,036	1,263,774	1,311,073
Labor Force Participation Rate	71.8%	71.5%	72.2%
Unemployment Rate	3.4%	4.1%	2.9%
Average Wage Per Job (USD)	$29,229	$34,280	$35,540
Education Attainment (Population 25 Years and Older)	**(%)**	**(%)**	**(%)**
High School Graduate or Higher	87.7	90.1	90.2
Bachelors Degree or Higher	26.1	27.9	28.6
Graduate or Professional Degree	8.3	8.7	9.4

Data: U.S. Census Bureau, American Community Survey; U.S. Department of Commerce, Bureau of Economic Analysis; U.S. Department of Labor, Bureau of Labor Statistics

Industry Overview

	1998	2004	2005
Total Employees	866,146	935,126	974,686
Total Payroll ($1,000s)	$22,199,933	$28,602,403	$30,970,696
Total Establishments	52,025	62,834	65,549
Establishments with 1–19 Employees	44,560	54,604	57,040
Establishments with 20–49 Employees	4,716	5,138	5,326
Establishments with 50–249 Employees	2,355	2,711	2,778
Establishments with 250–999 Employees	341	330	350
Establishments with 1,000+ Employees	53	51	55

Data: U.S. Census Bureau, County Business Patterns

Major Industries (Ranked by 2005 Employment; Payroll in $1,000s)				
Industry	1998 Employment	2005 Employment	1998 Payroll	2005 Payroll
Retail Trade	117,336	130,073	2,014,702	2,840,452
Manufacturing	124,504	116,003	3,923,759	4,624,262
Health Care and Social Assistance	83,229	108,171	2,278,267	3,475,642
Admin., Support, Waste Mngt., Remediation Services	78,929	93,585	1,437,965	2,267,711
Accommodation and Food Services	76,781	87,672	736,994	1,016,166
Construction	58,005	70,587	1,732,765	2,485,740
Professional, Scientific, Technical Services	43,350	64,467	1,618,657	2,761,145
Finance and Insurance	40,957	48,763	1,385,462	2,181,880
Wholesale Trade	44,727	45,994	1,515,979	2,009,505
Other Services (except Public Admin.)	45,158	45,166	936,360	1,153,359

Data: U.S. Census Bureau, County Business Patterns

Taxes and Business Climate

State and Local Taxes		
Combined Revenues ($1,000s)	**2003–4**	**2004–5**
Revenue from Property Taxes	1,668,988	1,792,451
Revenue from Sales and Gross Receipts Taxes	2,770,235	3,017,459
Revenue from Individual Income Taxes	1,692,035	1,926,697
Revenue from Corporate Income Taxes	145,005	188,845
Revenue from Other Taxes	344,962	378,512
Total Tax Revenue	6,621,225	7,303,964
Per Capita Taxes		
Property Tax Per Capita	689	716
Sales and Gross Receipts Tax Per Capita	1,144	1,205
Individual Income Tax Per Capita	699	769
Corporate Income Tax Per Capita	60	75
Other Taxes Per Capita	142	151
Total Taxes Per Capita	2,735	2,916

Data: U.S. Census Bureau; Anderson Economic Group, LLC

Business Climate Measures

Anderson Economic Group: 2007 Business Tax Ranking (1 is Best)	12
Forbes Magazine: 2007 Best States for Business Ranking (1 is Best)	2
Tax Foundation: 2008 Business Tax Climate Ranking (1 is Best)	17
ALEC-Laffer 2007 Economic Competitiveness Ranking (1 is Best)	1
2003–4 Employer Firm Births	7,912
2003–4 Employer Firm Terminations	6,086

Data: Anderson Economic Group; Tax Foundation; Forbes Magazine; U.S. Census, Statistics of U.S. Businesses; American Legislative Exchange Council

Voting Behavior and Elected Officials

Voter Registration and Turnout (%)

	1992	1996	2000	2004
Registered Voters Who Voted	77.1	63.4	68.6	72.6
Citizens Age 18+ Who Voted	65.1	49.9	50.8	57.7

Data: Dave Leip's Atlas of U.S. Presidential Elections

Presidential Election Results (Nationwide Winner Listed First)

2004	Popular Vote (%)	Electoral Votes
George W. Bush (Republican, Incumbent)	71.5	5
John Kerry (Democrat)	26.0	0
Other	2.5	0
2000		
George W. Bush (Republican)	66.8	5
Albert Gore (Democrat)	26.3	0
Ralph Nader (Green)	4.7	0
Other	2.2	0
1996		
William Clinton (Democrat, Incumbent)	33.3	0
Robert Dole (Republican)	54.4	5
H. Ross Perot (Reformist)	10.0	0
Other	2.4	0
1992		
William Clinton (Democrat)	24.7	0
George H. W. Bush (Republican, Incumbent)	43.4	5
H. Ross Perot (Independent)	27.3	0
Other	4.7	0

Data: Dave Leip's Atlas of U.S. Presidential Elections

Governor and U.S. Congressional Seats				
Governor	**Party**	**Year Term Began**	**Term**	**Max. Consecutive Terms**
Jon Huntsman	R	2005	First	3
U.S. Senators	**Party**	**Year Elected**	**Term Expires**	
Robert Bennett	R	1992	2011	
Orrin Hatch	R	1976	2013	
U.S. Representatives		**Republican**	**Democrat**	**Other**
		2	1	0

Data: National Governors Association; U.S. Senate, Office of the Clerk; U.S. House of Representatives

Business and Economic Agencies

Agency	Website Address
Utah Governor's Office of Economic Development	goed.utah.gov
Utah Small Business Dev. Center	www.utahsbdc.org
Utah Department of Commerce	www.commerce.utah.gov

Data: Various agency websites

Vermont

Vermont had a population of 623,908 people in 2006, making it the second least populous state. The state's population increased by 15,081 people from 2000 to 2006, and is projected to increase to 703,288 by 2025. This 0.6% projected annual growth rate compares to the projected national average of 0.8%. Per capita personal income in Vermont was $34,623 in 2006, up from $32,654 in 2005. For 2006, this was twenty-eighth lowest in the country and $2,006 below the national average. From 2000 to 2006 per capita income in Vermont grew at an average annual rate of 3.8%, compared to 3.5% nationally.

In 2005, the state's largest industry in terms of employment was retail trade, followed by health care and social assistance. The fastest growing industry was professional, scientific, and technical services, with 8.0% annual employment growth from 1998 to 2005. The state's workforce is generally more educated than other states—89.8% of the state's adult population has graduated from high school, compared to an 84.1% national average. Nationally, an average of 27.0% hold a bachelor

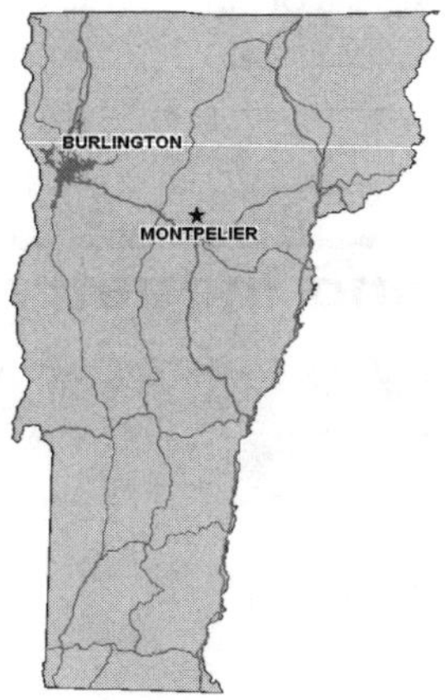

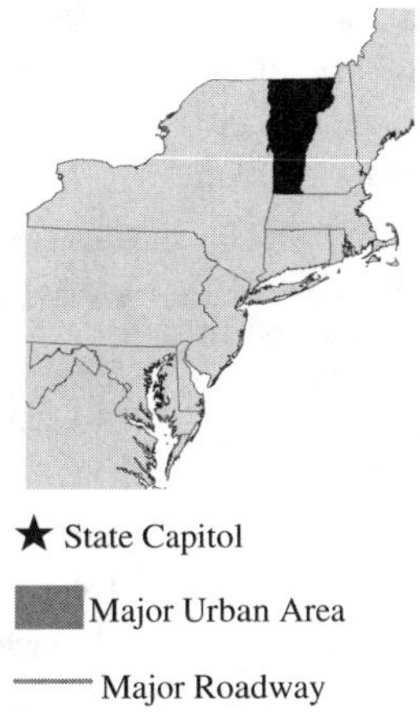

Demographic and Socioeconomic Profile

Demographics and Socioeconomic Figures			
Population and Households	**2000**	**2005**	**2006**
Total Population	608,827	602,290	623,908
Number of Households	240,634	248,825	253,808
Average Household Size	2.4	2.4	2.4
Age and Ethnicity			
Median Age	37.7	40.7	40.6
Population 18 Years of Age and Older	461,248	469,721	490,004
Population 65 Years of Age and Older	77,295	76,815	82,945
Caucasian Population	588,836	581,874	600,529
African-American Population	2,981	2,932	5,167
Hispanic Population	5,316	5,214	6,644
Asian Population	4,851	6,659	5,693
Foreign-Born Population (%)	3.8	3.6	3.9
Income			
Per Capita Personal Income (USD)	$27,680	$32,654	$34,623
Median Household Income (USD)	$40,856	$45,686	$47,665
Individuals Below Poverty Level	9.4%	11.5%	10.3%

Data: U.S. Census, American Community Survey; U.S. Department of Commerce, Bureau of Economic Analysis

degree or higher compared to 32.4% in Vermont. Nationally, 9.9% hold professional or graduate degrees compared to 12.8% in Vermont.

In fiscal year 2004–5, Vermont had total tax revenues of $2.6 billion. The largest share was generated from property taxes, followed by sales and gross receipts taxes. The per capita tax burden in Vermont was $4,155 for 2004–5, some $450 above the national average. In terms of business taxes, the state ranked fiftieth in a report from Anderson Economic Group. Forbes Magazine and the Tax Foundation ranked the state's business climate thirty-second and forty-fourth, respectively, while ALEC ranked Vermont fiftieth in its state competitiveness index. One is considered best for each ranking.

Population Projections

Year	2010	2015	2020	2025
Total Population	652,512	673,169	690,686	703,288
Median Age	40.6	41.1	41.5	42.8
Population 18 Years of Age and Older	520,140	541,204	554,847	563,723
Population 65 Years of Age and Older	93,442	113,487	136,449	158,159

Data: U.S. Census Bureau

Workforce and Industry Profile

Workforce

	2000	2005	2006
Civilian Labor Force	335,798	353,642	361,044
Labor Force Participation Rate	70.8%	70.9%	71.8%
Unemployment Rate	2.7%	3.4%	3.6%
Average Wage Per Job (USD)	$28,914	$35,070	$36,350
Education Attainment (Population 25 Years and Older)	**(%)**	**(%)**	**(%)**
High School Graduate or Higher	86.4	89.5	89.8
Bachelors Degree or Higher	29.4	32.5	32.4
Graduate or Professional Degree	11.1	12.3	12.8

Data: U.S. Census Bureau, American Community Survey; U.S. Department of Commerce, Bureau of Economic Analysis; U.S. Department of Labor, Bureau of Labor Statistics

Industry Overview

	1998	2004	2005
Total Employees	239,034	256,132	261,656
Total Payroll ($1,000s)	$5,907,989	$7,952,582	$8,284,548
Total Establishments	21,261	22,133	22,273
Establishments with 1–19 Employees	19,113	19,816	19,914
Establishments with 20–49 Employees	1,406	1,558	1,570
Establishments with 50–249 Employees	657	663	690
Establishments with 250–999 Employees	75	84	87
Establishments with 1,000+ Employees	10	12	12

Data: U.S. Census Bureau, County Business Patterns

Major Industries (Ranked by 2005 Employment; Payroll in $1,000s)				
Industry	1998 Employment	2005 Employment	1998 Payroll	2005 Payroll
Retail Trade	37,212	41,385	645,573	930,372
Health Care and Social Assistance	32,784	39,298	819,150	1,291,378
Manufacturing	44,836	37,170	1,495,644	1,655,015
Accommodation and Food Services	27,550	29,634	298,343	403,200
Professional, Scientific, Technical Services	9,228	15,821	353,212	587,749
Construction	12,699	15,083	385,573	623,572
Educational Services	12,254	13,692	217,795	327,266
Wholesale Trade	10,792	10,482	348,198	444,784
Finance and Insurance	9,370	9,632	355,166	482,077
Other Services (except Public Admin.)	8,675	9,604	153,936	208,873

Data: U.S. Census Bureau, County Business Patterns

Taxes and Business Climate

State and Local Taxes		
Combined Revenues ($1,000s)	**2003–4**	**2004–5**
Revenue from Property Taxes	950,456	1,056,355
Revenue from Sales and Gross Receipts Taxes	693,232	787,102
Revenue from Individual Income Taxes	429,817	500,464
Revenue from Corporate Income Taxes	62,228	68,962
Revenue from Other Taxes	150,450	161,878
Total Tax Revenue	2,286,183	2,574,761
Per Capita Taxes		
Property Tax Per Capita	1,531	1,705
Sales and Gross Receipts Tax Per Capita	1,116	1,270
Individual Income Tax Per Capita	692	808
Corporate Income Tax Per Capita	100	111
Other Taxes Per Capita	242	261
Total Taxes Per Capita	3,681	4,155

Data: U.S. Census Bureau; Anderson Economic Group, LLC

Business Climate Measures	
Anderson Economic Group: 2007 Business Tax Ranking (1 is Best)	50
Forbes Magazine: 2007 Best States for Business Ranking (1 is Best)	32
Tax Foundation: 2008 Business Tax Climate Ranking (1 is Best)	44
ALEC-Laffer 2007 Economic Competitiveness Ranking (1 is Best)	50
2003–4 Employer Firm Births	1,845
2003–4 Employer Firm Terminations	1,643

Data: Anderson Economic Group; Tax Foundation; Forbes Magazine; U.S. Census, Statistics of U.S. Businesses; American Legislative Exchange Council

Voting Behavior and Elected Officials

Voter Registration and Turnout (%)

	1992	1996	2000	2004
Registered Voters Who Voted	75.6	67.1	68.9	70.3
Citizens Age 18+ Who Voted	67.5	58.1	63.8	64.8

Data: Dave Leip's Atlas of U.S. Presidential Elections

Presidential Election Results (Nationwide Winner Listed First)

2004	Popular Vote (%)	Electoral Votes
George W. Bush (Republican, Incumbent)	38.8	0
John Kerry (Democrat)	58.9	3
Other	2.3	0
2000		
George W. Bush (Republican)	40.7	0
Albert Gore (Democrat)	50.6	3
Ralph Nader (Green)	6.9	0
Other	1.8	0
1996		
William Clinton (Democrat, Incumbent)	53.4	3
Robert Dole (Republican)	31.1	0
H. Ross Perot (Reformist)	12.0	0
Other	3.6	0
1992		
William Clinton (Democrat)	46.1	3
George H. W. Bush (Republican, Incumbent)	30.4	0
H. Ross Perot (Independent)	22.8	0
Other	0.7	0

Data: Dave Leip's Atlas of U.S. Presidential Elections

Governor and U.S. Congressional Seats				
Governor	**Party**	**Year Term Began**	**Term**	**Max. Consecutive Terms**
Jim Douglas	R	2007	Second	No limit
U.S. Senators	**Party**	**Year Elected**	**Term Expires**	
Bernie Sanders	I	2006	2013	
Patrick Leahy	D	1974	2011	
U.S. Representatives		**Republican**	**Democrat**	**Other**
		0	1	0

Data: National Governors Association; U.S. Senate, Office of the Clerk; U.S. House of Representatives

Business and Economic Agencies

Agency	Website Address
Vermont Chamber of Commerce	www.vtchamber.com
Vermont Department of Economic Development	www.thinkvermont.com
Vermont Small Business Dev. Center	www.vtsbdc.org
Vermont Secretary of State, Corporations	www.sec.state.vt.us/corps

Data: Various agency websites

Virginia

With a population of 7.6 million people, Virginia was the twelfth most populous state in the United States in 2006. From 2000 to 2006 the state's population increased by 564,369 people, and is projected to increase to 9.4 million by 2025. This 1.1% projected annual growth rate compares to the projected national average of 0.8%. The state's 2006 per capita personal income of $39,564 was higher compared to $37,974 in 2005 and ninth highest in the United States, some $2,935 above the national average. Per capita income in Virginia grew at an average annual rate of 4.1% from 2000 to 2006, compared to 3.5% nationally.

Virginia's largest industry in terms of 2005 employment was retail trade. The fastest growing industry was professional, scientific, and technical services, with 5.0% annual employment growth from 1998 to 2005. The second fastest growing industry was construction. The state's workforce is generally more educated than other states—85.4% of the state's adult population has graduated from high school, compared to an 84.1% national average; 32.8% hold a bachelor degree or higher (national average is 27.0%); and 13.2% hold professional or graduate degrees

★ State Capitol

Major Urban Area

Major Roadway

Demographic and Socioeconomic Profile

Demographics and Socioeconomic Figures			
Population and Households	**2000**	**2005**	**2006**
Total Population	7,078,515	7,332,608	7,642,884
Number of Households	2,699,173	2,889,688	2,905,071
Average Household Size	2.5	2.5	2.6
Age and Ethnicity			
Median Age	35.7	37.2	36.9
Population 18 Years of Age and Older	5,342,691	5,520,020	5,837,331
Population 65 Years of Age and Older	790,567	823,048	886,014
Caucasian Population	5,116,929	5,259,281	5,413,295
African-American Population	1,384,008	1,397,192	1,496,076
Hispanic Population	327,273	438,789	470,871
Asian Population	256,355	342,239	365,515
Foreign-Born Population (%)	8.1	9.9	10.1
Income			
Per Capita Personal Income (USD)	$31,087	$37,974	$39,564
Median Household Income (USD)	$46,677	$54,240	$56,277
Individuals Below Poverty Level	9.6%	10.0%	9.6%

Data: U.S. Census, American Community Survey; U.S. Department of Commerce, Bureau of Economic Analysis

compared to the national average of 9.9%.

Virginia's total tax revenue was $27.7 billion for fiscal year 2004–5, up from the 2001–2 total revenue of $25.0 billion. The largest share of tax revenue in 2004–5 was generated from property taxes, followed by individual income taxes. On a per capita basis, residents of Virginia paid taxes of $3,660, compared to the national average of $3,705 for 2004–5. In terms of business taxes, the state ranked nineteenth in a report from Anderson Economic Group. Forbes Magazine and the Tax Foundation ranked the state's business climate first and fourteenth, respectively, while ALEC ranked Virginia sixth in its state competitiveness index. One is considered best for each ranking.

Population Projections

Year	2010	2015	2020	2025
Total Population	8,010,245	8,466,864	8,917,395	9,364,304
Median Age	37.2	37.2	37.3	37.5
Population 18 Years of Age and Older	6,130,061	6,484,801	6,817,484	7,155,835
Population 65 Years of Age and Older	994,359	1,193,453	1,404,580	1,634,012

Data: U.S. Census Bureau

Workforce and Industry Profile

Workforce

	2000	2005	2006
Civilian Labor Force	3,584,037	3,921,951	3,998,569
Labor Force Participation Rate	67.6%	68.6%	68.9%
Unemployment Rate	2.3%	3.5%	3.0%
Average Wage Per Job (USD)	$35,172	$39,760	$41,450
Education Attainment (Population 25 Years and Older)	**(%)**	**(%)**	**(%)**
High School Graduate or Higher	81.5	85.4	85.4
Bachelors Degree or Higher	29.5	33.2	32.8
Graduate or Professional Degree	11.6	13.4	13.2

Data: U.S. Census Bureau, American Community Survey; U.S. Department of Commerce, Bureau of Economic Analysis; U.S. Department of Labor, Bureau of Labor Statistics

Industry Overview

	1998	2004	2005
Total Employees	2,700,589	3,054,816	3,060,127
Total Payroll ($1,000s)	$81,261,075	$114,893,068	$121,801,479
Total Establishments	172,182	188,989	193,067
Establishments with 1–19 Employees	147,954	160,922	164,708
Establishments with 20–49 Employees	15,065	17,549	17,796
Establishments with 50–249 Employees	7,933	9,138	9,150
Establishments with 250–999 Employees	1,080	1,196	1,239
Establishments with 1,000+ Employees	150	184	174

Data: U.S. Census Bureau, County Business Patterns

Major Industries (Ranked by 2005 Employment; Payroll in $1,000s)				
Industry	1998 Employment	2005 Employment	1998 Payroll	2005 Payroll
Retail Trade	381,550	424,451	6,814,272	9,551,693
Professional, Scientific, Technical Services	252,923	355,406	12,668,638	24,259,680
Health Care and Social Assistance	293,642	346,082	8,276,316	13,095,304
Manufacturing	368,397	290,052	12,148,259	11,987,037
Accommodation and Food Services	234,205	284,857	2,583,716	3,927,633
Admin., Support, Waste Mngt., Remediation Services	193,746	230,060	3,863,555	6,647,026
Construction	178,057	229,405	5,235,341	9,166,257
Finance and Insurance	131,159	163,718	5,444,898	10,660,107
Other Services (except Public Admin.)	141,679	163,099	3,105,675	4,576,441
Wholesale Trade	106,663	110,990	4,036,250	5,583,345

Data: U.S. Census Bureau, County Business Patterns

Taxes and Business Climate

State and Local Taxes		
Combined Revenues ($1,000s)	**2003–4**	**2004–5**
Revenue from Property Taxes	7,715,220	8,390,045
Revenue from Sales and Gross Receipts Taxes	7,249,089	7,640,559
Revenue from Individual Income Taxes	7,422,071	8,352,366
Revenue from Corporate Income Taxes	422,119	605,959
Revenue from Other Taxes	2,193,806	2,670,257
Total Tax Revenue	25,002,305	27,659,186
Per Capita Taxes		
Property Tax Per Capita	1,031	1,110
Sales and Gross Receipts Tax Per Capita	969	1,011
Individual Income Tax Per Capita	992	1,105
Corporate Income Tax Per Capita	56	80
Other Taxes Per Capita	293	353
Total Taxes Per Capita	3,342	3,660

Data: U.S. Census Bureau; Anderson Economic Group, LLC

Business Climate Measures

Anderson Economic Group: 2007 Business Tax Ranking (1 is Best)	19
Forbes Magazine: 2007 Best States for Business Ranking (1 is Best)	1
Tax Foundation: 2008 Business Tax Climate Ranking (1 is Best)	14
ALEC-Laffer 2007 Economic Competitiveness Ranking (1 is Best)	6
2003–4 Employer Firm Births	19,669
2003–4 Employer Firm Terminations	15,138

Data: Anderson Economic Group; Tax Foundation; Forbes Magazine; U.S. Census, Statistics of U.S. Businesses; American Legislative Exchange Council

Voting Behavior and Elected Officials

Voter Registration and Turnout (%)

	1992	1996	2000	2004
Registered Voters Who Voted	83.7	72.7	72.6	76.5
Citizens Age 18+ Who Voted	52.8	47.5	51.3	57.2

Data: Dave Leip's Atlas of U.S. Presidential Elections

Presidential Election Results (Nationwide Winner Listed First)

2004	Popular Vote (%)	Electoral Votes
George W. Bush (Republican, Incumbent)	53.7	13
John Kerry (Democrat)	45.5	0
Other	0.8	0
2000		
George W. Bush (Republican)	52.5	13
Albert Gore (Democrat)	44.4	0
Ralph Nader (Green)	2.2	0
Other	0.9	0
1996		
William Clinton (Democrat, Incumbent)	45.2	0
Robert Dole (Republican)	47.1	13
H. Ross Perot (Reformist)	6.6	0
Other	1.1	0
1992		
William Clinton (Democrat)	40.6	0
George H. W. Bush (Republican, Incumbent)	45.0	13
H. Ross Perot (Independent)	13.6	0
Other	0.8	0

Data: Dave Leip's Atlas of U.S. Presidential Elections

Governor and U.S. Congressional Seats				
Governor	**Party**	**Year Term Began**	**Term**	**Max. Consecutive Terms**
Timothy Kaine	D	2006	First	1
U.S. Senators	**Party**	**Year Elected**	**Term Expires**	
John W. Warner	R	1978	2009	
Jim Webb	D	2006	2013	
U.S. Representatives		**Republican**	**Democrat**	**Other**
		8	3	0

Data: National Governors Association; U.S. Senate, Office of the Clerk; U.S. House of Representatives

Business and Economic Agencies

Agency	Website Address
Virginia Chamber of Commerce	www.vachamber.com
Virginia Economic Development Partnership	www.yesvirginia.org
Virginia Small Business Dev. Center	www.virginiasbdc.com
Virginia State Corporation Commission	www.scc.virginia.gov/division/clk

Data: Various agency websites

Washington

Washington, located in the Pacific region of the United States, had a population of 6.4 million people in 2006, making it the fourteenth most populous state. The state's population increased by 501,677 people from 2000 to 2006, and is projected to increase to 8.0 million by 2025. This 1.2% projected annual growth rate compares to the projected national average of 0.8%. Per capita personal income in Washington was $38,067 in 2006, up from $35,730 in 2005. For 2006, this was sixteenth highest in the country and $1,438 above the national average. From 2000 to 2006 per capita income in Washington grew at an average annual rate of 3.1%, compared to 3.5% nationally.

In 2005, the state's largest industry in terms of employment was retail trade, followed by health care and social assistance. The fastest growing industry was professional, scientific, and technical services, with 3.3% annual employment growth from 1998 to 2005. The state's workforce is generally more educated than other states—89.0% of the state's adult population has graduated from high school, compared to an 84.1% national

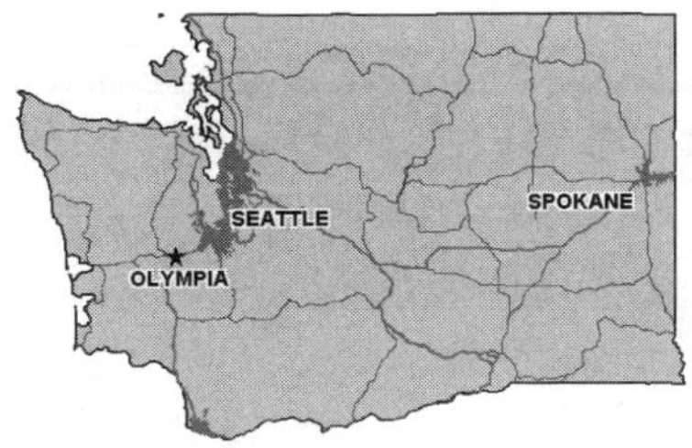

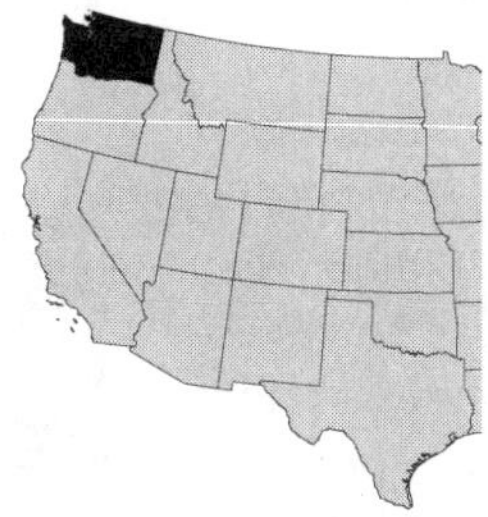

★ State Capitol

Major Urban Area

Major Roadway

Demographic and Socioeconomic Profile

Demographics and Socioeconomic Figures			
Population and Households	**2000**	**2005**	**2006**
Total Population	5,894,121	6,146,338	6,395,798
Number of Households	2,271,398	2,450,474	2,471,912
Average Household Size	2.5	2.5	2.5
Age and Ethnicity			
Median Age	35.3	36.7	36.7
Population 18 Years of Age and Older	4,384,341	4,668,831	4,867,922
Population 65 Years of Age and Older	662,162	683,774	736,716
Caucasian Population	4,815,072	4,988,017	5,148,130
African-American Population	185,052	202,286	217,868
Hispanic Population	439,841	541,722	580,027
Asian Population	320,979	405,030	423,976
Foreign-Born Population (%)	10.4	12.2	12.4
Income			
Per Capita Personal Income (USD)	$31,779	$35,730	$38,067
Median Household Income (USD)	$45,776	$49,262	$52,583
Individuals Below Poverty Level	10.6%	11.9%	11.8%

Data: U.S. Census, American Community Survey; U.S. Department of Commerce, Bureau of Economic Analysis

average. Nationally, an average of 27.0% hold a bachelor degree or higher compared to 30.5% in Washington. Nationally, 9.9% hold professional or graduate degrees compared to 10.7% in Washington.

In fiscal year 2004–5, Washington had total tax revenues of $23.0 billion. The largest share was generated from sales and gross receipts taxes, followed by property taxes. The per capita tax burden in Washington was $3,664 for 2004–5, just $41 below the national average. In terms of business taxes, the state ranked twentieth in a report from Anderson Economic Group. Forbes Magazine and the Tax Foundation ranked the state's business climate fifth and eleventh, respectively, while ALEC ranked Washington thirty-first in its state competitiveness index. One is considered best for each ranking.

Population Projections

Year	2010	2015	2020	2025
Total Population	6,541,963	6,950,610	7,432,136	7,996,400
Median Age	37.3	37.3	37.7	38.1
Population 18 Years of Age and Older	5,053,540	5,389,525	5,748,788	6,164,834
Population 65 Years of Age and Older	795,528	965,506	1,168,199	1,380,872

Data: U.S. Census Bureau

Workforce and Industry Profile

Workforce

	2000	2005	2006
Civilian Labor Force	3,050,021	3,270,480	3,326,524
Labor Force Participation Rate	68.3%	67.6%	67.4%
Unemployment Rate	5.0%	5.5%	5.0%
Average Wage Per Job (USD)	$37,090	$41,460	$42,910
Education Attainment (Population 25 Years and Older)	**(%)**	**(%)**	**(%)**
High School Graduate or Higher	87.1	88.8	89.0
Bachelors Degree or Higher	27.7	30.1	30.5
Graduate or Professional Degree	9.3	10.5	10.7

Data: U.S. Census Bureau, American Community Survey; U.S. Department of Commerce, Bureau of Economic Analysis; U.S. Department of Labor, Bureau of Labor Statistics

Industry Overview

	1998	2004	2005
Total Employees	2,134,598	2,268,913	2,316,296
Total Payroll ($1,000s)	$73,268,188	$90,154,182	$94,928,122
Total Establishments	161,473	171,529	175,658
Establishments with 1–19 Employees	142,096	150,587	154,332
Establishments with 20–49 Employees	12,485	13,527	13,633
Establishments with 50–249 Employees	6,136	6,560	6,847
Establishments with 250–999 Employees	667	744	745
Establishments with 1,000+ Employees	89	111	101

Data: U.S. Census Bureau, County Business Patterns

Major Industries (Ranked by 2005 Employment; Payroll in $1,000s)				
Industry	1998 Employment	2005 Employment	1998 Payroll	2005 Payroll
Retail Trade	288,387	321,048	6,107,356	8,064,049
Health Care and Social Assistance	269,465	317,975	7,767,349	12,130,929
Manufacturing	335,467	256,563	13,655,822	12,547,603
Accommodation and Food Services	195,249	214,805	2,165,493	3,182,478
Construction	143,168	164,391	5,224,593	7,492,851
Professional, Scientific, Technical Services	117,463	147,540	5,122,866	9,140,640
Admin., Support, Waste Mngt., Remediation Services	116,150	130,772	2,992,866	4,772,511
Wholesale Trade	120,196	128,315	4,704,938	6,384,947
Finance and Insurance	96,128	108,834	4,272,989	6,460,604
Other Services (except Public Admin.)	100,652	106,632	1,942,337	2,586,035

Data: U.S. Census Bureau, County Business Patterns

Taxes and Business Climate

State and Local Taxes		
Combined Revenues ($1,000s)	2003–4	2004–5
Revenue from Property Taxes	6,386,346	6,637,299
Revenue from Sales and Gross Receipts Taxes	12,999,301	13,825,212
Revenue from Individual Income Taxes	0	0
Revenue from Corporate Income Taxes	0	4
Revenue from Other Taxes	2,039,281	2,511,527
Total Tax Revenue	21,424,928	22,974,042
Per Capita Taxes		
Property Tax Per Capita	1,029	1,058
Sales and Gross Receipts Tax Per Capita	2,094	2,205
Individual Income Tax Per Capita	0	0
Corporate Income Tax Per Capita	0	0
Other Taxes Per Capita	329	401
Total Taxes Per Capita	3,452	3,664

Data: U.S. Census Bureau; Anderson Economic Group, LLC

Business Climate Measures

Anderson Economic Group: 2007 Business Tax Ranking (1 is Best)	20
Forbes Magazine: 2007 Best States for Business Ranking (1 is Best)	5
Tax Foundation: 2008 Business Tax Climate Ranking (1 is Best)	11
ALEC-Laffer 2007 Economic Competitiveness Ranking (1 is Best)	31
2003–4 Employer Firm Births	18,315
2003–4 Employer Firm Terminations	15,470

Data: Anderson Economic Group; Tax Foundation; Forbes Magazine; U.S. Census, Statistics of U.S. Businesses; American Legislative Exchange Council

Voting Behavior and Elected Officials

Voter Registration and Turnout (%)

	1992	1996	2000	2004
Registered Voters Who Voted	81.3	73.2	74.6	81.5
Citizens Age 18+ Who Voted	59.9	54.8	56.8	61.7

Data: Dave Leip's Atlas of U.S. Presidential Elections

Presidential Election Results (Nationwide Winner Listed First)

2004	Popular Vote (%)	Electoral Votes
George W. Bush (Republican, Incumbent)	45.6	0
John Kerry (Democrat)	52.8	11
Other	1.6	0
2000		
George W. Bush (Republican)	44.6	0
Albert Gore (Democrat)	50.2	11
Ralph Nader (Green)	4.1	0
Other	1.1	0
1996		
William Clinton (Democrat, Incumbent)	49.8	11
Robert Dole (Republican)	37.3	0
H. Ross Perot (Reformist)	8.9	0
Other	3.9	0
1992		
William Clinton (Democrat)	43.4	11
George H. W. Bush (Republican, Incumbent)	32.0	0
H. Ross Perot (Independent)	23.7	0
Other	1.0	0

Data: Dave Leip's Atlas of U.S. Presidential Elections

Governor and U.S. Congressional Seats				
Governor	Party	Year Term Began	Term	Max. Consecutive Terms
Christine Gregoire	D	2005	First	No limit
U.S. Senators	Party	Year Elected	Term Expires	
Maria Cantwell	D	2000	2013	
Patty Murray	D	1992	2011	
U.S. Representatives		Republican	Democrat	Other
		3	6	0

Data: National Governors Association; U.S. Senate, Office of the Clerk; U.S. House of Representatives

Business and Economic Agencies

Agency	Website Address
Association of Washington Business	www.awb.org
Department of Community, Trade, and Economic Development	www.cted.wa.gov
Washington Small Business Dev. Center	www.wsbdc.org
Washington Secretary of State	www.secstate.wa.gov

Data: Various agency websites

West Virginia

With a population of 1.8 million people, West Virginia was fourteenth least populous state in the United States in 2006. From 2000 to 2006 the state's population increased by 10,126 people, and is projected to decrease slightly by 2025. The −0.15% projected annual growth rate compares to the projected national average of 0.8%. The state's 2006 per capita personal income of $28,067 was higher compared to $26,435 in 2005 and second lowest in the United States, some $8,562 below the national average. Per capita income in West Virginia grew at an average annual rate of 4.2% from 2000 to 2006, compared to 3.5% nationally.

West Virginia's largest industry in terms of 2005 employment was health care and social assistance. The fastest growing industry was professional, scientific, and technical services, with 3.4% annual employment growth from 1998 to 2005. The second fastest growing industry was administration, support, waste management, and remediation services. The state's workforce is generally less educated than other states—81.0% of the state's adult population has graduated from high school, compared to an 84.1% national average; 16.5% hold a

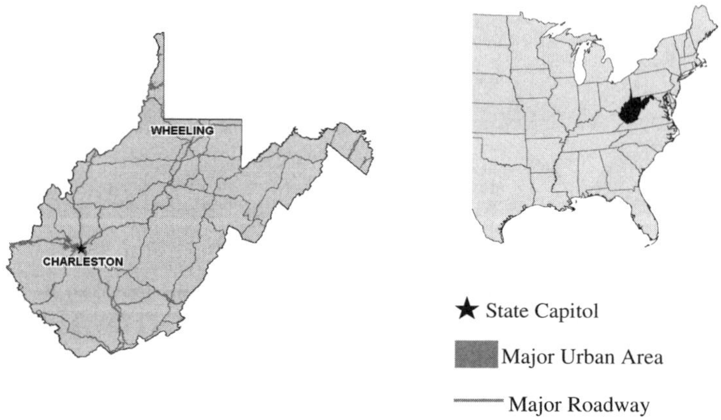

Demographic and Socioeconomic Profile

Demographics and Socioeconomic Figures			
Population and Households	**2000**	**2005**	**2006**
Total Population	1,808,344	1,771,750	1,818,470
Number of Households	736,481	740,702	743,064
Average Household Size	2.4	2.4	2.4
Age and Ethnicity			
Median Age	38.9	40.7	40.7
Population 18 Years of Age and Older	1,406,569	1,391,259	1,428,249
Population 65 Years of Age and Older	276,826	266,385	279,117
Caucasian Population	1,717,482	1,682,489	1,721,098
African-American Population	55,999	54,270	58,693
Hispanic Population	11,774	10,139	14,383
Asian Population	9,445	7,967	10,479
Foreign-Born Population (%)	1.1	1.1	1.2
Income			
Per Capita Personal Income (USD)	$21,899	$26,435	$28,067
Median Household Income (USD)	$29,696	$33,452	$35,059
Individuals Below Poverty Level	17.9%	18.0%	17.3%

Data: U.S. Census, American Community Survey; U.S. Department of Commerce, Bureau of Economic Analysis

bachelor degree or higher (national average is 27.0%); and 6.6% hold professional or graduate degrees compared to the national average of 9.9%.

West Virginia's total tax revenue was $5.6 billion for fiscal year 2004–5, up from the 2003–4 total revenue of $5.0 billion. The largest share of tax revenue in 2004–5 was generated from sales and gross receipts taxes, followed by individual income taxes. On a per capita basis, residents of West Virginia paid taxes of $3,074, compared to the national average of $3,705 for 2004–5. In terms of business taxes, the state ranked forty-sixth in a report from Anderson Economic Group. Forbes Magazine and the Tax Foundation ranked the state's business climate fiftieth and thirty-seventh, respectively, while ALEC ranked West Virginia fortieth in its state competitiveness index. One is considered best for each ranking.

Population Projections

Year	2010	2015	2020	2025
Total Population	1,829,141	1,822,758	1,801,112	1,766,435
Median Age	41.4	42.7	43.9	45.4
Population 18 Years of Age and Older	1,446,830	1,450,163	1,443,442	1,428,017
Population 65 Years of Age and Older	292,402	329,775	372,024	408,533

Data: U.S. Census Bureau

Workforce and Industry Profile

Workforce

	2000	2005	2006
Civilian Labor Force	808,861	793,757	806,996
Labor Force Participation Rate	56.5%	54.8%	55.6%
Unemployment Rate	5.5%	5.0%	4.9%
Average Wage Per Job (USD)	$26,887	$30,560	$31,440
Education Attainment (Population 25 Years and Older)	**(%)**	**(%)**	**(%)**
High School Graduate or Higher	75.2	81.2	81.0
Bachelors Degree or Higher	14.8	16.9	16.5
Graduate or Professional Degree	5.9	6.8	6.6

Data: U.S. Census Bureau, American Community Survey; U.S. Department of Commerce, Bureau of Economic Analysis; U.S. Department of Labor, Bureau of Labor Statistics

Industry Overview

	1998	2004	2005
Total Employees	547,234	568,619	565,499
Total Payroll ($1,000s)	$13,278,895	$15,608,156	$16,323,457
Total Establishments	41,703	40,837	40,735
Establishments with 1–19 Employees	36,537	35,454	35,419
Establishments with 20–49 Employees	3,330	3,471	3,425
Establishments with 50–249 Employees	1,628	1,704	1,667
Establishments with 250–999 Employees	184	181	199
Establishments with 1,000+ Employees	24	27	25

Data: U.S. Census Bureau, County Business Patterns

Major Industries (Ranked by 2005 Employment; Payroll in $1,000s)				
Industry	1998 Employment	2005 Employment	1998 Payroll	2005 Payroll
Health Care and Social Assistance	99,695	112,764	2,520,213	3,499,116
Retail Trade	89,474	92,369	1,348,903	1,658,688
Manufacturing	74,424	62,972	2,595,303	2,574,491
Accommodation and Food Services	52,369	58,510	514,087	652,685
Construction	29,587	29,842	785,188	1,045,632
Admin., Support, Waste Mngt., Remediation Services	23,736	29,472	441,041	637,526
Other Services (except Public Admin.)	26,797	26,151	398,111	483,169
Professional, Scientific, Technical Services	18,472	23,323	487,462	844,354
Mining	21,325	23,040	997,383	1,329,536
Wholesale Trade	23,082	21,134	689,794	785,543

Data: U.S. Census Bureau, County Business Patterns

Taxes and Business Climate

State and Local Taxes		
Combined Revenues ($1,000s)	**2003–4**	**2004–5**
Revenue from Property Taxes	979,034	1,008,409
Revenue from Sales and Gross Receipts Taxes	2,150,048	2,211,808
Revenue from Individual Income Taxes	1,068,212	1,171,987
Revenue from Corporate Income Taxes	181,515	463,249
Revenue from Other Taxes	588,696	695,293
Total Tax Revenue	4,967,505	5,550,746
Per Capita Taxes		
Property Tax Per Capita	540	558
Sales and Gross Receipts Tax Per Capita	1,186	1,225
Individual Income Tax Per Capita	589	649
Corporate Income Tax Per Capita	100	257
Other Taxes Per Capita	325	385
Total Taxes Per Capita	2,740	3,074

Data: U.S. Census Bureau; Anderson Economic Group, LLC

Business Climate Measures

Anderson Economic Group: 2007 Business Tax Ranking (1 is Best)	46
Forbes Magazine: 2007 Best States for Business Ranking (1 is Best)	50
Tax Foundation: 2008 Business Tax Climate Ranking (1 is Best)	37
ALEC-Laffer 2007 Economic Competitiveness Ranking (1 is Best)	40
2003–4 Employer Firm Births	3,558
2003–4 Employer Firm Terminations	3,236

Data: Anderson Economic Group; Tax Foundation; Forbes Magazine; U.S. Census, Statistics of U.S. Businesses; American Legislative Exchange Council

Voting Behavior and Elected Officials

Voter Registration and Turnout (%)

	1992	1996	2000	2004
Registered Voters Who Voted	71.5	65.6	60.8	64.7
Citizens Age 18+ Who Voted	50.6	44.9	46.1	53.3

Data: Dave Leip's Atlas of U.S. Presidential Elections

Presidential Election Results (Nationwide Winner Listed First)

2004	Popular Vote (%)	Electoral Votes
George W. Bush (Republican, Incumbent)	56.1	5
John Kerry (Democrat)	43.2	0
Other	0.7	0
2000		
George W. Bush (Republican)	51.9	5
Albert Gore (Democrat)	45.6	0
Ralph Nader (Green)	1.7	0
Other	0.8	0
1996		
William Clinton (Democrat, Incumbent)	51.5	5
Robert Dole (Republican)	36.8	0
H. Ross Perot (Reformist)	11.3	0
Other	0.5	0
1992		
William Clinton (Democrat)	48.4	5
George H. W. Bush (Republican, Incumbent)	35.4	0
H. Ross Perot (Independent)	15.9	0
Other	0.3	0

Data: Dave Leip's Atlas of U.S. Presidential Elections

Governor and U.S. Congressional Seats				
Governor	**Party**	**Year Term Began**	**Term**	**Max. Consecutive Terms**
Joe Manchin	D	2005	First	2
U.S. Senators	**Party**	**Year Elected**	**Term Expires**	
Jay Rockefeller	D	1984	2009	
Robert C. Byrd	D	1958	2013	
U.S. Representatives		**Republican**	**Democrat**	**Other**
		1	2	0

Data: National Governors Association; U.S. Senate, Office of the Clerk; U.S. House of Representatives

Business and Economic Agencies

Agency	Website Address
West Virginia Chamber of Commerce	www.wvchamber.com
West Virginia Development Office	www.wvdo.org
West Virginia Small Business Dev. Center	www.sbdcwv.org
West Virginia Secretary of State	www.wv.gov/sec.aspx?pgID=1

Data: Various agency websites

Wisconsin

Wisconsin had a population of 5.6 million people, making it the twentieth most populous state in 2006. The state's population increased by 192,831 people from 2000 to 2006, and is projected to increase to 6.1 million by 2025. This 0.5% projected annual growth rate is above the national average of 0.8%. Per capita personal income in Wisconsin was $34,476 in 2006, up from $32,922 in 2005. For 2006, this was $2,153 below the national average and the twentieth lowest in the country. The state's per capita income grew at an average annual rate of 3.2% from 2000 to 2006, compared to 3.5% nationally.

The state's workforce generally has less education than other states—88.4% of the state's adult population has graduated from high school, compared to an 84.1% national average; 25.1% hold a bachelor degree or higher (national average is 27.0%); and 8.4% hold professional or graduate degrees (national average is 9.9%). In 2005, the state's largest industry in terms of employment was manufacturing, followed by health care and social assistance. The fastest growing industry was also

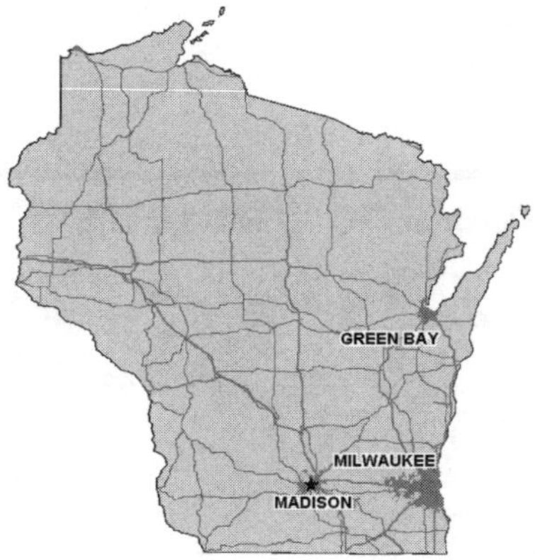

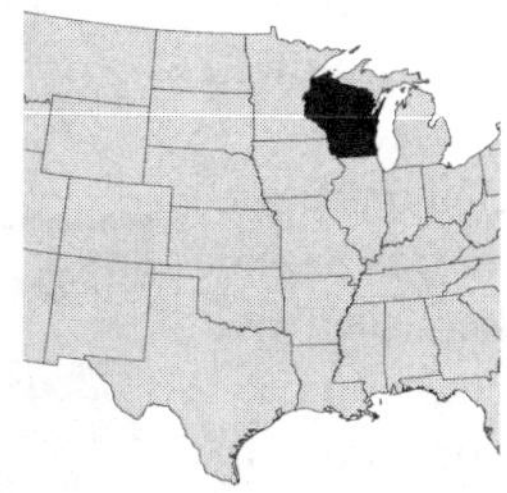

★ State Capitol

Major Urban Area

Major Roadway

Demographic and Socioeconomic Profile

Demographics and Socioeconomic Figures			
Population and Households	**2000**	**2005**	**2006**
Total Population	5,363,675	5,375,751	5,556,506
Number of Households	2,084,544	2,219,571	2,230,060
Average Household Size	2.5	2.4	2.4
Age and Ethnicity			
Median Age	36.0	37.9	37.6
Population 18 Years of Age and Older	3,996,289	4,085,023	4,241,563
Population 65 Years of Age and Older	702,668	674,464	721,873
Caucasian Population	4,773,553	4,734,357	4,859,689
African-American Population	300,355	307,950	328,376
Hispanic Population	191,049	242,287	256,304
Asian Population	83,077	107,517	110,778
Foreign-Born Population (%)	3.6	4.2	4.4
Income			
Per Capita Personal Income (USD)	$28,570	$32,922	$34,476
Median Household Income (USD)	$43,791	$47,105	$48,772
Individuals Below Poverty Level	8.7%	10.2%	11.0%

Data: U.S. Census, American Community Survey; U.S. Department of Commerce, Bureau of Economic Analysis

health care and social assistance, with 2.6% annual growth from 1998 to 2005.

In fiscal year 2004–5, Wisconsin had total tax revenues of $21.4 billion. The largest share was generated from property taxes, followed by sales and gross receipts taxes. The per capita tax burden in Wisconsin was $3,863 for 2004–5, some $158 above the national average, and a $149 increase from 2003–4. In terms of business taxes, Wisconsin ranked twenty-first in a report by Anderson Economic Group. The state's business climate was ranked forty-fourth by Forbes Magazine and thirty-ninth by the Tax Foundation. Wisconsin was ranked thirtieth by ALEC in its state competitiveness index. One is considered best for each ranking.

Population Projections

Year	2010	2015	2020	2025
Total Population	5,727,426	5,882,760	6,004,954	6,088,374
Median Age	38.1	38.5	39.6	40.7
Population 18 Years of Age and Older	4,408,282	4,539,380	4,636,998	4,711,673
Population 65 Years of Age and Older	771,993	881,745	1,025,542	1,183,596

Data: U.S. Census Bureau

Workforce and Industry Profile

Workforce

	2000	2005	2006
Civilian Labor Force	2,996,091	3,033,025	3,062,932
Labor Force Participation Rate	73.3%	70.8%	70.8%
Unemployment Rate	3.4%	4.8%	4.7%
Average Wage Per Job (USD)	$30,694	$35,660	$36,730
Education Attainment (Population 25 Years and Older)	**(%)**	**(%)**	**(%)**
High School Graduate or Higher	85.1	88.8	88.4
Bachelors Degree or Higher	22.4	25.0	25.1
Graduate or Professional Degree	7.2	8.1	8.4

Data: U.S. Census Bureau, American Community Survey; U.S. Department of Commerce, Bureau of Economic Analysis; U.S. Department of Labor, Bureau of Labor Statistics

Industry Overview

	1998	2004	2005
Total Employees	2,319,343	2,435,143	2,449,114
Total Payroll ($1,000s)	$64,912,499	$82,834,268	$85,781,279
Total Establishments	138,635	144,116	145,159
Establishments with 1–19 Employees	117,738	121,865	122,919
Establishments with 20–49 Employees	12,751	13,660	13,535
Establishments with 50–249 Employees	7,060	7,442	7,530
Establishments with 250–999 Employees	943	1,015	1,037
Establishments with 1,000+ Employees	143	134	138

Data: U.S. Census Bureau, County Business Patterns

Major Industries (Ranked by 2005 Employment; Payroll in $1,000s)				
Industry	1998 Employment	2005 Employment	1998 Payroll	2005 Payroll
Manufacturing	566,219	493,661	19,872,068	21,148,313
Health Care and Social Assistance	291,781	348,275	7,935,213	12,542,232
Retail Trade	309,194	317,423	5,228,682	6,626,134
Accommodation and Food Services	191,531	220,168	1,722,956	2,382,706
Finance and Insurance	126,572	135,409	4,930,640	7,125,232
Admin., Support, Waste Mngt., Remediation Services	116,764	132,266	2,130,335	3,014,260
Wholesale Trade	114,445	124,033	4,131,194	5,991,081
Construction	107,027	119,663	4,308,527	5,668,227
Other Services (except Public Admin.)	104,798	114,835	1,696,610	2,230,825
Professional, Scientific, and Technical Services	82,860	96,891	3,088,806	4,752,212

Data: U.S. Census Bureau, County Business Patterns

Taxes and Business Climate

State and Local Taxes		
Combined Revenues ($1,000s)	2003–4	2004–5
Revenue from Property Taxes	7,429,001	7,796,015
Revenue from Sales and Gross Receipts Taxes	5,915,255	6,107,888
Revenue from Individual Income Taxes	5,251,190	5,465,082
Revenue from Corporate Income Taxes	681,990	782,742
Revenue from Other Taxes	1,163,552	1,251,799
Total Tax Revenue	20,440,988	21,403,526
Per Capita Taxes		
Property Tax Per Capita	1,350	1,407
Sales and Gross Receipts Tax Per Capita	1,075	1,102
Individual Income Tax Per Capita	954	986
Corporate Income Tax Per Capita	124	141
Other Taxes Per Capita	211	226
Total Taxes Per Capita	3,714	3,863

Data: U.S. Census Bureau; Anderson Economic Group, LLC

Business Climate Measures	
Anderson Economic Group: 2007 Business Tax Ranking (1 is Best)	21
Forbes Magazine: 2007 Best States for Business Ranking (1 is Best)	44
Tax Foundation: 2008 Business Tax Climate Ranking (1 is Best)	39
ALEC-Laffer 2007 Economic Competitiveness Ranking (1 is Best)	30
2003–4 Employer Firm Births	11,744
2003–4 Employer Firm Terminations	10,521

Data: Anderson Economic Group; Tax Foundation; Forbes Magazine; U.S. Census, Statistics of U.S. Businesses; American Legislative Exchange Council

Voting Behavior and Elected Officials

Voter Registration and Turnout

	1992	1996	2000	2004
Registered Voters Who Voted	NA	NA	NA	NA
Citizens Age 18+ Who Voted	69.0%	57.4%	65.0%	72.4%

Data: Dave Leip's Atlas of U.S. Presidential Elections; Not Available

Presidential Election Results (Nationwide Winner Listed First)

2004	Popular Vote (%)	Electoral Votes
George W. Bush (Republican, Incumbent)	49.3	0
John Kerry (Democrat)	49.7	10
Other	1.0	0
2000		
George W. Bush (Republican)	47.6	0
Albert Gore (Democrat)	47.8	11
Ralph Nader (Green)	3.6	0
Other	0.9	0
1996		
William Clinton (Democrat, Incumbent)	48.8	11
Robert Dole (Republican)	38.5	0
H. Ross Perot (Reformist)	10.4	0
Other	2.4	0
1992		
William Clinton (Democrat)	41.1	11
George H. W. Bush (Republican, Incumbent)	36.8	0
H. Ross Perot (Independent)	21.5	0
Other	0.6	0

Data: Dave Leip's Atlas of U.S. Presidential Elections

Governor and U.S. Congressional Seats				
Governor	**Party**	**Year Term Began**	**Term**	**Max. Consecutive Terms**
Jim Doyle	D	2007	Second	No limit
U.S. Senators	**Party**	**Year Elected**	**Term Expires**	
Russell Feingold	D	1992	2011	
Herb Kohl	D	1988	2013	
U.S. Representatives		**Republican**	**Democrat**	**Other**
		3	5	0

Data: National Governors Association; U.S. Senate, Office of the Clerk; U.S. House of Representatives

Business and Economic Agencies

Agency	Website Address
Wisconsin Chamber of Commerce Foundation	www.wischamberfoundation.org
Wisconsin Housing and Economic Development Authority	www.wheda.com
Wisconsin Small Business Dev. Center	www.wisconsinsbdc.org
State of Wisconsin, Department of Financial Institutions	www.wdfi.org/corporations

Data: Various agency websites

Wyoming

Wyoming had a population of 515,004 people in 2006, making it the least populous state. The state's population increased by 21,222 people from 2000 to 2006, and is projected to increase to 529,031 by 2025. This 0.1% projected annual growth rate compares to the projected national average of 0.8%. Per capita personal income in Wyoming was $40,569 in 2006, up from $37,161 in 2005. For 2006, this was sixth highest in the country and $3,940 above the national average. From 2000 to 2006 per capita income in Wyoming grew at an average annual rate of 6.1%, compared to 3.5% nationally.

In 2005, the state's largest industry in terms of employment was retail trade, followed by health care and social assistance. The fastest growing industry was transportation and warehousing, with 6.1% annual employment growth from 1998 to 2005. The state's workforce is generally less educated than other states—90.2% of the state's adult population has graduated from high school, compared to an 84.1% national average. Nationally, an average of 27.0% hold a bachelor degree or higher compared to 22.7% in Wyoming. Nationally, 9.9% hold professional or

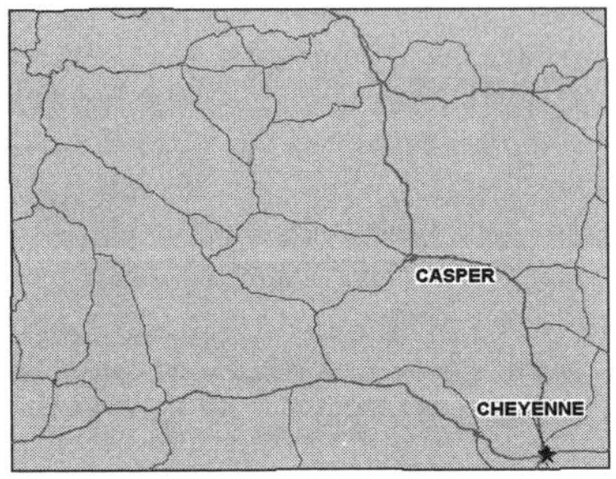

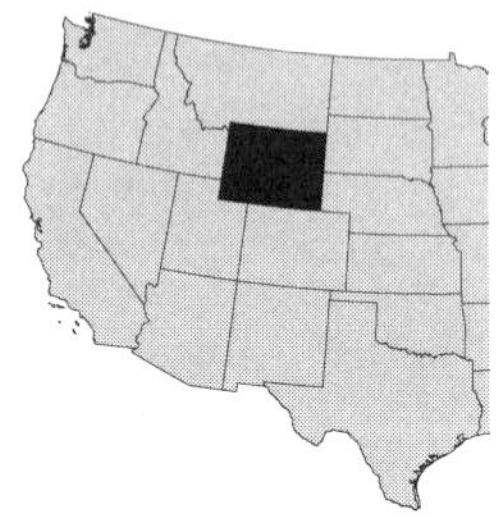

★ State Capitol

Major Urban Area

Major Roadway

Demographic and Socioeconomic Profile

Demographics and Socioeconomic Figures			
Population and Households	**2000**	**2005**	**2006**
Total Population	493,782	495,226	515,004
Number of Households	193,608	204,935	207,302
Average Household Size	2.5	2.4	2.4
Age and Ethnicity			
Median Age	36.2	39.1	37.5
Population 18 Years of Age and Older	365,685	382,349	394,074
Population 65 Years of Age and Older	57,467	59,221	61,630
Caucasian Population	454,095	457,681	472,937
African-American Population	3,126	3,317	3,686
Hispanic Population	31,384	33,437	35,732
Asian Population	2,972	3,148	4,656
Foreign-Born Population (%)	2.3	2.3	2.7
Income			
Per Capita Personal Income (USD)	$28,460	$37,161	$40,569
Median Household Income (USD)	$37,892	$46,202	$47,423
Individuals Below Poverty Level	11.4%	9.5%	9.4%

Data: U.S. Census, American Community Survey; U.S. Department of Commerce, Bureau of Economic Analysis

graduate degrees compared to 7.4% in Wyoming.

In fiscal year 2004–5, Wyoming had total tax revenues of $2.7 billion. The largest share was generated from taxes in the "other" category, followed by property taxes. The per capita tax burden in Wyoming was $5,275 for 2004–5, some $1,570 above the national average. In terms of business taxes, the state ranked thirty-sixth in a study from Anderson Economic Group. Forbes Magazine and the Tax Foundation ranked the state's business climate twenty-ninth and first, respectively, while ALEC ranked Wyoming fourth in its state competitiveness index. One is considered best for each ranking.

Population Projections

Year	2010	2015	2020	2025
Total Population	519,886	528,005	530,948	529,031
Median Age	39.5	40.9	42.4	44.3
Population 18 Years of Age and Older	403,613	412,506	418,436	422,797
Population 65 Years of Age and Older	72,658	88,842	109,655	128,605

Data: U.S. Census Bureau

Workforce and Industry Profile

Workforce

	2000	2005	2006
Civilian Labor Force	266,882	277,899	284,690
Labor Force Participation Rate	71.5%	70.7%	71.3%
Unemployment Rate	3.8%	3.7%	3.2%
Average Wage Per Job (USD)	$26,837	$32,940	$34,290
Education Attainment (Population 25 Years and Older)	**(%)**	**(%)**	**(%)**
High School Graduate or Higher	87.9	91.3	90.2
Bachelors Degree or Higher	21.9	23.2	22.7
Graduate or Professional Degree	7.0	7.7	7.4

Data: U.S. Census Bureau, American Community Survey; U.S. Department of Commerce, Bureau of Economic Analysis; U.S. Department of Labor, Bureau of Labor Statistics

Industry Overview

	1998	2004	2005
Total Employees	163,791	187,360	191,934
Total Payroll ($1,000s)	$3,980,094	$5,696,419	$6,202,411
Total Establishments	17,888	19,330	19,736
Establishments with 1–19 Employees	16,231	17,439	17,804
Establishments with 20–49 Employees	1,160	1,338	1,363
Establishments with 50–249 Employees	453	491	508
Establishments with 250–999 Employees	42	59	58
Establishments with 1,000+ Employees	2	3	3

Data: U.S. Census Bureau, County Business Patterns

Major Industries (Ranked by 2005 Employment; Payroll in $1,000s)				
Industry	1998 Employment	2005 Employment	1998 Payroll	2005 Payroll
Retail Trade	26,974	30,186	443,320	655,186
Health Care and Social Assistance	23,694	28,269	556,515	908,285
Accommodation and Food Services	22,882	25,765	236,920	345,459
Mining	16,257	19,443	748,353	1,182,693
Construction	13,265	16,372	383,677	598,206
Manufacturing	8,916	10,465	283,720	463,053
Other Services (except Public Admin.)	7,894	8,618	128,223	185,478
Transportation and Warehousing	5,313	8,057	141,255	309,655
Professional, Scientific, Technical Services	6,096	7,951	170,895	300,600
Finance and Insurance	6,130	7,108	200,139	264,363

Data: U.S. Census Bureau, County Business Patterns

Taxes and Business Climate

State and Local Taxes		
Combined Revenues ($1,000s)	2003–4	2004–5
Revenue from Property Taxes	683,963	890,710
Revenue from Sales and Gross Receipts Taxes	734,105	819,934
Revenue from Individual Income Taxes	0	0
Revenue from Corporate Income Taxes	0	0
Revenue from Other Taxes	827,197	961,209
Total Tax Revenue	2,245,265	2,671,853
Per Capita Taxes		
Property Tax Per Capita	1,352	1,758
Sales and Gross Receipts Tax Per Capita	1,451	1,619
Individual Income Tax Per Capita	0	0
Corporate Income Tax Per Capita	0	0
Other Taxes Per Capita	1,635	1,898
Total Taxes Per Capita	4,437	5,275

Data: U.S. Census Bureau; Anderson Economic Group, LLC

Business Climate Measures	
Anderson Economic Group: 2007 Business Tax Ranking (1 is Best)	36
Forbes Magazine: 2007 Best States for Business Ranking (1 is Best)	29
Tax Foundation: 2008 Business Tax Climate Ranking (1 is Best)	1
ALEC-Laffer 2007 Economic Competitiveness Ranking (1 is Best)	4
2003–4 Employer Firm Births	1,913
2003–4 Employer Firm Terminations	1,593

Data: Anderson Economic Group; Tax Foundation; Forbes Magazine; U.S. Census, Statistics of U.S. Businesses; American Legislative Exchange Council

Voting Behavior and Elected Officials

Voter Registration and Turnout (%)

	1992	1996	2000	2004
Registered Voters Who Voted	85.3	87.9	99.2	104.7
Citizens Age 18+ Who Voted	62.1	59.4	59.7	64.1

Data: Dave Leip's Atlas of U.S. Presidential Elections

Presidential Election Results (Nationwide Winner Listed First)

2004	Popular Vote (%)	Electoral Votes
George W. Bush (Republican, Incumbent)	68.9	3
John Kerry (Democrat)	29.1	0
Other	2.1	0
2000		
George W. Bush (Republican)	67.8	3
Albert Gore (Democrat)	27.7	0
Ralph Nader (Green)	2.1	0
Other	2.4	0
1996		
William Clinton (Democrat, Incumbent)	36.8	0
Robert Dole (Republican)	49.8	3
H. Ross Perot (Reformist)	12.3	0
Other	1.1	0
1992		
William Clinton (Democrat)	34.0	0
George H. W. Bush (Republican, Incumbent)	39.6	3
H. Ross Perot (Independent)	25.6	0
Other	0.9	0

Data: Dave Leip's Atlas of U.S. Presidential Elections

Governor and U.S. Congressional Seats				
Governor	**Party**	**Year Term Began**	**Term**	**Max. Consecutive Terms**
David Freudenthal	D	2007	Second	2
U.S. Senators	**Party**	**Year Elected**	**Term Expires**	
Michael B. Enzi	R	1996	2009	
John Barrasso	R	2007	2013	
U.S. Representatives		**Republican**	**Democrat**	**Other**
		1	0	0

Data: National Governors Association; U.S. Senate, Office of the Clerk; U.S. House of Representatives

Business and Economic Agencies

Agency	Website Address
Buffalo Chamber of Commerce	www.jacksonholechamber.com
Wyoming Business Council	www.wyomingbusiness.org
Wyoming Small Business Dev. Center	www.uwyo.edu/sbdc
Wyoming Secretary of State, Corporations	soswy.state.wy.us/corporat/corporat.htm

Data: Various agency websites

Ranking the States

Population Growth, 2006–25 Projected Average Annual Rate

Rank	State Name	Rate (%)	*Rank*	State Name	Rate (%)
1	Nevada	2.33	*26*	Montana	0.49
2	Arizona	2.32	*27*	Wisconsin	0.48
3	Florida	1.91	*28*	Rhode Island	0.43
4	Texas	1.44	*29*	Missouri	0.41
5	North Carolina	1.36	*30*	Massachusetts	0.40
T6	Utah	1.24	*31*	New Mexico	0.39
T6	Idaho	1.24	*32*	Maine	0.36
8	Washington	1.18	*T33*	Oklahoma	0.34
9	Oregon	1.08	*T33*	Kentucky	0.34
T10	Virginia	1.07	*35*	Indiana	0.33
T10	Alaska	1.07	*36*	Michigan	0.31
12	Georgia	1.06	*37*	Kansas	0.29
13	California	1.03	*38*	Mississippi	0.28
14	New Hampshire	0.99	*39*	Connecticut	0.27
15	Maryland	0.98	*40*	Alabama	0.23
16	Minnesota	0.89	*41*	Illinois	0.20
17	Tennessee	0.84	*42*	Pennsylvania	0.15
T18	Colorado	0.79	*43*	Wyoming	0.14
T18	Delaware	0.79	*T44*	South Dakota	0.13
20	South Carolina	0.76	*T44*	Nebraska	0.13
21	Vermont	0.63	*T46*	New York	0.06
22	Arkansas	0.60	*T46*	Ohio	0.06
23	Hawaii	0.59	*48*	Iowa	0.02
24	Louisiana	0.55	*49*	North Dakota	−0.13
25	New Jersey	0.52	*50*	West Virginia	−0.15

Youth Population (Percent under 18 Years of Age), 2006

Rank	State Name	Youth Population (%)	Rank	State Name	Youth Population (%)
1	Utah	31.06	*26*	Ohio	24.16
2	Texas	27.66	*27*	South Carolina	24.04
3	Idaho	26.89	*T28*	Tennessee	23.96
4	Alaska	26.82	*T28*	Iowa	23.96
5	Arizona	26.38	*30*	New Jersey	23.95
6	Georgia	26.19	*31*	Washington	23.89
7	California	26.14	*32*	Delaware	23.87
8	New Mexico	26.11	*33*	Kentucky	23.78
9	Mississippi	26.08	*34*	Wisconsin	23.66
10	Nevada	25.42	*35*	Virginia	23.62
10	Louisiana	25.40	*36*	Wyoming	23.48
12	Nebraska	25.19	*37*	New York	23.38
13	Kansas	25.13	*38*	Connecticut	23.34
14	Illinois	25.07	*39*	Oregon	23.17
15	Indiana	25.02	*40*	Hawaii	23.12
16	Oklahoma	25.01	*41*	Montana	23.09
17	South Dakota	24.81	*42*	New Hampshire	22.64
18	Arkansas	24.66	*43*	North Dakota	22.59
19	Colorado	24.61	*44*	Pennsylvania	22.57
20	Michigan	24.54	*45*	Massachusetts	22.50
21	Missouri	24.35	*46*	Rhode Island	22.24
22	Minnesota	24.34	*47*	Florida	22.21
23	North Carolina	24.33	*T48*	Vermont	21.46
T24	Alabama	24.26	*T48*	West Virginia	21.46
T24	Maryland	24.26	*50*	Maine	21.33

Percent of Individuals Below Poverty Level, 2006

Rank	State Name	Rate (%)	Rank	State Name	Rate (%)
1	Mississippi	21.1	T25	Idaho	12.6
2	Louisiana	19.0	27	Kansas	12.4
3	New Mexico	18.5	28	Illinois	12.3
T4	Arkansas	17.3	29	Pennsylvania	12.1
T4	West Virginia	17.3	30	Colorado	12.0
T6	Kentucky	17.0	31	Washington	11.8
T6	Oklahoma	17.0	32	Nebraska	11.5
8	Texas	16.9	33	North Dakota	11.4
9	Alabama	16.6	T34	Delaware	11.1
10	Tennessee	16.2	T34	Rhode Island	11.1
11	South Carolina	15.7	T36	Iowa	11.0
T12	Georgia	14.7	T36	Wisconsin	11.0
T12	North Carolina	14.7	38	Alaska	10.9
T14	Arizona	14.2	39	Utah	10.6
T14	New York	14.2	T40	Nevada	10.3
T16	Missouri	13.6	T40	Vermont	10.3
T16	Montana	13.6	42	Massachusetts	9.9
T16	South Dakota	13.6	43	Minnesota	9.8
19	Michigan	13.5	44	Virginia	9.6
T20	Ohio	13.3	45	Wyoming	9.4
T20	Oregon	13.3	46	Hawaii	9.3
22	California	13.1	47	New Jersey	8.7
23	Maine	12.9	48	Connecticut	8.3
24	Indiana	12.7	49	New Hampshire	8.0
T25	Florida	12.6	50	Maryland	7.8

Projected Change in Median Age of Population, 2006–25

Rank	State Name	Change in Median Age (Years)	*Rank*	State Name	Change in Median Age (Years)
1	Maryland	−0.4	*T25*	Michigan	2.1
2	Alaska	−0.2	*T25*	Ohio	2.1
3	North Carolina	0.2	*T28*	Kansas	2.2
T4	Colorado	0.6	*T28*	Vermont	2.2
T4	Virginia	0.6	*30*	Nebraska	2.3
T6	Georgia	0.9	*31*	Kentucky	2.5
T6	Hawaii	0.9	*T32*	Arkansas	2.7
T8	Connecticut	1.2	*T32*	Louisiana	2.7
T8	Indiana	1.2	*34*	Wisconsin	3.1
T10	Oregon	1.3	*T35*	Iowa	3.5
T10	Rhode Island	1.3	*T35*	Nevada	3.5
T10	Tennessee	1.3	*T35*	South Dakota	3.5
13	Washington	1.4	*38*	Alabama	3.7
14	Massachusetts	1.4	*39*	South Carolina	3.9
15	Texas	1.5	*40*	Arizona	4.2
16	Minnesota	1.6	*T41*	Idaho	4.3
T17	Illinois	1.7	*T41*	Maine	4.3
T17	New York	1.7	*43*	West Virginia	4.7
T19	Oklahoma	1.8	*T44*	Montana	4.8
T19	Pennsylvania	1.8	*T44*	North Dakota	4.8
T21	Missouri	2.0	*46*	Florida	5.0
T21	New Hampshire	2.0	*47*	Mississippi	5.2
T21	New Jersey	2.0	*48*	Delaware	5.3
T21	Utah	2.0	*49*	Wyoming	6.8
T25	California	2.1	*50*	New Mexico	7.7

Change in Per Capita Income from 2005–6

Rank	State Name	Change (%)	*Rank*	State Name	Change (%)
1	Louisiana	26.58	*26*	Pennsylvania	5.40
2	Wyoming	9.17	*27*	Illinois	5.32
3	Oklahoma	7.80	*28*	Maryland	5.26
4	New York	7.44	*29*	Arizona	5.15
5	New Jersey	6.95	*30*	Delaware	5.13
6	Washington	6.54	*31*	North Carolina	5.04
7	Connecticut	6.47	*32*	Colorado	5.00
8	Kansas	6.36	*33*	Iowa	4.91
9	West Virginia	6.17	*34*	Kentucky	4.82
10	Massachusetts	6.09	*T35*	Nebraska	4.72
11	Vermont	6.03	*T35*	Wisconsin	4.72
12	New Mexico	6.00	*37*	Missouri	4.50
13	Idaho	5.92	*38*	South Carolina	4.44
14	New Hampshire	5.80	*39*	Indiana	4.35
15	Hawaii	5.77	*40*	Ohio	4.30
16	Texas	5.72	*41*	Minnesota	4.27
17	Mississippi	5.71	*42*	Nevada	4.26
18	Montana	5.70	*T43*	Tennessee	4.21
19	Utah	5.65	*T43*	Rhode Island	4.21
20	Florida	5.63	*45*	Virginia	4.19
21	California	5.57	*46*	Maine	3.59
22	Oregon	5.54	*47*	Michigan	3.25
23	Arkansas	5.50	*48*	North Dakota	3.06
T24	Alabama	5.42	*49*	Georgia	3.01
T24	Alaska	5.42	*50*	South Dakota	1.87

Note: The significant change in Louisiana's per capita income is at least partially attributable to demographic shifts that occurred after Hurricane Katrina, which hit the state's largest city, New Orleans, in August 2005.

Change in Civilian Labor Force Size, 2000–6

Rank	State Name	Change (%)	Rank	State Name	Change (%)
1	Nevada	3.35	*26*	South Dakota	0.89
2	Arizona	2.92	*27*	New Jersey	0.88
3	Utah	2.42	*28*	Montana	0.87
4	Florida	2.24	*29*	Oregon	0.80
5	Idaho	2.06	*30*	Minnesota	0.77
6	Colorado	1.93	*31*	Kentucky	0.75
7	Georgia	1.87	*32*	Kansas	0.71
8	Virginia	1.84	*33*	Tennessee	0.68
9	Texas	1.76	*34*	Indiana	0.66
10	New Mexico	1.56	*35*	Iowa	0.64
11	Washington	1.46	*T36*	Pennsylvania	0.59
12	Alaska	1.40	*T36*	New York	0.59
13	Arkansas	1.34	*38*	Oklahoma	0.58
14	North Carolina	1.33	*39*	North Dakota	0.57
15	South Carolina	1.26	*40*	Nebraska	0.43
16	Vermont	1.22	*T41*	Illinois	0.37
17	Maryland	1.14	*T41*	Wisconsin	0.37
18	Wyoming	1.08	*43*	Ohio	0.36
T19	Rhode Island	1.01	*44*	Alabama	0.35
T19	California	1.01	*45*	Missouri	0.33
T19	Connecticut	1.01	*46*	Massachusetts	0.19
22	New Hampshire	1.00	*47*	West Virginia	−0.04
23	Maine	0.94	*48*	Mississippi	−0.09
24	Delaware	0.93	*49*	Michigan	−0.20
25	Hawaii	0.92	*50*	Louisiana	−0.34

Note: Louisiana's change in civilian labor force may be at least partially attributable to demographic shifts that occurred after Hurricane Katrina, which hit the state's largest city, New Orleans, in August 2005.

Population Age 25+ with Masters Degree or Higher, 2006

Rank	State Name	% of Population	*Rank*	State Name	% of Population
1	Maryland	15.65	*26*	Maine	8.94
2	Massachusetts	15.61	*27*	Florida	8.91
3	Connecticut	14.41	*28*	Missouri	8.67
4	New York	13.32	*29*	Montana	8.45
5	Virginia	13.24	*30*	Nebraska	8.42
6	Vermont	12.78	*31*	Wisconsin	8.39
7	Colorado	12.40	*T32*	North Carolina	8.28
8	New Jersey	12.36	*T32*	Ohio	8.28
9	New Hampshire	11.26	*34*	Kentucky	8.17
10	Rhode Island	11.25	*35*	Texas	8.05
11	New Mexico	10.88	*36*	Indiana	8.04
12	Illinois	10.81	*37*	South Carolina	7.86
13	Washington	10.69	*38*	Alabama	7.73
14	Delaware	10.54	*39*	Tennessee	7.51
15	California	10.35	*40*	Iowa	7.40
16	Oregon	9.99	*41*	Wyoming	7.38
17	Hawaii	9.84	*42*	South Dakota	7.25
18	Kansas	9.82	*43*	Nevada	7.24
19	Minnesota	9.64	*44*	Oklahoma	7.18
20	Pennsylvania	9.60	*45*	Idaho	7.12
21	Alaska	9.47	*46*	Louisiana	6.84
22	Utah	9.40	*47*	West Virginia	6.56
23	Arizona	9.24	*48*	North Dakota	6.47
24	Georgia	9.19	*49*	Arkansas	6.25
25	Michigan	9.18	*50*	Mississippi	6.13

Net Change in Establishments (Births Less Deaths), 2004–5

Rank	State Name	Change in Establishments	Rank	State Name	Change in Establishments
1	Florida	17,554	*26*	Connecticut	809
2	California	7,470	*27*	Montana	788
3	Texas	5,521	*28*	Louisiana	784
4	New York	5,498	*29*	Alabama	761
5	Virginia	4,531	*30*	Arkansas	640
6	Georgia	4,372	*31*	Rhode Island	630
7	North Carolina	2,973	*32*	Kentucky	587
8	Missouri	2,918	*33*	Kansas	547
9	Washington	2,845	*34*	New Hampshire	524
10	Arizona	2,731	*35*	Delaware	522
11	Illinois	2,415	*36*	New Mexico	519
12	Maryland	2,148	*37*	Hawaii	486
13	Colorado	2,081	*38*	Mississippi	466
14	Minnesota	2,052	*39*	Ohio	407
15	Pennsylvania	1,933	*40*	Maine	362
16	Nevada	1,881	*41*	South Dakota	340
17	Utah	1,826	*42*	West Virginia	322
18	Oregon	1,584	*43*	Wyoming	320
19	Tennessee	1,470	*44*	Iowa	278
20	South Carolina	1,455	*45*	Alaska	277
21	Indiana	1,333	*46*	North Dakota	270
22	Wisconsin	1,223	*47*	Nebraska	257
23	Idaho	1,059	*48*	Vermont	202
24	New Jersey	988	*49*	Michigan	−78
25	Oklahoma	913	*50*	Massachusetts	−1,307

Change in State and Local Taxes Per Capita, from 2003–4 to 2004–5

Rank	State Name	Change (%)	*Rank*	State Name	Change (%)
1	Alaska	21.94	*26*	Idaho	7.51
2	Wyoming	18.89	*27*	North Carolina	7.41
3	Arkansas	14.55	*28*	Arizona	7.28
4	Hawaii	14.29	*29*	Maryland	6.77
5	Indiana	13.70	*30*	Utah	6.62
6	Vermont	12.88	*31*	Ohio	6.46
7	West Virginia	12.19	*32*	Oklahoma	6.43
8	North Dakota	11.61	*33*	Missouri	6.38
9	Montana	10.94	*34*	Kentucky	6.25
10	New Mexico	10.70	*35*	Washington	6.14
11	Alabama	10.57	*36*	Massachusetts	6.07
12	Connecticut	10.14	*37*	Colorado	5.87
13	Nevada	9.86	*38*	New Hampshire	5.81
14	Louisiana	9.73	*39*	Mississippi	5.69
15	New York	9.66	*40*	Michigan	5.40
16	Virginia	9.52	*41*	Tennessee	5.28
17	Florida	9.08	*42*	Texas	5.03
18	California	9.05	*43*	Maine	4.99
19	Illinois	8.66	*T44*	Oregon	4.90
20	Rhode Island	8.40	*T44*	Georgia	4.90
21	Delaware	8.07	*46*	South Carolina	4.17
22	Pennsylvania	7.95	*47*	Nebraska	4.05
23	New Jersey	7.93	*48*	Wisconsin	4.01
T24	Iowa	7.53	*49*	South Dakota	3.14
T24	Minnesota	7.53	*50*	Kansas	1.27

About the Data

The majority of the data presented in this book comes from government agencies, including the Census Bureau, the Department of Labor, and the Department of Commerce. These agencies provide the most reliable estimates available at the time the data is released. However, as new information becomes available, these agencies will occasionally refine their estimates. As a result, researchers should be aware that data may vary slightly based on when it was retrieved.

Below is more information on the sources used for each section of the state profiles.

Demographic and Socioeconomic Data. The population, household, age, and ethnicity data is from the U.S. Census Bureau's American Community Survey for 2005 and 2006, as well as the 2000 Census Summary File 1 and Summary File 3. The household income and poverty data is also from these sources, while the per capita income data in this section is from the U.S. Department of Commerce's Bureau of Economic Analysis (BEA), table SA1-3. Population projections are from the Census Bureau's April 2005 interim projections consistent with Census 2000.

Workforce and Industry Data. Educational attainment data is from the U.S. Census Bureau's 2005 and 2006 American Community Survey and the 2000 Census Summary File 3. Labor force data is from the U.S. Department of Labor's Bureau of Labor Statistics' (BLS) Local Area Unemployment Statistics, and are annualized figures without seasonal adjustment. The data on average wages per job were obtained from the Bureau of Labor Statistics' Occupational Employment Statistics program. The industry data on employment, payroll, and establishments is from the U.S. Census Bureau's County Business Patterns from 1998, 2004, and 2005.

Tax and Business Climate Data. Data for state and local tax revenues was collected from survey of State and Local Government Finances, and provided by the Census Bureau's Government's Division. In general we include tax revenue from state and local sources to allow valid comparison among states. Anderson Economic Group, LLC calculated the per capita taxes using July population estimates from the Census Bureau, as available at the time the data was collected. Employer firm birth and employer firm termination data was collected from the Census Bureau's Statistics of U.S. Businesses, County Business Patterns.

Measures of business climates are from annual reports by Anderson Economic Group, *Forbes* Magazine, the American Legislative Exchange Council, and the Tax Foundation. Please see the glossary for a description of how each group assesses a state's business climate. Further information is available on the websites of *Forbes* Magazine, the American Legislative Exchange Council, the Tax Foundation, and Anderson Economic Group.

Voter Behavior and Elected Official Data. The data on voter registration and turnout, as well as the presidential election results, is from Dave Leip's Atlas of U.S. Presidential Elections, available at www.uselectionatlas.org. This site was also useful in verifying data for the gubernatorial and congressional section, data for which was collected from a variety of sources, but mainly the websites for the National Governor's Association, the United States Senate, and the United States House of Representatives.

Business and Economic Agencies. This information was collected by Anderson Economic Group. The first agency listed for each state is a state-level chamber of commerce, or similar. The second agency listed is the state's economic development agency or office. Third listed is an agency that promotes and provides resources for small businesses in each state, and lastly listed is the agency or office that businesses should contact for information on registering and filing to do business in the state.

These agencies are only a few of many that are available in each state. There are many local chambers of commerce and economic development organizations that can serve as excellent resources as well.

Glossary of Terms

African-American Population. Persons having origins in any of the Black racial groups of Africa. It includes people who indicate their race as "African American or Black," or provide written entries such as African American, Afro-American, Kenyan, Nigerian, or Haitian.

Definition: U.S. Census Bureau, American Community Survey

ALEC-Laffer 2007 Economic Competitiveness Ranking. A ranking of economic competitiveness in all 50 states based on the equal weighting of each states rank in marginal personal income tax rate, marginal corporate income tax rate, progressivity of the personal income tax system, property tax burden, sales tax burden, tax burden from all remaining taxes, estate tax or inheritance tax, tax policy changes in 2005–6, debt service as a share of tax revenue, public employees per 10,000 residents, quality of the legal system, state minimum wage, workers' compensation costs, right-to-work state, tax or expenditure limit, and an education freedom index.

Definition: American Legislative Exchange Council

Anderson Economic Group 2006 Business Tax Burden Ranking. A ranking of business tax burdens in all 50 states. This ranking measures actual taxes paid by businesses in 2005 as a percentage of profits earned within each state's borders. "Business" taxes are defined as taxes with an initial incidence on a business, rather than an individual. Included are corporate income, gross receipts, value-added, and property taxes; but not taxes on employee wages, residential property, or consumer spending.

Definition: Anderson Economic Group, LLC

Asian Population. Persons having origins in any of the original peoples of the Far East, Southeast Asia, or the Indian subcontinent including, for example, Cambodia, China, India, Japan, Korea, Malaysia, Pakistan, the Philippine Islands, Thailand, and Vietnam. It includes "Asian Indian," "Chinese," "Filipino," "Korean," "Japanese," "Vietnamese," and "Other Asian."

Definition: U.S. Census Bureau, American Community Survey

Average Household Size. The total number of occupants in a household, divided by the total number of households units.

Definition: U.S. Census Bureau, American Community Survey

Average Wage Per Job. Average wage and salary disbursements are wage and salary disbursements divided by the number of wage and salary jobs (total wage and salary employment). Wage and salary disbursements consists of the monetary remuneration of employees, including the compensation of corporate officers; commissions, tips, and bonuses; and receipts in kind, or pay-in-kind, such as the meals furnished to the employees of restaurants. It reflects the amount of payments disbursed, but not necessarily earned during the year.

Definition: U.S. Department of Commerce, Bureau of Economic Analysis

Bachelors Degree of Higher. Respondents who have completed a bachelors, masters, or professional degree were classified as having a "bachelors degree or higher." Associates degrees were included in this category only if the coursework could be transferred into a complete bachelors degree.

Definition: U.S. Census Bureau, American Community Survey

Caucasian Population. The U.S. Census Bureau defines "Caucasian" as a person having origins in any of the original peoples of Europe, the Middle East, or North Africa. It includes people who indicate their race as "White" or report entries such as Irish, German, Italian, Lebanese, Near Easterner, Arab, or Polish.

Definition: U.S. Census Bureau, American Community Survey

Civilian Labor Force. All persons 16 years of age and older residing in the 50 states and the District of Columbia who are not inmates of institutions (for example, penal and mental facilities and homes for the aged) and who are not on active duty in the Armed Forces. This is equal to the universe used by the Census Bureau for labor force data.

Definition: U.S. Bureau of Labor Statistics

Corporate Income Tax. Taxes on corporations and unincorporated businesses (when taxed separately from individual income), measured by net income, whether on corporations in general or on specific kinds of corporations, such as financial institutions. Some other business activity taxes, such as Michigan's Single Business Tax (a value-added tax), are also included in this category.

Definition: U.S. Census Bureau, Quarterly Summary of State and Local Government Tax Revenue; Anderson Economic Group, LLC

Employees. The total number of persons on establishment payrolls employed full or part time who received pay for any part of the pay period that includes the twelfth day of the month.

Definition: U.S. Department of Labor, Bureau of Labor Statistics

Employer Firm Births and Deaths. Births are establishments that have zero employment in the first quarter of the initial year and positive employment in the first quarter of the subsequent year. Deaths are establishments that have positive employment in the first quarter of the initial year and zero employment in the first quarter of the subsequent year.

Definition: U.S. Census Bureau, Statistics of U.S. Businesses

Establishment. The physical location of a certain economic activity—for example, a factory, mine, store, or office. A single establishment generally produces a single good or provides a single service. An enterprise (a private firm, government, or nonprofit organization) can consist of a single establishment or multiple establishments.

Definition: U.S. Census Bureau, County Business Patterns.

Forbes Magazine: 2007 Best States for Business Ranking. A ranking of the business climates of all 50 states based on 30 metrics in 6 main categories: business costs, economic climate, growth prospects, labor, quality of life, and regulatory environment.

Definition: Forbes, The Best States for Business

Foreign-Born Population. The foreign-born population includes all people who were not U.S. citizens at birth. Foreign-born people are people who indicated they were either a U.S. citizen by naturalization or that they were not a citizen of the United States. Immigration status is not relevant in determining the foreign-born population.

Definition: U.S. Census Bureau, Summary of Social, Economic, and Housing Characteristics

Graduate Degree or Higher. This category includes people who hold at least one graduate degree. A graduate degree includes master of arts, master of science, field specific master's degrees, professional, and doctorate degrees.

Definition: U.S. Census Bureau, American Community Survey

High School Graduate or Higher. This category includes people whose highest degree was a high school diploma or its equivalent (e.g., passed the test of General Educational Development), people who attended college but did not receive a degree, and people who received an associate's, bachelor's, master's, or professional doctorate degree. People who reported completing the twelfth grade but not receive a diploma are not included.

Definition: U.S. Census Bureau, American Community Survey

Hispanic Population. Since the 2000 census, the U.S. Census Bureau has defined "Hispanic" as any population identifying themselves as "Spanish," "Hispanic origin," or "Latino." Some respondents identified with all three terms, while others may have identified with only one, or none of the three terms. In addition, all write-in responses to the "other Spanish/Hispanic/ Latino" category were coded as "Hispanic," beginning with the 2000 Census. Currently, the U.S. Census Bureau defines "Hispanic" as a population that may be of any race. This handbook used all census classifications of "Hispanic" or "other Hispanic."

Definition: U.S. Census Bureau, Summary of Social, Economic, and Housing Characteristics

Household Income. The sum of all monetary income received in a calendar year by all household members 15 years old and over, including household members not related to the householder, people living alone, and other nonfamily household members. Household income may include nonwage income as well.

Definition: U.S. Department of Labor, Bureau of Labor Statistics

Individual Income Tax. The U.S. government classifies income taxes as taxes on individuals measured by net income and taxes on special types of income (e.g., interest, dividends, income from intangible property, etc.).

Definition: U.S. Census Bureau, Quarterly Summary of State and Local Government Tax Revenue, Quarterly Summary of Technical Documentation

Median. The middle value in a distribution, with an equal number of values above and below the median (sometimes called "midpoint").

Number of Households. A household includes all people subsiding in a housing unit. A household may consist of family members and or lodgers, foster children, wards, or employees who share the housing unit. A person living alone in a housing unit is also counted as a household. The count of households excludes group quarters.

Definition: U.S. Census Bureau, American Community Survey

Other Taxes. Taxes that are not listed separately or specifically accounted for in a tax category. These taxes most commonly include inheritance and estate taxes; taxes on recording, registering, or transferring documents; and taxes on the value or quantity of natural resource extraction. Also included here, though listed separately by the Census Bureau, are motor vehicle license taxes.

Definition: U.S. Census Bureau, Government Finance and Employment Classification Manual; Anderson Economic Group, LLC

Personal Income. The sum of wages by place of residence, rental income of persons, personal dividend income, personal interest income, and personal current transfer receipts.

Definition: U.S. Department of Commerce, Bureau of Economic Analysis

Popular Vote. The number of votes from citizens, independent of the electoral college.

Definition: U.S. National Archives and Records Administration

Poverty. Poverty thresholds are determined by the amount of income necessary for self-sustenance. Poverty thresholds determine the government's official poverty definition and may vary based on family size and age of family members. Thresholds are adjusted annually for inflation, but they do not vary geographically.

Definition: U.S. Census Bureau

Poverty Rate. The number of people in a given area living under the poverty threshold divided by the total number of people in that area. *(See poverty).*

Definition: U.S. Census Bureau

Property Tax. General property taxes, relating to property as a whole, taxed at a single rate or at classified rates according to the class of property. Property may refer to real property (i.e., land and structures), or personal property (i.e., automobiles and boats).

Definition: U.S. Census Bureau, Quarterly Summary of State and Local Government Tax Revenue, Quarterly Summary Technical Documentation

Sales and Gross Receipts Taxes. Taxes on goods and services, measured on the basis of the volume or value of their transfer. Depending on the good, sales taxes may be based upon gross receipts or gross income accrued from the sale of the good, or as an amount per unit sold (gallon, package, etc.). The Census Bureau also includes related taxes based upon use, storage, production, importation, or consumption of goods and services. Few states levy gross receipts taxes, which are included in this category by Census Bureau convention.

Definition: U.S. Census Bureau, Quarterly Summary of State and Local Government Tax Revenue, Quarterly Summary Technical Documentation

State and Local Taxes. In Census Bureau data, "State and Local Taxes" include the state-imposed taxes collected or received by the state and subsequently distributed to local governments. Locally collected and retained tax amounts are excluded from the data.

Definition: U.S. Census Bureau, Quarterly Summary of State and Local Government Tax Revenue, Quarterly Summary Technical Documentation

Tax Foundation: 2008 Business Tax Climate Ranking. A ranking of business tax climate in each state that takes into the corporate tax, individual income tax, sales tax, unemployment tax, and property tax into consideration, and the scores for these factors are weighted based on the relative importance or impact of the tax to a business.

Definition: Tax Foundation

Taxes. Taxes are comprised of all compulsory contributions exacted by a government for public purposes, except employer and employee assessments for retirement and social insurance purposes, which are classified as insurance trust revenue. Included are all receipts from licenses and compulsory fees, in addition to those that are imposed for regulatory purposes and those designed to provide revenue.

Definition: U.S. Census Bureau, Quarterly Summary of State and Local Government Tax Revenue, Quarterly Summary Technical Documentation

Tax Revenue. Revenue from taxes generated in a given area, includes related penalty and interest receipts but excludes protested amounts and refunds.

Definition: U.S. Census Bureau, Quarterly Summary of State and Local Government Tax Revenue, Quarterly Summary Technical Documentation

Total Payroll. The total amount of money paid to employees in wages.

Definition: U.S. Department of Labor, Bureau of Labor Statistics

Total Population. All people, male and female, child and adult, living in a given geographic area.

Definition: U.S. Census Bureau, American Community Survey

Unemployment. All noninstitutionalized civilians 16 years old and over are classified as unemployed if they (1) were neither "at work" nor "with a job but not at work" during the reference week, and (2) were actively looking for work during the 4 weeks prior to the reference week, and (3) were available to accept a job.

Definition: U.S. Bureau of Labor Statistics

Unemployment Rate. The proportion of the total number of persons considered "unemployed" to the total civilian noninstitutional population 16 years and over (*See unemployment).*

Definition: U.S. Bureau of Labor Statistics

Index